STAKEHOLDERING

STAKEHOLDERING

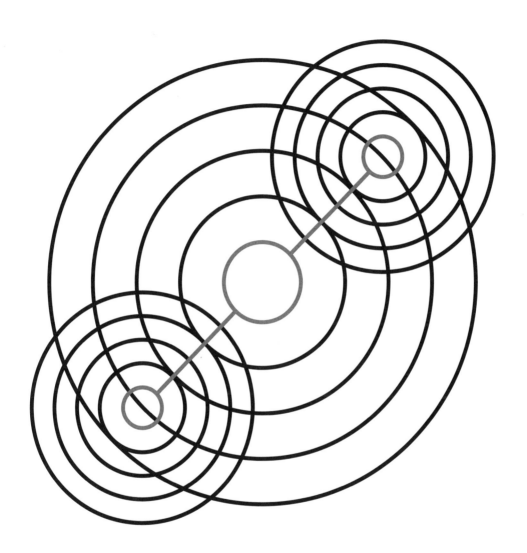

DIPLOMATIC SKILLS FOR
SUCCESSFUL PROJECTS

Jan Van der Vurst

 LANNOO
CAMPUS

This book was originally published as *Stakeholdering*, LannooCampus, 2019.

D/2019/45/334 – ISBN 978 94 014 6252 5 – NUR 801

COVER DESIGN   STEVE REYNDERS
INTERIOR DESIGN   BANANANAS.NET
TRANSLATION   IAN CONNERTY

© Jan Van der Vurst & Lannoo Publishers nv, Tielt, 2019.

LannooCampus Publishers is a subsidiary of Lannoo Publishers,
the book and multimedia division of Lannoo Publishers nv.

LannooCampus Publishers
Vaartkom 41   P.O. box 23202
3000 Leuven   1100 DS Amsterdam
Belgium   Netherlands
WWW.LANNOOCAMPUS.COM

For Marinette,
who means so much more to me
than the entire universe and beyond

TABLE OF CONTENTS

STAKEHOLDERING

There were two reasons for writing this book: budget responsibility and job satisfaction.

Anyone who wants to achieve something of significance within a complex organisation is dependent to a significant degree on the goodwill of other people to make constructive collaboration possible. Or at least to ensure that they do not actively work against you. Whether or not things actually turn out the way you planned is another matter, because others also have their own agenda and their own objectives. Not all agendas are compatible. This can sometimes give rise to a lack of clarity, friction, delays and double work. Which, in turn, can cost a sackful of money.

As a professional or a manager, you know your job through and through. You devise solutions that can make a difference both for your organisation and for your customers. The fact that you can develop these solutions and make them work gives you moments of intense satisfaction.

It is frustrating when others cast doubt on (or even ignore) the quality and the usefulness of your contribution. And it is equally frustrating when your knowledge, your ability and your desire to improve things are unable to find proper expression or fail to receive the recognition they deserve.

If you want to implement a project efficiently and effectively, so that both you and your organisation can reap the full benefits of your work, you will need to find a way to deal with other third parties, your stakeholders, in a targeted and reasoned manner. You will need to find methods that will turn these others into allies, so that they will also be able to benefit from what you are trying to achieve.

Developing diplomatic skills is the best way to do this. Diplomacy demands tact and respect. It means having a real interest in the things that are important for your stakeholders, so that you can find the ideal approach that will allow you to bring everyone's different interests into line. It is an active process of searching together, of influencing and being influenced. It is a process driven by rational analysis and by a method of implementation that is as systematic as the managing of your project. All these things, taken together, are what we call stakeholdering.

Stakeholdering is a methodology that unites fire with water. Stakeholdering offers you a rational approach to non-rational processes, which, even though they are directed more by instinct than by reason, nonetheless follow their own dynamic, so that they can be predicted and managed.

Two of these non-rational elements are central to this dynamic: the urge to defend and extend your own territory and the phenomenon of power.

These are also two elements that are difficult to control, but which can make a huge difference to the successful realisation of your projects.

In chapters 1 and 2 you will gain insights into the nature of territories: how they originate, how they are defended and extended (including the pitfalls this often entails) and how you can best deal with them.

In order to be able to operate in an environment populated by stakeholders and their agendas, the first thing you need to do is to map out the landscape. Who is able to influence the project? What is the attitude of each stakeholder towards the project at the present time? Who are the key players and who do you need to make closer alliances with? This process will be examined in detail in chapter 3.

The next task is to forge partnerships with the key players you have identi-fied. Chapters 4 and 5 will show you exactly how to do this.

If you are hoping to complete a project of some size, somewhere along the way you will inevitably come into contact with power figures. They can often have a decisive impact on your success or failure. Dealing with power is never simple, because it is a subject that affects us all emotionally, irrespective of whether you exercise power or are simply subject to it. It is a dynamic that is rooted deep within our human instinct. Chapter 6 will explore that nature of power and how you can best approach it.

Chapter 7 outlines a number of detailed interventions to illustrate how you can avoid difficulties with stakeholders or, alternatively, how you can get your project back on track if, for whatever reason, it at some point gets derailed.

I wish you good reading, good luck and plenty of inspiration!

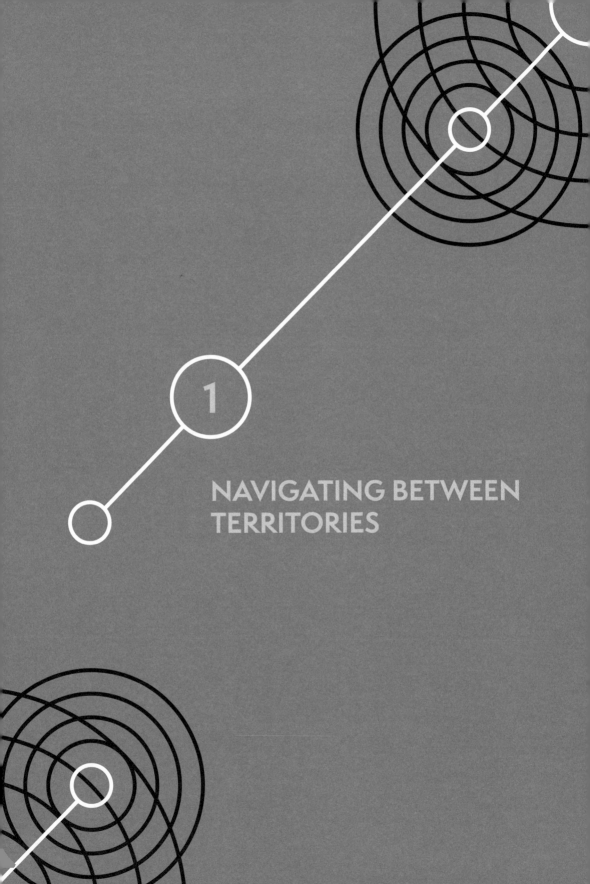

1

NAVIGATING BETWEEN TERRITORIES

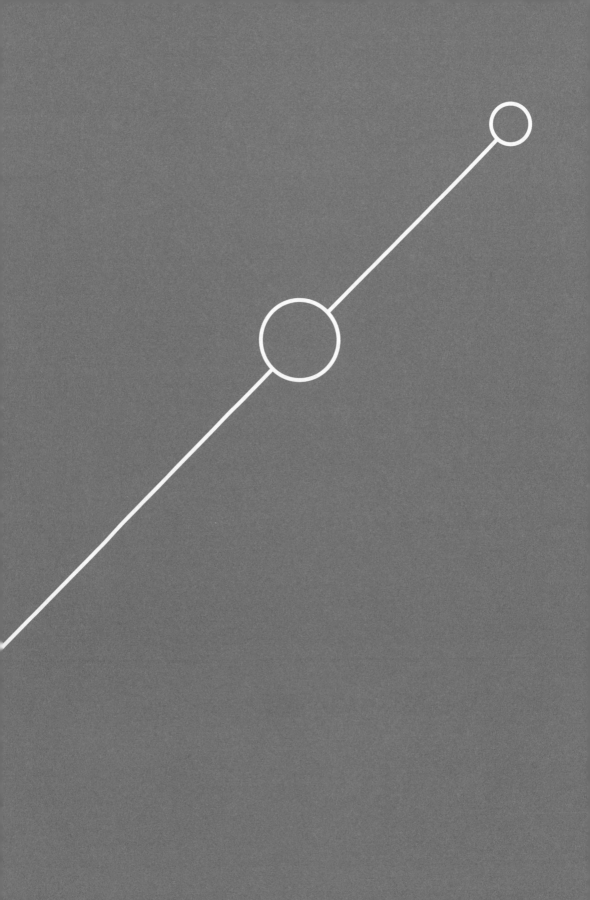

The main reason for setting up the European Union was to avoid repeating the horrors of the two world wars. Countries were tied to each other economically and, later, also monetarily. This benefited the prosperity and security of each country, whilst at the same time creating a dependence on each other that made serving their combined collective interests a necessity.

There are few objectives more important than these. Even so, we know that in practice things do not always run as smoothly as might reasonably be expected. The EU is an economic union, but not a political one. As a top European official once put it: 'Europe remains a collection of individual states.' Each of them has its own objectives, its own government, it own elections and its own opposition parties, who are all too ready to complain about Europe's 'interference' when it suits them.

There is a constant need to strike a balance between national autonomy and European collectivism. And it often happens that the former takes precedence over the latter. Some countries want to be in the euro area; others do not. Some are willing to accept African refugees; others are not. Some are happy to follow the provisions of jointly agreed European legislation; others prefer to play fast and loose with democratic principles and values. Some countries even leave the union altogether. But through it all, the European ship needs to be kept stable, afloat and moving forwards – because there is a lot at stake.

Europe will not be able to achieve this important objective by trying to force sovereign states to do things (or not do things) through diktats from Brussels. This would be wholly counterproductive. Nor is it possible to simply agree to everyone's separate wishes and see how things turn out, since this would risk bringing the entire European construction crashing to the ground. Instead, it is necessary to constantly steer a middle course between all the different interests, both collective and particular, so that it continues to be possible to find new balances that make the ultimate objective – a Europe that is economically strong and at peace – more rather than less secure.

How can you do this? Above all, through diplomacy.

Fortunately, getting things done within organisations is slightly less complex. But the basic dynamic remains the same: you need to achieve an objective that serves not only the company's interests but also your own interests and those of your team. And because you never work in a vacuum, your success will always depend on the cooperation of other teams, departments and interest groups. If you are leading a project that seeks to introduce change, you know that this will have consequences for how people are used to doing things, something that is seldom comfortable for those involved. You also know that you will often be accused of 'interfering' in things that are 'none of your business', so that you will need to find ways of getting these critics on your side, if you want to avoid the project becoming bogged down in endless delays. Last but not least, you also know that it is going to cost a lot of energy to deal with all this resistance.

About diplomacy

As a rule, diplomacy and company politics are not among the favourite pastimes of experts, professionals and managers. Quite the reverse: most of them hate these things with a vengeance and look on them with contempt: 'A waste of time, pursued only by people who are concerned with the superficial rather than the essential. It has nothing to do with the real work. Worse still, it even gets in the way of the real work, slowing it down and sometimes even making it impossible. If you really want to know: politics is a field that every right-minded professional should avoid. He has better things to do with his time.'

Jeffrey Pfeffer, a professor at the renowned Stanford University, was probably the first academic to take politics within organisations seriously and carry out systematic research into its nature.[1] What he soon discovered was that most people have very mixed feelings when it comes to political or diplomatic skills.

When he asked employees whether internal politics help organisations to function more efficiently or not, only 42 percent said that it had a positive effect. So does this mean that senior management should attempt to ban politics from their companies? 50 percent think that it should mean precisely that. Would people then be happier if politics played no role in their place of work? 60 percent agreed that they would. And now comes the really big leap in the figures: does politics of this kind exist in most organisations?

A resounding 93 percent are convinced that it does. An almost equally resounding 90 percent believe that you need to possess these political skills to get ahead in the organisation.

These figures reflect what we have already said about mixed feelings: people would prefer not to have politics in their company but it is there whether they like it or not, and you need to be good at it if you want to make a successful career. In other words, politics is a necessary evil. With the emphasis on 'necessary'.

Given these circumstances, it is hardly surprising that in competency manuals you always find a section on 'political skills' as a domain that you need to develop and manage. If you then look a little further, you will usually find the following description of the various sub-domains:[2]

- Being able to manoeuvre calmly and effectively in complex political situations.
- Being sensitive for the way in which people and organisations function.
- Anticipating potential landmines and being able to amend your route and plans to deal with them.
- Regarding internal politics as a necessary part of organisations and adjusting to it accordingly.

This book wants to serve as a pilot, to show you how to navigate your way through the treacherous waters you will need to cross if you wish to reconcile the collective interest with your own best interests. It will explain how you can avoid problems and pitfalls, making use of favourable currents and opportunities to arrive at your final objective safe and sound. This will often mean that your course does not follow a straight line from A to B, but will have to wind its way through the obstacles you will inevitably encounter along the way. It demands skill to be able to do this and it brings great satisfaction when you are able to do it successfully.

As the central thread running through this exploratory voyage of discovery, we will make use of the concept of 'territories': understanding what they are, why they exist, how they manifest themselves and, above all, how you can best deal with them. Only then will you be able to lay the solid foundations you need for the success of your project. As you will see, looking at matters from a territorial perspective helps to explain a lot of the things that happen in organisations. Yet strangely enough, very little is ever written or said about this key aspect of organisational systems. This is probably because territorial behaviour, in general, has negative connotations: the implication is that organisations would be better off without it. But this is most definitely not the case, as we shall see in the following pages! Territorial behaviour is built into our DNA. Denying its existence is like denying that the earth moves around the sun. Worse still, this misplaced reticence would also deny you access to a remarkable powerful dynamic that you can use to achieve your goals.

2 THE TERRITORIAL IMPULSE IS UNIVERSAL

There is no getting around it. It is simply the way things have been since the end of the 19th century: football teams that play at home have a huge advantage. Everywhere in the world. At all times. Okay, there may be some variations from country to country, but if you compare the total number of games won at home against the total number of games lost, the general picture is indisputable: there is a clear home advantage, ranging from just over 80 percent in countries like Albania and Bosnia-Herzegovina to between 60 and 65 percent in major footballing nations like Portugal, Spain, France, England, The Netherlands and Belgium, to 'just' 55 percent in Northern Ireland and the Baltic states.

This phenomenon is not quite so easy to explain as it might seem. In theory, the location of the game should make no difference at all: the ball is the same shape, the pitch is the same size and the number of players is the same, no matter where you play. Even so, the difference – and it is a big difference – remains. So what is the answer? Every local journalist and barroom pundit no doubt has his (or her) own explanation, but it may be wiser (if perhaps less fun) to rely on the insights of a good statistician.

Richard Pollard[3] is just such a statistician. He has made the most complete investigation to date of football results, while several of his other colleagues have done something similar, some of them with regard to other team sports, both inside Europe and beyond. This is what they have concluded.

If you ask the football supporters, the answer is crystal-clear: they – and no-one else – make the difference. How numerous they are, how close together they stand, how hard they scream and shout, and, above all, how much they sing. Sounds reasonable? Maybe. But how can you explain that home advantage still persists, even when there are only a handful of supporters? Or when clubs are forced to play behind closed doors as a punishment (usually for some form of misbehaviour by those same supporters!). And how is this mysterious supporters' benefit supposed to work? Are supporters an advantage for the home team or a disadvantage for the away one? Do they make their own players stronger? Or do they influence referees' decisions (a subject we will return to later)? They won't like to hear it, but a detailed analysis of the role of supporters in helping to create home advantage is wholly inconclusive. There is nothing to confirm that they make the difference they would like to think.

Might the distance the away team has to travel be the deciding factor? Does spending x hours in a coach, train or plane mean that they arrive at the game more tired than the players of the home side? Again, it sounds plausible. But again, the statistics – both for international and domestic pre-match travel – do nothing to support this contention. Travel does not make the difference.

So what about the sheer familiarity of your own home ground? After all, the home team trains there every day and plays there every second week. The players know the exact dimensions of the pitch, the distance to the terraces, the places where their most die-hard supporters stand. Their club flags and emblems are all around them and sometimes they even play with a specially made club ball. Could this be the elusive decisive factor? Might it explain, for example, why home advantage strongly declined in both Italy and England following the break in competition caused by the Second World War? Sadly, no: for the third time in a row, it is difficult to show empirically that familiarity with the surroundings – feasible though it seems – is the key to home team success. And the same applies to special tactical guidelines give by the home team managers.

Two factors that do make a difference...

There is, however, clear empirical evidence to show that referees play a demonstrable role in the creation of home advantage. To give you some idea: in a single season in the English Premier League referees gave 698 yellow cards to visiting players against just 512 for players from the home team. Similarly, home sides were awarded 42 penalties against a paltry 26 for the visitors.[4] When other referees were shown video material of the same phases of play, but without sight or sound of the crowd, this tendency to favour the home team disappeared almost completely.[5] 'Do you see what we mean?' say the supporters with pride. 'That's all our doing!' 'Do you see what we mean?' say FIFA with equal triumphalism. 'That is why we desperately need the VAR!'

For the theme of this book, it is the second factor favouring home advantage that is potentially more interesting. What is this X-factor? It is all a matter of testosterone. Seriously, this is not a joke. The level of testosterone in players is significantly higher before a home match than it is for a training session or for an away fixture. And the level is highest of all when the home game is against a team regarded as one of the home team's biggest rivals.[6] The most likely explanation for this is that the territorial impulse – the urge to defend your own territory – is as old as mankind itself. What we have, we hold – at all costs. You want to take it from us? 'Come and have a go, if you think you're hard enough!'

This kind of territoriality is perhaps best known among animals. There are many species that delineate a specific area sufficiently large to guarantee both adequate food for the group and the best possible conditions in which to pro-create. In addition, territories also have a regulatory social function: if they are clearly defined and marked, it creates clarity for all animals of the same species. Animals not belonging to the group will usually keep their distance, in order to avoid conflict. Conflict demands the use of extra energy that can be better used to find a more effective way to obtain the resources needed for survival.[7]

The biological roots of this territorial behaviour are also to be found in our human genes. After all, we are just another mammal used to living in groups. The ways in which we define and defend our territories is perhaps a little more sophisticated than leaving trails of urine and fighting tooth and nail with rivals who want to steal our women. At least, it sometimes seems more sophisticated. But in essence, what is at stake is much the same.

Imagine the scene. A residential estate in a pleasant rural area. At the heart of the estate Violet Avenue leads on to Primrose Lane. Sounds picturesque? It is – apart from one small problem. Both roads are shortcuts between two motorways. As a result, thousands of cars pass each day, especially during the morning and evening rush hours. To make matters worse, there are now roadworks. The junction of both roads is closed off with red and white warning tape and there are signs everywhere to divert the approaching traffic. The top layer of tarmac has already been scraped off for replacement, so that even if the road was open you would currently need a tank to get through without damaging your vehicle. But for some people that doesn't matter. Several times a day, a driver jumps furiously out of his car, tears down the tape and pushes the signs to one side, before furiously announcing to any bystanders who may be watching: 'This is my route and I will drive on it if I want to!'

This driver has established the basic components of a territory: the feelings of ownership ('This is my route') and autonomy ('I will drive on it if I want to'). You will note that these feelings are only experienced within his own perception of things. In reality, the road does not belong to him but to the local council and he cannot drive on it because further on there are still more signs – not to mention big potholes in the surface – that make it impossible. Even so, his own experience of the situation is sufficient to give rise to primeval territorial behaviour in all its glory!

This kind of territoriality is universal. On a large scale, it applies to the borders between countries, who will fight to hold on to every square metre of their ground. This is getting close to the concept of territory amongst animals. But we clever humans have developed plenty of other variations. There is the field of action: my job and my function description ('Hey, Fred, what are you doing? That's my task!'). There is the field of relationships: my partner and my children ('Nobody has the right to interfere with the way I raise my kids!'). There is even the field of ideas ('That was my idea first and no-one is going to steal it!').

... also in professional organisations

It is impossible to go to work every day and do things that have no involvement with others. There is always interaction. Where does your work come from? What happens to it once you have finished it? Who can you turn to for help, if you need it? Not knowing these things would be like a torture that is sometimes used in prisons. You dig a hole (preferably a large one) and then fill it up again with the earth you have just dug out of it. Then you repeat the process. Ad infinitum. And you do it completely alone.

No, this is not really possible – at least, I hope not for your sake!

We work by definition in networks, which means that we are constantly involved with others and with their territories. This is certainly the case in project organisations, where project teams are often drawn from the members of different departments, so that the managers of those departments also have a finger in the collective pie. Every project therefore has implications for many other people within the organisation, which means that they are also 'interested parties'.

It is regrettable that the territorial aspect of working together has so far been so inadequately researched, since it is an aspect that can help to explain many other collaborative phenomena. We all know that territories play a role, but we tend to regard them like we regard politics: as something irrational, based purely on emotions and ultimately leading nowhere constructive. This is a shame, because it is essentially the same as saying that territories don't belong, that we would be better off without them. According to this logic, they are no more than a tiresome marginal matter.

If we qualify territories in this manner, there is a danger of two things happening: we risk reducing the amount of energy we currently devote to deciphering and understanding other people's territories and we are even more likely than is currently the case (we have all done it) to negatively label territorial behaviour as defensive. People's reaction will quickly become: 'Territories? Don't have anything to do with them!' That would be a pity, since territories open up numerous possibilities that allow us to become many times more effective, if only we can learn how to properly read their underlying dynamics.

THERE ARE DIFFERENT KINDS OF TERRITORIES

To start with, a definition: a territory is an area of your life that matters, in which you experience independence and feel free to take the initiative. In short, we regard a territory as our property. There are two major fields where this applies: the private domain and the public arena.

The private domain

We all have our own private territory. It is, almost quite literally, the area that we have delineated to safeguard our personal privacy and security. This area probably includes your home and perhaps some other specific place where you can shut yourself off from the outside world. It might be a man cave, or the room where your computer is, or the place where the children go to do their own thing.

This is something you can see in children from an early age. Sometimes it might be a special blanket they love to crawl under. Or under the table. Or behind the sofa. From the age of six or seven years, our little darlings actually start to mark out these territories. This becomes even more evident once they learn how to write: suddenly, there is a notice on their bedroom door, instructing: 'KEEP OUT – OR ELSE!' (it is hard to expect too much subtlety at this age). They claim a place where they can keep 'their' things and be as messy as they like. Moreover, it is a place where other members of the family, except perhaps the household pets, can only enter with their explicit permission and where mum and dad should definitely keep their ideas about neatness and tidiness to themselves. Even if you risk breaking your ankle every time you need to enter their room (possibly to rescue your hopelessly lost cat, which you haven't seen for the past week), it is not recommended to suggest that they might like to 'tidy things up a bit'. And you are effectively committing parental suicide if (God forbid!) you decide to start clearing things up yourself.

Everyone needs a *private hideaway*. This is essential, and it remains so your whole life long. The strength of this need can be measured by the intensity of emotions people display when their hideaway is entered uninvited by others or taken away from them, so that it no longer provides the security they crave.

Hopefully, this has never happened to you but perhaps you have heard the story from others: having your private territory invaded is one of the most traumatising aspects of burglary. It is bad enough to be robbed of your prized possessions, but the idea that strangers have been in your home is somehow even worse. Your private sanctuary has been defiled.

At the other side of the legal spectrum, depriving prisoners of their own private space can be used as a punishment technique in prisons. In a jail, privacy is non-existent. There is nowhere you can go to be alone. This can have a remarkably destabilising effect on the people who experience it. There is, quite literally, no place where they can hide.

In addition to a private hideaway, we also all have an absolute need for *personal space*. This is something everyone can relate to. We feel uncomfortable when people get too close. We want our bubble of physical integrity to be respected and we have a highly sensitive compass that tells us when things risk getting out of hand.[8]

Imagine a waiting room with a long row of chairs against the wall. If someone comes in and sits on a chair at one end of the row, you can guess without too much difficulty where the next person is most likely to sit. It will certainly not be the chair directly next to the first person, nor will it be the chair at the opposite end of the row. It will most probably be a chair somewhere in the middle: far enough to be safe, but close enough not to seem unfriendly. What's more, this also leaves enough space for the third person who enters to sit between the second person and the other end of the row. This pattern will continue until there comes a point when the next person to enter has no option but to sit immediately next to someone else. You can see this same phenomenon every day in waiting rooms, trains, buses and even in public lavatories, not just for the gents, but also for women (who can see from the 'vacant-engaged' signs on the doors which toilets are occupied and which are not).

We like to keep our distance, but not to the extent that this distance makes us feel excluded. It is almost like the measured steps of a dance, a dance which is built into our genes. Everyone at the right interval. Close enough, but no further. And if circumstances dictate that it is physically impossible for these 'rules' to apply – for example, in a crowded lift – we do something very strange: we avoid all interaction, as though the other people in the same space do not exist. We shut ourselves up in our own being. No eye contact and very definitely no speaking.

People who have travelled to different parts of the world will know just how culturally sensitive 'keeping the right distance' can be. If you approach someone from Japan the way you might approach an Italian, you are likely to create a potentially embarrassing situation, especially for your Japanese friend. You don't believe me? Just look at the footage of the first meeting between President Trump and Prime Minister Abe. It is a classic example of the invasion of someone's private space – in this case, Abe's – and the discomfort it can cause.

But let us now briefly return to the animals and the biological roots of this need for distance. Animals will always try to create a space around them that is large enough to flee from predators. If this space is made smaller, they feel threatened by possible attack. Psychologically, it is not so very different with humans. We all know that in discussions it is not a good idea to back your conversation partner into a corner. If you do, he (or she) will either respond with irrational arguments in defence of his (or her) position or will clam up completely – neither of which is conducive to good dialogue. And you can be certain that they will be looking to get their revenge somewhere down the line. No matter how good and sensible your arguments are, it is important to offer your negotiating partner a way out, a possibility to end or leave the discussion without any loss of face, especially if you know that you will need to deal with the same person again in the future.

This is something that Vera had failed to understand. She was a remarkably intelligent woman, but had one particularly irritating characteristic: she didn't know when to stop arguing, even if her conversation partners had already conceded her point and were willing to follow her. Even if two arguments were enough to win the day, she always used five – just to prove that she was right. This led to a reaction that puzzled Vera: having initially agreed with her, people suddenly changed their minds and started opposing her again. She was so overwhelming with her tsunami of arguments that her conversation partners no longer had the space to decide for themselves to go along with her willingly. Instead, they were forced into it – and none of us responds favourably to force.

For the subjects covered by this book, the need for a physical personal space is probably the least important aspect of territoriality. In contrast, the highest degree of privacy and personal space is to be found in the intimacy of our own thoughts, feelings and mental images. We all know how irritating it can be when someone tries to read your newspaper over your shoulder on a train, but the idea that someone might read our private diary or text messages is positively unbearable. The world inside your head is the most personal and private of all worlds. This becomes clear, for example, in our courses on influencing techniques. Most people have a problem with the basic concept. The idea that their behaviour or their thoughts could be influenced against their will makes them rebellious. Suggest that they can use these techniques on others, okay. But suggest that someone might justifiably use these same techniques on them? No way!

As we shall see later, this is one of the biggest obstacles to the successful implementation of change processes. Introducing a new process often requires people to think in a different way. But thinking in a different way is not something that most people are keen to do, and certainly not when they feel they are being forced – or, even worse, seduced – into it against their will.

The public arena

In addition to a personal aspect, territories also have a social aspect that brings us much closer to our subject. It relates to interaction, to the things that happen between people. Once again, we need to distinguish between two different elements: psychological space and the sphere of action.

We can define the psychological space somewhat abstractly as the influence that every member of a group exercises on the thoughts, feelings and behaviour of the other group members. In essence, this means the extent to which a person is capable of attracting and directing the attention of others without it being obvious. Although this capacity varies from person to person, we are all aware from our experience of meetings that there is often an implicit 'competition' between the participants to capture and keep the focus of attention. Once again, this behaviour is based on a fundamental underlying need: the need for recognition as a person in your own right. This is something we all desire.

What's more, it is a desire that has been evident throughout history. You are always going to get more attention if you are the only person wearing a jewel-encrusted golden crown, with a sceptre in your hand. And it is the same with popes in their white vestments and beauty queens in their bathing suits. And with judges in their gowns and doctors in their white coats. And even with managers who have their own corner office or people who drive a big car. In all these cases, so much is immediately 'obvious' that no further explanation is necessary. Here is someone to whom you should give your attention and to whom you should listen.

These visual signs of status are not the only way to attract and keep people's attention. You can also do it through your behaviour.

This was the tactic adopted by the Israeli Prime Minister Benjamin Netanyahu when he addressed the General Assembly of the United Nations in 2012. The point he wanted to make was that in his opinion the Iranian nuclear programme posed a serious threat to world peace. Of course, he could have made his speech in the traditional manner: walk to the podium, remove your notes from your inside pocket, deliver the text with the right timing and inflection, wait for the polite applause, return to your seat and make way for the next speaker. But Netanyahu chose to do something different. He still made a speech, but to support his arguments he used a visual aid: a childishly simply drawing of a bomb. On this bomb he marked with a thick red line just how far it was safe to let the Iranians go before it would be necessary for the outside world to intervene. In this way, he also made clear that if the outside world didn't do it, Israel would. The use of this visual medium was so out-of-the-ordinary in the UN that the media quickly picked it up, so that the speech was reported in many countries. Which is exactly what Netanyahu wanted: to get the attention of people everywhere.

A year later, he was back at the UN, speaking from the same podium. In the intervening period, the United States had concluded a nuclear deal with Iran, a deal which was not to Netanyahu's liking. Again, he managed to capture everyone's attention, this time by saying nothing for 23 seconds while looking grim-faced around the chamber, before announcing: 'We cannot remain silent.'

Visible symbols of status attract attention. So, too, does unusual and unexpected behaviour. But there is no need to adopt Netanyahu's 'in your face' approach to have the desired effect. Having a good reputation is often enough.

People listen to experts who are known to have had plenty of good ideas in the past or who represent prestigious consultancy bureaus with a proven track record. The lower your position in the pecking order of things, the less likely your idea will be favourably received – no matter how good it is.

This was the frustration that Lena experienced. For a long time, she had been hammering on about the need for her department to change course, if it did not wish to be left behind. She had made the same point in several presentations, supported by an impressive battery of facts and figures. The response of her colleagues? At best, an approving nod of the head but no real action. At worst, a rolling of the eyes and a 'here we go again' look on their faces. Until, that is, the company appointed an expensive consultant, who said precisely what Lena had been saying for years. Almost overnight, everyone started singing a very different tune. Suddenly, change was 'essential' and could 'no longer be delayed'. This was good for the department, which at least now seemed to be moving in the right direction. But not so good for Lena, who received none of the credit. After all, she was only a junior manager. And a woman as well...

The importance of psychological space can be demonstrated by the effect it has on people when it is removed. Consider, for example, the case of Keith, a professor in social psychology. His lectures are special, for a number of different reasons. One of them is the fact that he likes to conduct live experiments with his students in the lecture hall, so that they can experience at first hand a number of the psychological principles involved, before then moving on to the nuts and bolts of the theoretical framework. Giving lectures in this way demands a lot of additional preparation, but Keith doesn't mind, because he regards teaching as perhaps the most interesting of his many activities. But woe betide the student who dares to use a smartphone during one of his lectures. Whenever this happens, the otherwise mild and unassuming Keith flies into a rage that is as awesome as it is unexpected. The miscreant is sent from the hall, with a sombre 'See me later' still ringing in his ears. Keith finds it intolerable that the psychological space he creates to influence – and, in this case, improve – the thoughts of his students is not being properly respected.

Keith's reaction is no different from the irritation that most of us feel when someone interrupts us in mid-sentence or when our conversation partner decides that he suddenly has to send a text message that simply cannot wait. But let's be clear on this point: interaction between people is more than just a non-stop fight to gain the most 'air time'. This would be unworkable. At certain moments, people are willing to give up some of their space, but in most cases only if there is the prospect of them getting something in return. For instance, they may be willing to listen to what someone else has to say and even allow themselves to be influenced by it, providing what is said is something they can also use to their own benefit. In other words, a fair deal.

The second important aspect of territoriality in the public arena is the *sphere of action*. Again, let's start with a definition. The sphere of action is the domain or area in which you are active and in which you feel entitled to act, use your expertise, make decisions, take responsibility and exercise control. In an organisation, this is your job, the thing that you are good at, the thing where you are in charge, at least up to a certain point. Part of this arrangement is usually formalised within a job description, but the most important part relates to the extent to which you regard the tasks involved as being 'yours'.

This is what makes micro-management so onerous for junior employees. We have all met managers who insist on determining both the 'what' and the 'how' of every job, right down to the finest detail, and then monitor the implementation at close range. Managers of this kind leave almost no room within their employees' sphere of action for independent thought and initiative. If this persists, the only solution for the employees is to mentally switch off, which is clearly in no-one's interest. Perhaps they will continue to do their jobs, allowing the interference of their managers to flow over them like water off a duck's back, but their heart will no longer be in it. As a result, they will seek new spheres of action, often away from their work, which offer them sufficient autonomy to make them feel happy and appreciated.

This was the kind of problem faced by Alan. He was the director of a state-run agency and had responsibility for four different departments. He wanted to be able to use his people more flexibly, so that an official working in department A could easily be seconded to work on a project in department B, C or D. This would significantly increase overall effectiveness.

The only real problem was the attitude of one of Alan's heads of department. Chris was willing to cooperate with the integration plan, but only if everything that one of his people did in another department or everything that someone from another department did in his department was routed through him, so that he could give his prior approval. Alan could see that this simply would not work. Such an unnecessary level of control would take up so much time that it would form a bottleneck in the whole system. To solve the problem, Alan decided to take his heads of department and their deputies for a weekend in the country. After a detailed consultation session, he dealt with the situation as follows:

1 As a management team, he explained, we are currently losing too much impact because our different departments are working as separate silos.
2 There is much to be gained by making it possible for staff to be employed flexibly across departmental boundaries.
3 This means that the employees seconded in this manner must be able to make their contributions independently. It was at this point that Chris said: 'No, there must be a proper mechanism of control.' He could already see the risk that his personal territory might be significantly reduced in size.
4 Alan let other members of the group respond to Chris's intervention, so that the group pressure on Chris gradually built up.
5 When he judged that this pressure was great enough, Alan proposed a compromise solution: there would be no control mechanisms, but instead he would introduce an inter-departmental notification procedure, which would make clear what percentage of his time an official spent working on projects in other departments and what exactly he was doing there.

This was an elegant solution: the sphere of action of the individual officials was expanded, which benefited the organisation as a whole, while Chris's sphere of action was still kept sufficiently large to avoid any loss of face. Result: everyone happy.

Spheres of action are just like any other form of territory: people will fight to defend them. Nobody likes to have their autonomy restricted in an area they regard as being 'theirs'. This is one of the main causes of difficulty in project work. As a project leader, you will inevitably find yourself impinging on the territories of others, often several at a time! The key to success consists of allowing these others to experience your 'interest' in their domain as something that actually strengthens their autonomy, rather than weakening it. How can you do this? That is what the rest of this book is about.

Additional comment 1

The smaller the sphere of action, the more fiercely it will be defended.

Once upon a time, there was a conference centre. A renovated castle. Delegates were received in style and were served refreshments during the coffee breaks by middle-aged waiters dressed in dinner jackets and white gloves. The only thing that these gentlemen needed to do was to pour coffee out of a pot and into the cups. Even so, they did their best to ensure that it was done in exactly the right way at exactly the right time.

One day, the waiters were extremely offended when the delegates – perhaps as a gesture of help or perhaps to speed up proceedings – decided to pour their own coffee before the waiters arrived. In fact, their displeasure went so far that the centre's manager (to his credit) sent a formal letter to the customer who had organised the conference, requesting that in future his delegates should show proper respect to the ability of his catering personnel!

Additional comment 2

The sphere of action consists exclusively of tasks that the person concerned has freely chosen to accept.

Attempting to impose a sphere of action on someone, who is therefore unable to feel ownership for the tasks involved, never works. As a former president of the World Bank once said: 'In the whole of recorded history, there is no single example of anyone who ever washed a rental car!' Anyone who works with procedures knows this principle to be true: even if the procedures deal with important matters like personal security or business integrity, successful compliance with the procedures in the long term is only possible on the basis of the personal commitment of those concerned. The feeling of autonomy is crucial in this respect. The freedom to choose whether or not to accept a task is a necessary prerequisite before that task can become a part of a person's territory. We will see later how best to deal with this important dynamic.

4 THERE ARE GOOD REASONS FOR TERRITORIAL BEHAVIOUR

People are busy with their territory all day long. Like Peter. He wakes up each morning in his bed (or at least on his side of the bed). Because he is concerned about *his* physical condition, he does his daily exercises before eating his breakfast. A glance at his watch tells him that it is time to set off to work, so he drives in his car through his home town to arrive at his office. During the morning meeting, he presents his new sales strategy and answers the questions of his colleagues and his management. At the end of the day, he drives home to his family and watches *his* favourite programme with *his* wife on television, explaining to her in passing *his* views on the current political situation in America. At 11 o'clock, he climbs the stairs, cleans *his* teeth and slides once again under the sheets on *his* side of the bed. Throughout the entire day, he has made a distinction between what is *his* and what belongs to others.[9]

It is staggering how much energy we invest in our territory. We would not do this without good reason. Fortunately, there are reasons a-plenty – the most important of which are identity, security and freedom. And let's face it: reasons don't come much more important than that!

Identity

Who we are is the result of a balancing act. Everyone wants to be a unique person. A special someone, different from everybody else, the possessor of an inalienable individuality. At the same time, we need a social identity. We want to be accepted by others, to be part of a group, more than just an isolated unit. Both these motivations are constantly at work, interacting with each other.

Identity is very important to us, because it ensures that our behaviour displays coherence, both for ourselves and for others. It would be difficult to live with the notion that our behaviour, our ideas and our values could fluctuate from minute to minute without us having any real control over the situation. A degree of flexibility? That's fine. But total chaos? No, thank you. This is where our sense of identity can help us. It brings a degree of order to the confusion of life and, above all, makes us aware that we are the masters of what we think and do. This realisation brings with it a huge benefit: predictability. It allows us to set a clear course – and this is reassuring, not only for ourselves but also for our environment. When our behaviour is (up to a point) predictable, this reduces uncertainty about our person and makes possible the growth of trust. Trust in ourselves, trust in others, and trust in others for us. In this way, people can enter into secure relationships, which helps us to meet our need to belong. In short, it gives us a social identity.

Viewed in these terms, it is hardly surprising that the various classification systems for defining human character are so in vogue, not only in the popular press but also in the professional literature. We want to know who we are and we are happy if the system we use for finding out is not too complex or nuanced. In fact, the clearer, the better. A handful of labels is sufficient for our purposes. We are extravert or introvert, red or blue, Gemini or Taurus. Academics can turn their nose up at this kind of simplistic analysis, but the fact that these easy-to-understand models continue to be so popular shows that they meet a real need: the need to get a grip on what makes people tick, what makes them behave the way they do. This is the only way to make something highly complex more manageable and more predictable. Or that, at least, is the feeling it gives us.

This attempt to frame people within a set of typologies can have some interesting side effects. As soon as we identify ourselves with a label, we allow ourselves to behave in the manner the label suggests, which at the same time conveniently absolves us from other forms of behaviour ('I'm an introvert, so don't expect me to say a lot during the meeting'). In this way, we confirm the content of the label. What's more, people from our environment will behave towards us in a certain way to reflect this, providing the label with yet further confirmation ('Don't ask him to go to the meeting; he's an introvert'). As a result, the label becomes a self-fulfilling prophecy. And, of course, this is also how others behave towards us.

You have probably heard of the Pygmalion effect: we behave towards others in accordance with the image we have of them, so that we unconsciously confirm that image. If I 'know' that some of my team are not particularly well motivated and if I receive crucial information that I don't have time to share with all my team members before an important meeting, there is a strong likelihood that I will only inform those who I believe are well-motivated and will not tell the others. Naturally, these others will then feel pushed to one side and will become even less motivated – but I 'knew' that already.

In this way, without realising it, I have triggered in them behaviour that conforms to the image I had of them in advance. And what is the (unintended) purpose of this action on my part? To create a sense of predictability and continuity, which in turn provides a feeling of control. This latter aspect is not unimportant, because it contributes to the feeling known by psychologists as self-efficacy. This is the feeling that allows us to believe, in a particular context, that we are able to bring the tasks allocated to us to a successful conclusion. There is a huge difference between having this feeling and not having it. If we are convinced that we can do something successfully, this increases the actual chances of success by 28 percent. And that is just one of the effects.[10]

If we regard something as belonging to our territory, we are quick to identify with it. We become someone by doing something, by having our own ideas about things and by discovering things (have you ever noticed how conversations often go like this: 'And then *she* said this and that, but *I* said...' or 'Ah yes, *I* said, but *I* think that...'). These are all ways to build up our identity, allowing us to construct the feeling that we are unique and therefore valuable enough to be valued and accepted by others.

This is the second aspect of identity: social identity. As mammals, we humans live in groups. This offered huge advantages during our evolutionary development: hunting in groups provided more food, defending in groups kept the big, bad world at bay, cooperating in groups improved chances of survival, especially in times of hardship. All these things are built into our genes. It is therefore important for us to belong to a group and to demonstrate this desire to others. In fact, it is so important that we are sometimes prepared to surrender part of our individual identity to achieve it. We support our favourite football team dressed in the club colours; we follow the dress code at work; we go to family gatherings with the obligatory present, which is not too big and not too small, so that we don't look out of place. And in all these contexts, we enjoy conversing with the other members of our group in a way that denigrates the members of other groups: how disgusting the rival team's purple kit is (although it matches the appalling way they play the game); how short-sighted the strategy of your main business competitor is (although what can you expect from the kind of people they employ?); how much better your side of the family is ('My in-laws are terrible snobs – but don't tell my wife I said that!').

This creates a new field of tension: by definition having an identity means that you are different from others. Whenever there is an 'us'; there is also inevitably a 'them'. And the more 'we' feel threatened, the more 'they' will become the focus for our suspicion and displeasure. At least, that is what will happen unless you make a serious effort to move beyond 'us' and 'them' to create a common territory or, failing that, a situation of respectful co-existence. Exactly how you can do this is something else we will be looking at later in the book. The field of tension most likely to affect your projects is the territorial rivalry that exists between different teams and departments. They each have their own identity, each insist on doing their own thing and each expect that their ownership will be respected.

A feeling of security

Like the entire financial sector, banks and insurance companies have seen a major switch towards greater automation and digitalisation in recent years. The impact has been most strongly felt on the branch office networks and has particularly affected the staff who in the past used to serve as cashiers.

But sometimes it is the technical staff who are also affected. In one bank, the management's desire for more far-reaching automation caused a veritable earthquake of discontent in their IT department. It was decided to change the bank's operating systems by buying in existing IT packages from outside, as a result of which the jobs of the bank's own software programmers would lose much of their technical content, effectively reducing them to a role as support and maintenance engineers for the new programmes. Most of the programmers had already worked for more than 15 years in IT and suddenly saw the source of their job satisfaction being threatened. The project leader charged with implementing this change met with huge resistance and a lack of understanding from his colleagues. Information sessions explaining the need for the change helped little. Why? Because as far as the technical staff were concerned, something essential was being jeopardised: their professional identity. In other words, who they were as professionals, the reason why they were worth the wages the bank paid them, their professional pride and their feeling that they were able to create something good that worked effectively, something that benefited business and the bank as a whole. Just as importantly, this was also an identity that (rightly) brought them considerable prestige beyond the banking world.

If you operate within your own territory, you are on familiar ground. This might be a physical environment like your office, or your trusted colleagues, or your field of expertise, or your favourite music in your earphones, or even your own secret fantasy world. It is always a place where you can relax and feel comfortable, because you are in total control. You don't need to feel on your guard. There are no surprises. You can see everything and are master of the situation. If something changes, it is because you want it to change. This is your 'home front', where you can lick your wounds and recharge your batteries. You know that it is always there for you and (hopefully) always will be, providing cover for your back in difficult times. It is a constant source of solace and reassurance that is yours without ever really needing to make any great effort. In short, it is the much despised but oh-so essential 'comfort zone'.

Have you ever heard of Harlow's experiments with apes? Perhaps not; it was way back in the 1950s when he conducted them.[11] But they still have some interesting lessons to teach. What did he do exactly? He made two artificial ape mothers. The first was made from rough wire. The second was precisely the same, but the wire was covered with a soft fabric.

However, there was one other important difference: the wire mother was fitted with a milk bottle; the fabric mother was not.

Step 1. Question: which of the two mothers is most likely to attract a baby ape? The soft and cuddly fabric mother, of course. The wire mother was only approached when the baby was hungry and even then only temporarily. Once the milk bottle was empty, it was straight back to soft and cuddly mum before you could say Jack Robinson.

Step 2. Harlow built a monster in one of his experimental spaces: an ogre complete with huge eyes, a working jaw full of sharp teeth, flailing arms and an ear-piercing howl. He placed the baby ape next to this monster. Not surprisingly, the baby reacted with panic. Not to worry: fabric mum was also in the same space, so that baby ran over and clung to her for dear life, hardly daring to look around at the monster for more than a minute. But once that minute was past, and although still holding on tight to soft mum, the baby gradually began to show interest in the monster.

Step 3. The baby ape is now placed in a space full of strange objects. If there is no soft mother in the space, the baby looks around in confusion, before eventually laying down on the ground. End of story. But if there is a soft mum present, the baby first pays her a brief visit and then goes exploring amongst the objects, repeating this process at fairly regular intervals until the exploration is complete.

Like the baby ape, we all need a soft mum, a place where we feel comfortable and safe. Not just physically, but also in our head. And the more turbulent things are, the greater this need becomes. Turbulence means unpredictability and the possibility of losing control. If we no longer have a focus of calm to compensate for this, there is a risk that two things will happen: first, we will end up exhausting ourselves with worry; second, we will fail to make use of the opportunities that every period of turbulence creates (or as Hillary Clinton once said: 'Never waste a good crisis').

This offers some interesting perspectives for project managers. If the changes involved in the project you are running threaten to undermine many of the certainties (foci of calm) of some of your stakeholders, you need to offer them something in return that they can hold on to. Often, it is enough to give them plenty of information at a previously agreed set of times via a previously agreed set of channels, so that the level of predictability can be kept as high – and as comforting – as possible.

What should you communicate? Almost everything. Certainly why the change is necessary, but also the 'what' and the 'how'. How will things change for them? What will the new structure look like? What steps will be taken to implement the change? When and in what order? How will colleagues be trained to deal with the new situation? How will the evolution of this new situation be monitored? How (and by whom) will their questions be answered? And so on...

How much should you communicate? Much more than is strictly necessary. Everything seven times (as in the Bible) is a good rule of thumb. If you want people to approach the new situation positively, you need to give them sufficient security and confidence in what you are planning. And the more these plans impact on their familiar certainties, the greater this need becomes (like the IT-ers in the bank we mentioned above).

The social identity that territories can provide meets our human need to feel connected with others.

But in addition to connectedness, autonomy is also another essential source of internal motivation,[12] because it answers another universal human need: the need to feel that we have a grip on our own situation. This is probably the most important factor in creating a sense of self-esteem.

An international production company is faced with a massive safety problem. There have been 26 fatal accidents at work in the past three years, a situation that clearly cannot be allowed to continue. But what to do? The management introduces a number of corrective measures, one of which is the worldwide roll-out of a new health and safety training programme. Everyone in the company – many thousands of people, from senior managers right down to the office cleaners – will be required to follow the programme. Organising this programme will need a strong project manager and the company's choice falls on Rick, an Australian who has earned his spurs in 'compliance' (the strict implementation at company level of existing legislation in matters such as, for example, environmental protection). There is often very little room for manoeuvre with compliance: you either comply with the law or you don't. Things tend to be black and white, not grey.

Assisted by a consultancy bureau, Rick designs a training programme, including a train-the-trainer trajectory, because the intention is that the programme will be rolled out in the same manner in every country where the company operates. Viewing things from his compliance perspective, he can all too easily imagine that different countries will want to do things in different ways – and this is what he wants to avoid. Unfortunately, what Rick fails to recognise is that this programme revolves around changing people's attitudes and behaviour toward safety, which are both things that cannot be imposed. Change of this kind has to come from within. People must want it for themselves. You can't really blame Rick for failing to understand this. After all, he is a jurist, not a psychologist, and he is under huge pressure to complete the implementation of the programme within a year.

Much of what Rick does is good. No-one disputes the usefulness of the programme, because the facts – 26 deaths in three years – speak for themselves. Likewise, the proposed content of the programme is met without too many frowns and raised eyebrows. But the real problem is that there is no flexibility to maximise the return on the training by adjusting it to reflect local cultural conditions and working practices. This is a point where Rick leaves no room for manoeuvre: for him, it is 'My way or the highway'. As far as he is concerned, local freedom to judge and to act is out of the question. Unfortunately, in this way he also removes one of the essential territorial building blocks that is crucial for success in every country: autonomy.

The result is as you might expect. Some countries pretend to play the game and report to the project office that the programme has been implemented as instructed, but actually do things their own way (it is a long way between Brazil and Australia, and the likelihood of anyone coming over to check is small). Others resist the instructions and try to win support for their position from the company's senior management. Perhaps inevitably, this confusing situation eventually costs Rick his job, even though there is still a lot at stake for the company (human lives) and notwithstanding the fact that the hard-working and enthusiastic Rick has acted with the best of intentions. But one thing is certain: if you flagrantly impinge upon the territory of your local colleagues, who are just as committed as you are but who know the local situation and their people so much better, you are unlikely ever to be able to realise your plans, no matter how high the stakes are. Ninety-nine times out of a hundred a mentality that says 'That's the way it is and that's the way it will stay because that's the way I want it' is a recipe for disaster.

There is an important point that needs to be emphasised here: in a work context freedom does not mean that you can do whatever you want just because you want it or because you want to give free expression to all your whims and wishes. Every project is subject to limits and boundaries of some kind. Sometimes these are easy to objectify and justify. Budgetary restraints are a good example. Freedom then means that you accept these limitations, because you can see their purpose and validity. Deciding to support these limitations is a decision that you are free to take. In other words, it is a decision in which you can exercise your autonomy.

The fundamental importance of freedom and autonomy and the willingness of people to defend the territories that guarantee them these values have been demonstrated by the world's psychologists time after time. One of the most influential set of experiments in this respect was conducted by Martin Seligman of the University of Pennsylvania[13] – although if he wanted to conduct similar experiments today, he would need to find a different way of doing it and one that involved significant less cruelty to animals (sensitive readers have been warned).

So what exactly did Seligman do? Imagine a steel cage separated into two sections by a partition wall. This wall does not reach to the top of the cage, but forms a serious barrier for getting from one side to the other. The floor on one side is made from metal. The floor on the other side is made from wood (a non-conductive material). It was in this setting that Seligman carried out four different tests.

In test 1, he put a rat on the metal floor, through which he passed a series of electric shocks, varying in intensity, interval and duration. In other words, the shocks were unpredictable. Of course, they were also painful, as a result of which the rat attempted to escape from them by jumping up from the floor. Eventually, one of these jumps took the rat by chance over the barrier and onto the wooden floor, where the shocks ceased. The rat was then returned to the steel floor and the process was repeated. The shocks were inflicted and the rat jumped to avoid them, but this time the animal found its way more quickly to the safety of the wood-floored compartment. After the same process was repeated several times, the rat knew immediately what to do: even before the shocks started, it jumped deliberately over the barrier. It had learnt how to take its fate into its own hands.

Test 2 was even more unpleasant (both for the rat and for modern sensibilities). This time, the entire floor was made of metal and the barrier had been removed. The rat was again subjected to a series of unpredictable electrical shocks and again jumped to avoid them. This time, however, the poor animal eventually discovered that there was no escape from the pain, no matter how hard it tried. As a result, it simply crawled into a corner of the cage and allowed itself to be further inflicted with shocks. Seligman referred to this condition as 'learned helplessness': the rat has discovered that its fate is no longer in its own hands and understands that any further effort on its part to escape is futile. It accepts the inevitable.

Test 3 involved two distinct phases. During the first phase, Seligman again induced learned helplessness in the rat. Having achieved this, he then introduced a potential means of escape by reinstalling the barrier and the wooden floor. To begin with, the rat simply continued to lie in its corner, accepting the electric shocks. Seligman then moved it to the other 'safe' side of the barrier to allow it to briefly recuperate, before returning it to the metal floor and the shocks. Would the rat now realise that there was a means of escape and start jumping at the barrier? Not at first: it crept back into its corner and accepted the bolts of pain as before. Eventually, however, after Seligman had repeated this process many, many times, the animal finally began to realise that it had a way out and eventually jumped to safety. But it took a long, long time for it to shake off its learned helplessness and become aware that it was once again in control of its own welfare.

Test 4 reversed the order of test 3. The rat was first taught how to escape and only then reduced to a state of learned helplessness. What would happen if it was then returned to the cage where the escape option was available? This time the learning process was a quick one: the rat jumped over the barrier to safety in a flash – demonstrating that the rat's (or, by extension, a person's) original condition (learned helplessness or not) has an important influence on the response to a given situation later on.

In the margin, it is worth noting that this last point suggests the importance of people's first work experience. When you start your first job, you arrive in a context in which you are susceptible to many different influences. If, right from the very beginning, your willingness to show initiative is encouraged and rewarded, this will have a positive impact on your belief in your own ability and on your job satisfaction in the long term. If, on the other hand, your first work experience involves you slavishly doing what other say you have got to do, this will have a correspondingly negative effect.

Of course, psychologists have not only carried out experiments of the Seligman variety on animals but also on human guinea pigs – although thankfully without the electric shocks!

One of the most well-known of these experiments was conducted on children. Most children like to solve puzzles, until the moment arrives when the puzzles are deliberately made too difficult for them to solve. No matter what they do, no matter how hard they try, they just can't make the puzzle work. In short, their efforts bring no result and so a mini-version of learned helplessness sets in. But there is more to it than that. Not only do the children lose interest, but their level of intellectual ability falls dramatically from the level of the fourth grade of primary education (their actual age) to the level of nursery school children. To make matters worse, it remains that way for some time (although fortunately not for too long!).[14]

An experiment carried out by Yale University on an elderly population of test subjects produced equally startling results.[15] The researchers selected two roughly comparable groups from among the residents of a retirement home. Both groups were treated well and both were systematically provided with a series of pleasant surprises: an extra special breakfast, a visit to the movies, flowers in their room, etc. The only difference was that one group had to accept what the researchers offered, whereas the second group was allowed an element of choice: what kind of breakfast, which film, what flowers.

Both groups were followed for a period of 18 months. It was established that by the end of the experiment the group with the choice was significantly more active and happier than the other group. More importantly, more of them were still alive! The human desire for freedom and autonomy is not a marginal phenomenon.

If territories can provide people with feelings of self-esteem, security and a belief that their fate is in their own hands, is it any wonder that they are marked 'Keep out!' and are defended tooth and nail by their guardians? With so much at stake, would you be any different? Honestly?

5 THERE ARE DIFFERENT KINDS OF TERRITORIAL BEHAVIOUR

Territorial behaviour falls into three different categories: (1) extending; (2) marking; (3) defending.

1 Extending

Territorial behaviour often has a bad press, because it is associated in the popular mind with actions that we seldom find pleasant, not in ourselves and certainly not in others. The marking of a territory and its defence are often seen as negative actions. They exude negative energy. The need to defend ourselves is already unpleasant enough, but if others start to behave defensively towards us, then the fat really is in the fire, because there is a possibility that our own autonomy will be restricted. If they say 'Keep off our patch!', this means that we are no longer able to go where we please. This leads to frustration, which in turn encourages a first form of territorial behaviour: the strong desire we all have to extend the boundaries of our own territory.

Back to basics: a territory is something we regard as our property (material or otherwise), in which we feel safe in our freedom and autonomy. It is our most valuable possession and motivation, so much so that it is almost impossible to imagine that we should not wish to extend it as often and as far as we can. How otherwise would we have been able to learn things in childhood and beyond? How would we have been able to develop our interest in our hobbies? In the past, what would have driven explorers to discover the world? What drives us today to go on Facebook, pursue a career, build a house?

Without our human need to continually explore new territories, there would be no innovation, no progress and no civilisation. The existence of territories satisfies three of the fundamental criteria that lead to internal motivation and impel people to keep moving forward. We have already discussed the first two: the need for connectedness and the need for autonomy. The third is the need for growth, the origins of which are to be found in life itself.

Because the desire to extend our territory is a powerful impulse in all of us, this inevitably creates a field of tension, since at some point our expanding territories are bound to collide. This, too, is simply a fact of life, but a fact that leads on to a question: how can we best order this field of tension and make use of its strength to further our projects? This is something we will look at presently. But before we do, it makes sense to first say something more about the two other forms of territorial behaviour.

2 Marking

Martha was leading a fusion trajectory for the Belgian and Dutch divisions of a chemical company. The systems and technologies of both divisions had already been adjusted and amalgamated successfully. Martha's task was to assist with the creation of a common culture. With this in mind, a leadership integration programme was started up.

All the leaders in both divisions were brought together in groups, so that they could get to know each other better. The idea was that this would help them to develop a common language and common forms that would give structure to the new company entity. The process was progressing remarkably well. Initial scepticism had been replaced by growing enthusiasm. Three months after the start of the trajectory, part of the quarterly board meeting was devoted to a first status report. As project leader, Martha was obviously invited to attend. The directors of the different departments explained how the fusion was being experienced by their staff and what expectations they had for the subsequent phases. This was followed by a lively exchange of views, during which Martha momentarily forgot her consultancy role and offered one of the directors the floor, so that he could further express his interesting ideas. Less than a second later she was interrupted by the CEO, who, courteous as he was, pointed out that it was *him* – not her – who was running the meeting. In this way, the territory was marked. He had made clear their respective positions in a manner that left no-one in doubt about who was the alpha male in this particular 'herd'. This is the purpose of marking: to set flags around the boundary of your domain.

There are many ways to do this. Some of them are very familiar. Every day we all receive mails with a digital signature at the bottom. If you read 'Dr. Francis Jones, Head of the Maintenance Department', you are immediately warned that 'Maintenance is my domain, where I'm in charge' and 'Don't try getting smart with me: I'm the one who's a doctor!'

Marking makes evident to the outside world precisely what belongs to you and what makes you so different from everyone else. However, the process is underpinned by our need to see ourselves as unique beings. It is a reflection of our natural desire to strengthen our feeling of self-esteem. Sometimes, however, this can find its expression in interesting and even amusing ways. It is often the case that some people need to additionally emphasise their formal ownership, depending on the extent to which they feel uncertain about it. At the other extreme, some people's ownership is so self-evident that they have no need for formal declarations of intent. Have you ever noticed how many people high up in organisations generally make less use of formal titles than those, say, in middle management? Like the rest of us, these top dogs still like to confirm their individuality – this is a universal impulse – but they do it in other ways.

When people know their position in the power pecking order, there is no need to advertise it too strenuously. It will become obvious through their presence at crucial meetings (but not at irrelevant ones), the relationships they have with key stakeholders and, above all, by the fact that they are approached differently than their more average colleagues. Okay, sometimes they will also have the biggest car in the car park and an office with a view on the top floor: after all, they are only human! We will explore these and other manifestations of power in a later chapter.

It often happens that territories are not marked with a flashy display of titles and personal characteristics, but are functionally marked instead. This involves the marking out of the area over which you think you have control.

A colleague once told me how his department was responsible for invoicing a major telecom company. As is often the case, a work order was drawn up for the declarable hours and expenses, based on the contract in which everything had been neatly set out. In practice, however, this seemingly simple procedure involves a number of different parties. There is the authorising officer, the purchasing department responsible for the contract and the finance department responsible for making the necessary calculations and payment – to name but three.

The settlement of the first invoice seemed to drag on for ages. Enquiries with the finance department got no further than a curt 'We're dealing with it'. It was only a month and a half later that it became clear what was going on. The authorising official has refused to sign off the invoice because he had recalculated the travel distances involved and discovered that my colleague had invoiced twelve and a half kilometres *too few*! This is the kind of infuriating micro-management we mentioned earlier on: a manager who wishes to make his mark by checking every document in advance and every claim in arrears, right down to the last word and euro cent.

By delaying payment of the invoice in this way, he wanted to make clear in a very tangible way that he was the person who checked and monitored everything. This was *his* responsibility. When my colleague later enquired through informal channels what was actually happening here, things became a little more understandable. The department of the authorising official was currently in the middle of a reorganisation and there was a great deal of uncertainty about the future roles that people would play. In this kind of situation, it is not so surprising that people stake their claims for their own territory, not only to signal this to the outside world, but also to give them something to cling onto. And the greater the uncertainty, the more likely you

are to come across this type of behaviour. In this particular case, the consequences were not too dramatic.

Sometimes, however, things can turn out much worse. The IT department
of an insurance company was right in the middle of a major change process.
There was a chance that a number of functions would disappear. Some staff
tried to safeguard their jobs by not revealing certain information in their
possession. By holding on to this information, they could ensure that many
of the most crucial procedures had to be routed through them, which slowed
down the operation of the entire organisation. It goes without saying that
this did nothing to safeguard their position – quite the reverse – and actually risked doing serious harm to the company, as a result of which everyone
would lose out.

Let's be clear on this point: there is nothing wrong with marking your territory. It creates clarity, which in turn creates calm. What's more, the clear delin-
eation of 'who owns what' can help to avoid unnecessary conflicts: everyone
knows precisely where they can tread and where they can't. This is the value
of having clear function and role descriptions in all your projects.

To round off this section, here is an interesting – and not wholly irrelevant –
anecdote from the world of nature. Seagull colonies are generally highly
populated. Not a problem, you might think, were it not for the fact that seagulls have the unfortunate habit of eating each other's eggs. Not surprisingly,
mummy seagulls are not happy with this and don't just sit around waiting for
it to happen. They are ready and willing to fight to protect their eggs. However, this demands the use of a lot of extra energy, which they then can't use to
build their nests or go in search of food. To help avoid this unnecessary waste
of energy, they have developed a series of five calls that must dissuade their
hungry colleagues from gobbling up their eggs. The calls range from something like 'Watch out, pal! This is my nest' to 'If you don't stop now, you're
going to get my beak right up your backside!'

Something similar happens with wolves. Each pack marks the boundaries
of its territory with scent. Other wolves can smell this and, as a rule, do not
encroach. Once again, the idea is to avoid territorial conflict, so that energy
can be saved for the more important task of hunting.

One of the reasons for marking your territory is to avoid conflict. In other words, it serves a preventative function. On the other hand, we have already seen that people also have a strong urge to expand their territory. This means that border conflicts frequently cannot be avoided. When this occurs, your territory is in danger and needs to be defended. This generally happens in two distinct phases. First there is a warning to stay away. Then there is the actual conflict, if the warning does not work. Just like the seagulls.

In the first instance, the intensity with which a territory is defended will depend on an assessment of the invader's intentions.

Linda is an excellent and extremely dedicated office coordinator. One of her many tasks is to welcome guests. Sometimes these guests are individuals; sometimes they come in groups. You can count on Linda to treat them like royalty, right down to the smallest of details. No-one could do it better.

Fred was a new trainee in the same office. He was bursting with energy and enthusiasm, anxious to help and keen to learn. On his first day, he noticed that the chairs in the meeting room had not been put back properly and so he straightened them up. Nothing wrong with that, you might think – except for the fact that this was Linda's territory. Of course, she soon noticed. When she had a chance to speak to him alone, she went up to Fred and told him with a smile and a wink: 'Fred, the way the office looks is my task. Just so you know.' No more than that. She recognised that there were no bad intentions behind Fred's action and that he could hardly be expected to know everything on his first day. Even so: 'Good agreements make good friends.'

If a territory is threatened or invaded, it is vitally important to react immediately, while the problem is still manageable. At this stage, the reaction is unlikely to be emotionally charged, so that it is possible to agree how to resolve the situation. However, the longer you wait before reacting, the longer you will feel irritated and the more emotional your eventual reaction will become. If you let things go this far, your reaction will be purely defensive, made from a position of weakness rather than strength. This results in a kind of self-fulfilling prophecy. If you show weakness, you can expect a swift and sharp counterattack. In other words, full scale war. When this happens, both sides risk losing. Why? Because the other person does not react to the content of your message, but to its emotionality. This makes it harder to find a solution that can satisfy you both.

With this is mind, we will now look at what expensive consultants call 'expectation management'. This is another domain where speed is recommended, both to mark your territory and defend it.

This was where Harry went wrong. He had been invited to a meeting by one of his internal clients, who said he wanted Harry to do something for him. Helpful as he was, Harry went along to the meeting to see what his client expected of him. It turned out to be quite a lot. He was asked to develop a new system that would do a thousand and one different things, but with a budget and within a time frame that were both extremely tight. Harry knew instantly that this was an impossible task and he should have said so immediately. But he didn't. His desire to be helpful – his service orientation, if you like – held him back. Two months later, the client sent an angry letter to Harry's manager, expressing his disappointment that Harry had failed to honour his commitment. 'Commitment? What commitment?!' said Harry. 'I committed myself to nothing. He knew as well as I did that what he was asking was totally unrealistic.' Which was true, of course. But no longer relevant.

So what happened here? From within his own territorial position, the internal client gives Harry a task. If Harry fails to immediately set his own boundaries, the client assumes that Harry is now part of his territory. This means that he – the client – believes that he is now the owner of the task he has set Harry. When it later becomes clear that Harry has not completed the task as the client expected, this is interpreted as a violation of his territory, which is something the client cannot allow to pass unpunished. Hence the angry mail. Harry had neglected to immediately mark his own territory – and now he paid the price.

There are countless ways to defend your territory in a professional environment. Most of them are not consciously planned. You do not sit behind your desk to devise your defence 'strategy'. Your defensive response is nearly always intuitive and spontaneous. The specific form will vary from person to person and situation to situation. What has worked for you in the past? What have you seen work for other people? It is useful to be able to read the defensive behaviour of others, so that you can assess how best to deal with it. The following summary might help you. You are not looking for one-off reactions, but for tactics that your stakeholders regularly use.

Put a cross in the relevant box when you regularly see a stakeholder use one of the following gambits.

		Stakeholder 1	Stakeholder 2	Stakeholder 3	Stakeholder 4
1	He is the only channel for important information.				
2	He uses faits accomplis to make decisions in advance, so that others are pushed onto the defensive.				
3	He talks or writes about a subject frequently, so that he can absorb it into his territory.				
4	He keeps his good staff out of the spotlight, so that there is little chance they will headhunted by other departments.				
5	He wants to take all crucial decisions on his own.				
6	Rivals are given no access to information.				
7	He keeps problems to himself, to avoid the need for others to help him.				
8	To support his extravagant claims, he uses a lot of data that is difficult to check.				
9	He frequently drops the names of key authority figures.				
10	He frequently puts authority figures in cc.				
11	He frequently refers to external authorities that confirm his point of view.				
12	He has frequent face-to-face contact with senior management.				
13	He monopolises communication with key internal and external figures by failing to put his colleagues in cc.				
14	He abides by the rules so strictly that it is impossible to work with him.				

15	He fails to provide the things that other people need to be successful or makes sure that they are delivered late.				
16	He repeatedly offers to help others, but then does nothing.				
17	He says that he would like to cooperate, but that 'they' (authority figures) are holding him back.				
18	He often finds excuses not to be present at crucial decision-making moments.				
19	He brands newcomers and consultants as lacking in relevant knowledge.				
20	He ignores people, even though they are involved in the projects he is working on.				
21	He uses highly complex jargon, so that others feel inferior and stupid.				
22	He attacks people in areas that have nothing to do with his projects, so that the credibility of those people is corroded.				

Whenever you are confronted with defensive stakeholders or with conflicts, you need to be aware that their defensiveness is nearly always caused by their uncertainty. The most promising route to a solution is therefore to make this uncertainty discussable, so that you can search together to see what can be done to resolve the situation. Chapter 7 will outline a good methodology to make this possible.

Avoiding the unnecessary waste of energy

You can also avoid lots of potential conflicts by agreeing explicitly and in advance the basic parameters of your collaboration with others. You can use the following model for this purpose. It is simple, but very robust.[16]

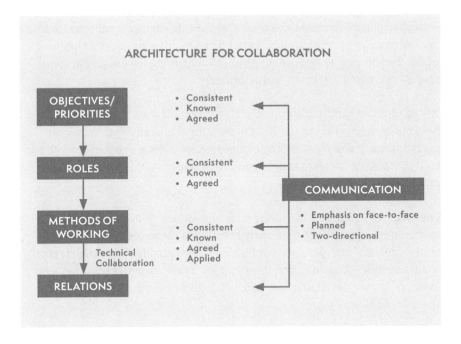

The first element about which all those involved need to agree is the objectives of their common task. Each area of attention is important. The objectives must be clear and accepted by everyone. Everyone also needs to see how these objectives fit within the wider picture of the organisational strategy as a whole.

In addition to objectives, priorities also need to be clearly formulated. What is the order of importance for these priorities and what are the reasons for this order? Again, absolute clarity and acceptance by all is essential. Sometimes, it is not only necessary to say what the task includes, but also what it does not include, and why.

The nature of the objectives will define the nature of the roles. There needs to be an obvious and logical connection between both elements. Who will do what and what are the underlying expectations? Full transparency and universal acceptance continue to be crucial. This can relate to individual roles or to the roles of specific groups. In larger projects, the respective roles of the project group and the steering group must be clearly delineated.

The allocation of roles is closely related to the allocation of resources. Expectations can only be met if resources are adequate and correctly assigned. As with all the other elements, the reasoning for this allocation must be clearly understood and unanimously accepted. The key criterion is the extent to which the role and its associated resources contribute towards the achievement of the stated objectives and priorities.

It is against this same background of objectives and roles that agreement also needs to be reached about methods of working. This can relate to specific procedures, but equally to more general processes (How will decisions be taken? How will the collaboration be given concrete form? How and when will reports on progress be made?).

The final element deals with interpersonal relations. When there is clarity and acceptance for all the previously mentioned elements, many of the potential causes of interpersonal conflict are automatically eliminated. It is only when people are known to find it very difficult to work with each other – for example, because of an existing personal dislike – that this aspect requires special attention.

When dealing with this model, it is vital that you do so hierarchically. This means that each element must be defined in relation to the previous element. In practical terms, this also means that when you experience problems in one domain, it is often worthwhile to search for the causes in the preceding domain. Imagine, for example, that you are having problems relating to your agreed operational arrangements (which are situated at the level of working methods). There is often an immediate tendency to try and solve the problem within the domain in which it occurs. In this case, that would lead to the clear and unambiguous repetition of the procedures that had been agreed. But this will have little effect if there is still a lack of clarity at the higher level of roles and expectations. Until this aspect is solved, the energy you invest in clarifying and re-clarifying of the procedures will all be wasted.

It makes sense to discuss this model (and their role within it) with all your different teams. However, you also need to be aware that work environments are subject to near-constant change. For this reason, it is important to have good communication in place for each team and each level of the model. This communication needs to be clearly structured in terms of its nature, frequency and the participants (who, what, why, when and where). Communication should for preference be face to face and on no account should it be delayed until problems arise. Plan regular time-out sessions to discuss the manner and progress of the collaboration, using the model as your framework. You should regard this as preventative maintenance for your teams.

Remember that your teams' work can also be affected by all different kinds of 'outsiders', your external stakeholders. Regularly involve the most important of these stakeholders in your preventative maintenance sessions. Check that your expectations still match theirs and ensure that everyone's combined efforts are still leading the project in the right direction. Chapter 7 will explain how you can best do this.

Additional comment

For complex projects it is often useful to describe the different roles – and therefore the different territories – in very specific terms. If you are familiar with project management, you will also be familiar with the RASCI methodology. This involves defining for your most important processes who will play what role in the decision-making. This means that for each step of the project you clearly delineate the people who are (R)esponsible (for the implementation), (A)ccountable (for the final decision-making), must give (S)upport, must be (C)onsulted and must be (I)nformed (who, when and how).

To prevent the boundaries between territories from becoming too vague, it is important that only one person is appointed for the (R) and (A) roles. If your initial project discussions reveal that this is difficult to achieve, you need to divide this process step into smaller sub-units, until the one-person solution does become feasible. People do not always like this, because in some cases clarity can also mean a limitation of their radius of action. Even so, it is necessary if you wish to avoid the possibility of imprecise boundaries leading to conflict and loss of energy later on in the project.

6 DEVELOPING A COMMON TERRITORY AS THE KEY TO SUSTAINABLE COLLABORATION

Because you never work in a vacuum, whatever you do will inevitably bring you into contact with the territories of other people. Sometimes these others are individuals; sometimes they are groups. Sometimes, you will know them personally; sometimes there are so many of them or they are so far away that it will be impossible for you to know them. But they are there all the same, each with the same territorial needs as your own: the needs to expand, mark and defend. This means that there are many potential sources of border conflict, which usually involve the use of a lot of energy with very little result.

The most elegant and productive way to deal with this situation is to build a common territory, in which everyone has his or her own area, but nonetheless feels sufficiently connected to the greater whole and is therefore prepared to invest in it. This can apply at all levels: between nations, between companies, between departments and even between individuals in the same team.

Sharing a common territory with other stakeholders implies that you feel connected with what is important to them, and vice versa. Psychologists refer to this as a shared feeling of psychological ownership. The reasons for investing time and energy in the development of this feeling have been well researched and the benefits are considerable.[17]

For example, it has been demonstrably proven that a shared feeling of psychological ownership leads to greater engagement, greater job satisfaction, a greater sense of contributing to something important, a greater sense of self-esteem and a stronger feeling of connectedness with the organisation as a whole. What's more, it also saves you a huge amount of energy, since it means you are no longer dealing with people who are indifferent or even hostile towards your project, but with fellow stakeholders who share the same common vision for success.

It goes without saying that people will always take care of themselves. 'Looking after No.1' is a natural reflex. Being prepared to invest in the general good requires an extra effort. If you look at shared ownership from a project perspective, the key question is: how can I make sure that others are prepared to put their shoulders behind my project? The answer is: not because they must, but because they want to, and preferably with whole-hearted enthusiasm. In other words, you need to find a way that will make people feel that they are co-owners of your project, so that they will actually do more on its behalf than is strictly necessary. How can you do this? The remaining chapters in this book will explain the various routes step by step.

The basic precondition for co-ownership is that there has to be a reason for it that is seen as being beneficial by everyone involved. This means that you first need to ask yourself in what ways other people's investment in your project will be rewarded with added value that is meaningful to them. And once you have the answer, you need to spell it out in very clear terms.

An example. Within a consumer goods company, a new team has been set up to deal with 'Product Stewardship', a task for which they have a worldwide responsibility. Their work involves monitoring that the materials used in the manufacturing of their products comply with all the relevant legal provisions, so that customers can rely on the quality and sustainability of those products. This is important not only for the customers but also for the company, bearing in mind the huge impact these matters can have on economic reputation and viability. If the company fails to comply with applicable legislation, this has serious economic implications: the products concerned would need to be withdrawn from the market and the damage to the company's image would probably take years to repair.

To do their work properly, the members of the team need information that must be provided by the company's many factories all around the world. For these factories, the process of gathering this information is costly and time-consuming, without it contributing directly to the realisation of their own immediate targets and objectives. In other words, the stewardship team is completely dependent on the goodwill of others. In these circumstances, their first priority is therefore: how can we persuade our overseas colleagues to cooperate in the manner we need? Once this willingness to cooperate has been indicated, the new priority then becomes: how can we make sure that they honour this commitment, in the knowledge that this conflicts with other priorities of their own, on which their performance will be judged?

From experience, the members of the Product Stewardship team know that simply appealing to the general good of the company will not have the desired effect. Their colleagues in the factories are well intentioned towards the company, but the request for information is too remote, too abstract and of too little direct concern. As a result, when the team tries to get their message across, most people nod approvingly and make the appropriate noises, but not much more than that.

If we want to galvanise people into action, we often have a tendency to rely on factual data and rationality. The assumption is that if we give people a sufficient amount of the right information, they will see the value of taking action for themselves. If only it was that easy!

Governments organise information and awareness campaigns with great regularity, in the hope of persuading their citizens to change aspects of their behaviour. This can range from road safety, to healthier eating habits, to dealing sensibly with the internet, and so on. Research suggests that the average level of real behavioural change in response to these campaigns is around 5 percent – which is not hugely encouraging.[18] That being said, if you are talking in terms of a population in millions, this 5 percent still represents a significant number of people – although in view of the huge cost of these campaigns, more would be nice. It does, however, mean that on a much smaller scale the effect is negligible. Campaigns that go no further than the provision of information make use of what the communication specialists call 'cold knowledge' – facts, figures and logical argument. Hardly surprising, then, that this fails to enthuse the masses.

So how are things at the opposite end of the spectrum? A few years ago on Belgian television, a recording made with a secret camera in a slaughterhouse was broadcast on the national evening news, to show people just how appallingly some animals were being mistreated before the final moment of their death. The cruelty was obvious and it was difficult to keep on watching. Millions of people were shocked and the effect on public opinion was palpable. This is 'hot knowledge': still based on facts, figures and reason, but with an added emotional link between the information and its recipients.

In fact, on this occasion the impact was so great and so immediate that within weeks several articles in the legislation relating to slaughterhouses had been amended in the Belgian Parliament. Such was the level of public disgust at what they had seen. Curiously enough, there were also a number of people who were disgusted by the level of disgust. They couldn't understand what all the fuss was about. Surely we all know what goes on inside a slaughterhouse? True, we all know that the purpose of a slaughterhouse is to kill animals, but you don't really know what that means until you see the images. It is this visual aspect that brings the message home and prompts people to action. And that is the difference in effect between cold and hot knowledge.

In a work context, it is difficult to find images of the 'slaughterhouse' variety to spur your colleagues into activity. And it isn't really necessary. The others involved will always ask themselves the key question: 'What's in it for me?' If you want to attract their attention and support, you need to answer that question as precisely and as invitingly as possible. To do this, you also need to ask yourself a few questions before you first discuss with them their possible contribution to the project:

'After I have given my presentation, made my proposals, laid my plans on the table, etc.:

1   What tangible benefit do *they* now have that they did not have before my intervention?
2   As a result, what will they now be able to do (knowing is not enough)?
3   What difference will that make for them?'

It is striking how seldom these questions are asked by project managers. Striking, but perhaps not surprising. The managers know their projects so well and are so convinced of their value that they assume everyone can see the same thing when this or that project is explained to them. Too many managers approach the subject exclusively from their own perspective: they know that their project is important, so its importance must be equally obvious to others. Consequently, a willingness to collaborate must automatically follow. Mustn't it? Unfortunately, that is often not the case – as the Product Stewardship team also discovered.

In order to motivate people to act, you have to make clear in a highly concrete manner what is at stake for *them*. There are two ways you can do this: (1) Make clear what they have to gain if they participate; (2) Make clear what they have to lose if they don't participate.

A number of years ago, Daniel Kahneman was awarded the Nobel Prize for Economics. Together with his colleague Amos Tversky, he made a significant contribution towards our understanding of the mechanisms that lead to economic decisions, and in particular the role that non-rational processes play in this context.[19]

One of their experiments was based on the theme of energy savings in private homes. The selected two residential areas that were comparable on the basis of a number of key criteria. In one area, they went from door to door with a list. Their message: 'If you take the measures we suggest on this list, you can be certain that you will enjoy an energy saving worth at least 350 euros year after year.' They then asked if they could record the readings on people's energy meter.

In the other area, they again went from door to door with the same list, but this time with a different message: 'If you take the measures we suggest on this list, you can be certain that you will avoid an energy loss worth at least 350 euros year after year.' Again, they asked if they could record the readings on people's meters.

After the winter, all the houses were re-visited and new meter readings were taken. This gave an objective picture of both the actual energy use and the effect of the two different messages, one promising a gain and the other promising the avoidance of a loss. Which of these messages do you think had the biggest impact on people's behaviour?

The results showed that the desire to avoid a loss was twice more powerful as a motivator than the prospect of a gain. In this context, the word 'motivator' must be taken literally, as something that moves people to take a particular course of action.

This immediately suggests a possible application in the field of project management. If you want to secure the cooperation of others, you cannot only tell them what they stand to gain by supporting your venture, but also what they risk losing if they remain reluctant to take part. Try to formulate this in terms that mean something concrete to them. A more cynical approach might involve you musing in the course of your discussions about the kind of impact your project could have on their reputation promotion, bonus, etc. The more you are able to quantify these potential gains and losses, the stronger your appeal will be. Of course, you don't need to calculate these things down to the last euro cent. A rough approximation or likely probability will usually be enough to get most people thinking.

Alternatively, it is often sufficient simply to express processes that are not working the way you would like in figures, so that they become more visible than might previously have been the case. This sudden awareness can frequently create a willingness to act. Here are a few examples.

An audit bureau with a chronic shortage of staff was finding it difficult to attract the number of new recruits it needed. This was surprising, since the number of job applications they received was actually quite high. When they examined the different steps of their recruitment process to see what the reasons for this might be, they soon discovered a number of crucial failings, all of which were related to poor communication. Things started going wrong right from the start. When a candidate submitted an application, it took far too long before the company first contacted him or her. There was not even an acknowledgement of receipt! It was the same again after they did eventually get around to sending a response: it took a further age before the candidate was invited for an interview. And if the interview was successful? You've guessed it: more weeks of delay before the good news was finally broken. By this time, the candidate had usually found work somewhere else. In the tight labour market for financial personnel, sloppy communication of this kind can be fatal. Good people simply have too many other good options. They don't need to wait.

Action to rectify this slowness only took place when the bureau took the trouble to start quantifying its communication shortcomings. How many applications did they receive? How many of these applications were converted into actual recruitments? What was the average number of days between each step in the recruitment process? How did these figures compare with their most important competitors? Once these figures were available, it soon shook the Recruitment & Selection department out of their previous complacency. They, like everyone else, could now see the need for change. New target figures were set and a strategy for reaching them developed. By making specific officials responsible for implementing the strategy and by setting a tight timeline, it was possible to achieve a rapid improvement in the situation.

Compiling statistics and setting objectives can help you a long way, but they are not always sufficient to awaken a sense of responsibility towards your project in some people, especially if you are expecting them to actively take part.

In a factory producing medicines, the management decided to set five critical result parameters for each department. Five was chosen as a maximum, to ensure that sufficient focus could be maintained. Each of the variables is measured on a weekly basis and a video screen has been installed next to the coffee corner, so that staff can examine the results at their leisure. The figures are displayed graphically in relation to the agreed objectives. Many people pass this spot in the course of the working day and the majority of them glance at the graphics. In addition, each department also holds a stand-up meeting for its personnel once a week, where the team leaders have a maximum of five minutes to comment on the week's results and indicate any corrective action that needs to be taken, which is then noted down on a whiteboard, with the name of the responsible member of staff written alongside. The strength of this approach lies in the manner in which it makes performance, necessary improvements and responsibilities visible and embeds them into the daily work routine.

A final example concerns another pharmaceutical company. In this company, each project team is given its own 'hutch', which serves as its home base. One of the many things attached to the walls of this space is a board that displays a matrix with the names of the team members and the agreed actions for which they are responsible. If an action is completed within the timeframe envisaged, the action is marked with a green sticker. Otherwise, it is marked with a red one. At the weekly project meeting, a run-through of the matrix is a fixed point on the agenda. This kind of 'naming and shaming' method is quite severe, but is reasonably (one might even say ruthlessly) efficient. The knowledge is certainly 'hot' for those concerned!

Additional comment

When you need cooperation and want to sketch out what is at stake for others, you must avoid using the kind of sales pitch that only focuses on benefits. If you want to appear credible, it is very important that you also say what it will cost them (time, money, manpower), but also making clear what support you are able to offer.

If you don't mention potential costs, there is a chance that their initial 'yes' at your first meeting might later turn into a final 'no', once they have done their homework more thoroughly.

'Would you like to take part in an educational programme about AIDS that is starting in the near future?' This question, with one variable, was put to two comparable groups of people. One group was told: 'If you want to take part, please fill in this form.' The other group was told: 'If you want to take part, forget about the form. Only fill it in if you don't want to take part.'

There was no significant difference between the two groups in terms of the number who wanted to take part. But that was not the purpose of the test. It is one thing to say you want to take part, but another to actually turn up when the programme starts. Here there was a difference, and what a difference: 49 percent of the first group turned up, but only 17 percent of the second group.[20]

This might seem like magic but it isn't. It is one of the mechanisms that Richard Thaler (another behavioural scientist who was also awarded the Nobel Prize for Economics) calls 'nudging': a small push in the back that almost automatically leads to the desired behaviour. The mechanism that produced the startling results in the test described above is known as 'internal consistency'. In its abstract formulation, this refers to the almost obsessional compulsion that people have to behave in a manner that is consistent with what they have previously said or done – in this case, simply filling in a form. Here is another example.

A sunny summer terrace on a market square. People are enjoying the wonderful weather, a refreshing drink and each other's company. At a certain moment, a woman who is part of the experiment goes to the toilet and leaves her handbag unattended. A second person, who is also part of the test team, walks onto the terrace, picks up the bag, and runs off with it. The people at the next table see what is happening, but fail to react.

This was the first variant of the experiment. In the second variant, the woman, before leaving for the toilet, asks the people at the next table if they would mind keeping an eye on her handbag while she is gone. Enter the thief for a second time. But now the reaction of the bystanders (or rather bysitters) is totally different. One of them runs after the thief, catches hold of him and insists that he should return the handbag. So why the difference? In this second case, the man at the next table had given a commitment to guard the bag. The urge to be internally consistent told him: 'If you said you will guard it, you have to guard it!'

This mechanism is a powerful one and almost 100 percent predictable, providing three conditions are met: the commitment must be voluntary, public and active. The mechanism does not work when imposed or is only in people's thoughts.

When you need the support of a stakeholder and have created in him a willingness to do something, it is of vital importance that you do everything you can to make sure that he effectively takes the first tiny practical step towards doing what you need him to do. This step should be as small and as easy as possible, so that the initial level of engagement and its associated threshold are both very low. This is what was happening in the example of the AIDS programme we mentioned earlier. The only difference between the two groups was that the first group was asked to do something. And it was a minimal something, something that anyone can do in just a few seconds: fill in a form. This required almost no time or effort, but it was sufficient to ensure that three times more people actually turned up to take part in the programme in comparison with the second group, who had also said 'yes' but had not been asked to take any additional confirmatory action.

What does this show? It shows that if you need someone's collaboration, it is important to think about the smallest possible first active step that the person concerned can take to move in the direction you want. This step must be practical, feasible, active and capable of rapid completion. Explain the step carefully but also ask what you can do to make this step as easy as possible. By adding this question, you appeal to a different dynamic that is also deeply ingrained in the human psyche and one that works almost as automatically as internal consistency. I am talking, of course, about reciprocity. If you want someone to do something for you, do something for him or her first.

The first step is the most important, but there is still a long way to go. You need to ensure that the level of engagement is systematically increased. This is something that you largely have in your own hands. The key is to make sure that whenever you see the other person taking a further step in your direction, you reward this action immediately. This reward consists in the first instance of letting the person know that you have noticed their action, thanking them for it, and explaining how it has already contributed to your project. A short time later, ask them about the possibility of taking a second small step, referring back to the first one they have already made and again asking what you can do to make this second step as easy as possible. You need to repeat this method of systematic asking and rewarding for as long as it takes, gradually building up the scale of the steps each time.

There are a number of good reasons for adopting this strategy. One of the most important is that people always respond better to a personal appeal, the results of which are immediately observable and the effects of which are certain to occur.

This sounds fairly theoretical, but a practical example will serve to explain. Imagine that you want to convince a friend to stop smoking. You can start by appealing to him directly. This fulfils the first of the conditions: the appeal is a personal one. But after that, things start to get difficult. You might tell him, for example, that he needs to take better care of his health, because smoking risks damaging it beyond repair. Yet even though this information is correct, the effects against which you warn will not be immediately apparent or real to your friend. What's more, he might be one of the lucky ones who are never confronted with those effects. For him, what is both real and immediate is the feeling of pleasure he gets when he lights up a cigarette. In other words, the impulse to smoke is greater than the impulse not to smoke.

This is one of the reasons why the early anti-smoking campaigns of the past were generally unsuccessful: people did not feel as though they were being personally addressed and/or that the risks against which they were being warned simply lay too far in the future or might not even materialise at all.

But let's get back to the people whose help you need, if you want to be successful. Imagine that they have already indicated their initial willingness to take a first step in the direction you want. They have also told you what you can do to make that first step as easy as possible. It is then vital to implement this facilitating action as quickly as you can. And the same applies to the reward once they have taken the step: it needs to be instant. If you can continue to react with the same speed as the project progresses, you will not only allow your stakeholders to see the immediate effect of the things they do, but also give them the certainty that these things are making a positive contribution to the project outcome. The more frequently you do this, the more automatic the process becomes.

Additional comment

Louise is the head nurse in a unit caring for AIDS sufferers. She is generally a mild-mannered person, but one of the things that can really drive her up the wall is when one of her patients phones her up in the middle of the evening to inform her blithely: 'Louise, I think you've got a problem. I've run out of medicine and I forgot to ask you for a new prescription during my last consultation visit!' What most annoys Louise about this kind of situation is the fact that the patient is imposing on her a territory that is actually his own, but for which he now pushes all the responsibility in her direction! This is not the way to secure other people's engagement. Remember that one of the most important conditions is that the engagement must be voluntary. Okay, a stakeholder might be appointed by a management decision to take part in a project, but that is just a starting point. He has been given a hire car; it is not his own car. As long as things stay that way, there is little chance that he will ever take the car to the carwash, never mind that he will actually wash it himself. By using the techniques outlined above, you need to make him feel that the car is also his.

TAKE AWAY

1   If you enter someone's territory, ask their permission first.
2   If someone enters your territory, let them know immediately.
3   Make sure that territories and roles are clear and meaningful in both directions.
4   Make sure there is regular consultation at previously agreed fixed moment, so that people's differing expectations can continue to be matched.
5   If you need the collaboration of others, make clear what they have to gain by agreeing to cooperate, but also what they might lose if they do not.
6   Focus on encouraging people to take the smallest possible step in the direction you want and do all you can to make that step as easy as possible.
7   Reward the behaviour you want immediately and consistently.

2

BE ON YOUR GUARD AGAINST GUERRILLA TACTICS THAT CAN LIMIT YOUR TERRITORY

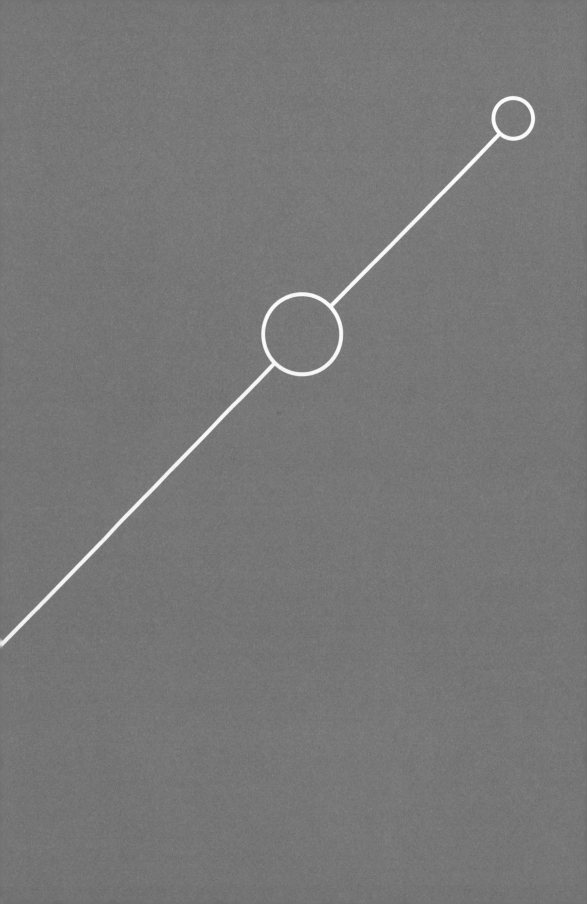

1   Everyone needs their own territory. A place where you feel safe, a place
    that is yours, a place where you can do what you want. A place where, to
    use a technical term, you have the right to self-determination. This is of
    vital importance, not only for nations and peoples, but also for each and
    every one of us as individuals. Part of this territory will be physical, such
    as a room. Part of it will be functional, like a job. An important part of it
    will also be immaterial, ranging from your own world of thoughts to the
    freedom of expression you allow yourself on Facebook. Having a territory
    is essential because it determines to a large extent who you are. In view of
    this, it is hardly surprising that you defend it strenuously when it comes
    under fire.

2   People are natural explorers. We are curious to discover new things. We
    wish to broaden our horizons as much as possible. We want to surf on new
    trends, buy new clothes, go on holiday to new lands, meet new people, try
    new flavours of pizza and perhaps every once in a while even try a new job.
    What's more, we want to make progress, get ahead in the world. We like to
    be appreciated, to receive praise for what we have done, whether it is from
    our new manager at work or from our next door neighbour's admiring
    glance at our perfectly mown lawn.

    Unless it is possible to find a previously unexplored territory, this desire
    for exploration and expansion will inevitably lead us into border conflicts
    with other territories and their occupants. We will invade their space or
    they will invade ours, resulting in both cases in the fear that some of our
    territory (and therefore our autonomy) will be lost.

3   If territories are clearly defined and formally marked in a visible manner,
    the likelihood of border conflict can be significantly reduced, not in the
    least because in these circumstances there are mechanisms to deter and
    punish territorial invasion. There is not much chance that a customer
    will go behind the bar to pull his own pint, and if he does he will soon be
    told in no uncertain terms not to do it again, or else he will be banned
    from the pub! This kind of unspoken prohibition is found at all levels of
    life. It applies to goalkeepers who know not to handle the ball outside the
    penalty area, just as it applies to politicians in a democracy who need to
    respect the separation of powers.

4   In contrast, if the boundaries of a territory over which a person has control
    are vague or impermanent, this increases the likelihood of border conflict,
    because it effectively creates a kind of no-man's-land, a grey area in which
    it is no longer clear whether you are taking over someone else's territory
    or they are taking over yours.

Feelings in this no-man's land are often equally vague and contradictory.
The excitement of the explorer heading off into the unknown merges with
irritation at the thought of what others might be doing behind your back
while you are gone. There is often nothing you can put your finger on, but
even so...

When you set off on your new voyage of discovery, you are driven on by
your enthusiasm and your élan. It is a wonderful feeling, nothing could
be finer. So why do you still have these vague doubts? Why is part of you
reluctant to press on? Are you uncertain about what – or who – you might
meet? You might say: 'Well, if I tread on anyone's toes, they'll just have to
tell me. Then we'll see what happens. It's as a simple as that.'

Unfortunately, it is seldom as simple as that. There is a good chance that
the other person, the one whose toes you may be treading on, is already
brooding on some ill-defined source of discontent, even if he says things
like: 'There is no point in overreacting like a drama queen. Perhaps nothing is going on. Let's just keep calm. Time will tell.' People don't always say
what they mean.

Territorial boundaries are often unclear. The feelings generated by territorial
expansion or defence are equally so, as too (unsurprisingly) are the tactics
used in both processes. And it makes no difference which side of the dispute
you are on: it is the same for all involved. These tactics look like ordinary
forms of interaction, but in reality they are weapons. Wolves in sheep's
clothing, whose seeming innocence makes them ideal for a surprise guerrilla
attack on you and your territory. These attacks are often indirect and seem to
come from nowhere, so that they are often over before you even realise what
is happening. But they always leave their mark and their destructive power is
often considerable, if not total.

In contrast to military guerrillas, the decision to use this or that guerrilla
tactic in territorial conflicts is seldom the result of reflection, evaluation
and rational consideration. To a large extent it is intuitive behaviour, which

makes use of the ways of doing things we best know from our own experience or have seen work for others to achieve the effect we now want.

Throughout our lives, we have all learnt how to establish a place for ourselves: in our family, at school, amongst our friends, at work, etc. We all do this in the manner that best suits us as individuals. It is one of the first lessons we learn as a child: everything that brings us closer to our goal is worth repeating, over and over again. This process of repetition almost literally sets out a pathway – a path of action – through our brain, and the more we repeat a particular type of behaviour, the more clearly defined that pathway becomes. This refines our behaviour, so that we get better and better at it: the more we use it, the easier it becomes to achieve what we want. This entire process takes place spontaneously, which is why it feels instinctive. Territorial behaviour is automatically given shape and form within the behavioural strategies that over the years we have made our own and which also work automatically.

In essence, there is only one good way to deal with (potential) territorial conflicts: take note of your vague feelings, give them a name, discuss them with the other conflicting party (or parties) and negotiate over the crux of the matter: namely, the claimed or defended territory. Unfortunately, we frequently fail to do this, so that if or when the discussion phase is reached it all too often focuses on the guerrillas and their tactics, rather than on the main issue. Consider, for example, the situation of Paula.

Paula is director of one of the R&D departments at the regional headquarters of a chemical company. She is a postgraduate in chemistry and joined the company some 10 years ago at the age of 40. Her department carries out applied research for three key customers. She has three other colleagues with a similar function, who each in turn have two or three key clients for whom they carry out specific research.

In addition to her operational job, Paula also sits on the board of two national umbrella organisations, is active in lobby work, and plays a role in helping to determine the long-term strategies that can be of value to the chemical industry as a whole.

Four months ago, Paula suddenly found herself working for a new boss. Edith is 42 years old, has a bachelor degree in mathematics, and joined the company straight from university. She has systematically worked her way up through the ranks to become a senior director, a success she owes primarily to her excellent

68

operational skills. Her most recent triumph was the development and implementation of a cost-saving programme based on the streamlining of processes between projects. Two jobs ago she occupied the position that Paula now holds. Since Edith's new appointment, things have not been going well for Paula.

Paula: 'I feel that Edith is always putting me under pressure ("Prove this, prove that."). It's like she is constantly looking over my shoulder. What's more, she only seems to be concerned about the operational aspects of my work, showing little or no appreciation for my wider strategic and conceptual abilities. At the start, I tried to ignore the pressure, just put it to one side and get on with my work. But it didn't help, because Edith continually insists on new figures and short-term deadlines. I have talked with her about it, about the pressure I feel and how hard I find it because she takes no account of my representational tasks and my strategic contributions. She answered: "I hear what you are saying and will try to build up a good working relationship with you, even though you and I come from two completely different worlds."'

'In the same conversation she told me that Eddy, one of the most promising members of my team, was not going to get the promotion I had recommended, because, in her words, "these youngsters can't expect to have promotions handed to them on a plate." She completely ignored my recommendation, even though I am convinced that Eddy deserves the promotion on the basis of his hard work and expertise.'

Since this conversation, the situation has deteriorated still further. Some of their colleagues are beginning to wonder what is going on between the pair of them and can't understand why Edith reacts in such a hostile manner to Paula in meetings.

By now, Paula is feeling pretty rotten. In fact, she is furious with Edith: 'Who the hell does she think she is? A bachelorette who has climbed the ladder thanks mainly to her flattery and short skirts.' Adding cynically: 'It's good to know that you don't need intelligence to make your way in this company.' She realises that this is just her frustration talking, but she can see no way out of the current impasse. She has reached the point where she is considering resignation, but is worried that finding another job of the same calibre at her age won't be easy. Her other concern is that the pressure Edith is putting her under will one day cause her to make a professional error, so that Edith will have the perfect excuse to give her a bad performance appraisal, which might even lead to her dismissal. This would be a disaster for Paula.

In this case, the territorial battleground is clear: Paula wishes to keep her autonomy, while Edith wants to limit it. However, they never discuss this most crucial aspect of the situation openly, as a result of which their collaboration becomes increasingly coloured by negative emotions. Once you become trapped in this kind of dynamic, you can be certain that the tension will continue to increase, until it eventually leads to open conflict and a breach that possibly cannot be repaired. This is what happened with Paula and Edith. Paula was transferred to a different department, which at least relieved the pressure she felt she was under, but nonetheless left her with a feeling that she had somehow failed. But the same was true of Edith, because she had lost one of the best members of her team.

If you want to make the process of expanding and defending territories more manageable, you need to be able to identify and name the tactics that are so often used (albeit unconsciously and unintentionally) to achieve the participants' different objectives. If you can track down and isolate these tactics, you will be able to disarm them of their emotional intensity, allowing you to control them better. So let's now have a look at some of the guerrilla tactics that you are most likely to encounter.

1 DEFINING

Consider the following: 'Because you know better than I do how important speed is during this phase of the project, I look forward to receiving the necessary figures from you tomorrow.' Or: 'Because you are someone who doesn't bow and scrape to authority figures, I think you are the best person to deal with this situation.'

Both these statements seem like compliments. And perhaps they are. But at the same time, if you accept them, they are also an invasion of your territory, because they impinge on your freedom of action. You can no longer wait until next week to provide the figures and in the next meeting with management you are almost forced into a critical position.

What makes this kind of guerrilla technique so powerful is the fact that it is dressed up as flattery. It praises and appeals to your positive qualities: your sense of responsibility and professionalism in the first example and your strength of character and honesty in the second example. This makes it difficult for you to react with 'Sorry, I just don't have the time' or 'No, I'm really a bit of a boot-licker.'

It is also worth noting that the first example adds an extra layer of seduction, beginning as it does with 'Because you know better than I do…' In this way, the speaker immediately puts you on a pedestal, positions you at a higher level than himself. In short, it is an appeal to your vanity, and it is hard not to feel flattered.

Appealing to socially desirable behaviour is not the only reason why this particular guerrilla tactic is so insidiously potent. It also exploits the natural human tendency to behave (or want to behave) in a consistent manner, which allows us to create a sense of coherence in our life. Imagine how frustrating it would be to realise that other people can make no sense of your behaviour. And it is even worse if you can make no sense of it, either.

If someone defines you as being coherent and consistent by labelling you as a person with admirable qualities, the pressure to behave in a way that conforms to this image is huge. When you have defined yourself in a particular manner, this makes the pressure even greater. We have all been there. You are walking along a busy shopping street and suddenly you are approached by a smiling young man or woman with a clipboard in their hand: 'Would you mind sparing a few minutes to answer some questions?'

In an experiment conducted by Bolkan and Andersen[1] only 29 percent of those asked were willing to be questioned. But if the first question was 'Do you regard yourself as helpful?', then followed by the request to take part in the survey, the response rate shot up to 77 percent!

Or what about this example, which will infuriate the privacy fanatics. If you ask people in a straightforward manner if they are willing to let you have their e-mail address in return for a free sample of the latest soft drink sensation, some 33 percent are barmy enough to agree. But if you precede this with the question 'Are you an adventurous person?', the number of people prepared to broadcast their private details to the world now skyrockets to an equally amazing 77.5 percent.

These figures clearly demonstrate the seductiveness of this kind of technique. They appeal to our sense of power, to our drive to expand our territory.

At the same time, it is clear that there is something manipulative about them, and where there is manipulation, irritation and resentment are usually not far behind. These tactics make us acutely aware of the vulnerability of our autonomy. They challenge our freedom of action to do what we have chosen to do for ourselves. Of course, we manage to convince ourselves that we belong to the 22.5 percent who would never fall for such trickery – we all need to maintain our sense of self-esteem – but who are we really kidding?

During a project meeting, Ralph let one of his company's external partners have it with both barrels. His criticism was scathing to the point of embarrassment. He shouted. He screamed. He banged the table. At one point, he even found it hard to stay in his chair. A short extract from his tirade: 'What the hell do you and your company think you are doing? How have you got the nerve to tell us that this kind of work is acceptable? Do you think you can get away with anything, just because you're an external partner? Well, if that's the case, you've got another think coming, sunshine!'

Everyone in the room was stunned. Nobody knew where to look or what to say. After an uncomfortable silence, the chairman suggested moving on to the next point on the agenda, but not before Ralph had added that he was 'very passionate' about his work.

This use of self-definition as a guerrilla tactic works in two directions. By referring to your own noble intentions, you extend your own behavioural territory: it gives you the 'right' to do things that would not normally be acceptable in a professional environment. At the same time, you also take away territory from others: how could they possibly hold things against you when your motives for your actions are so well intentioned? Clever? Maybe. But the irritation and resentment it causes will linger.

As with all guerrilla tactics, you need to be careful if you want to use self-definition as a territorial weapon. Although in the first instance your stakeholders won't be able to touch you for it, it will nonetheless create a vague feeling of unease, a sense that something is not quite right. And if you use the tactic in a planned and systematic way, there is a real danger that this feeling will grow, so that their confidence in you will be damaged. In chapter 5 you will read how this can fundamentally undermine the cornerstones that make any successful collaboration possible.

If others try to use this tactic against you, there are a number of things you can do:

1   Paranoia is a poor counsellor

Be aware that this weapon is seldom used in a planned and intentional manner. So don't automatically assume that the other person is deliberately attempting to nibble off a piece of your territory. If you make this mistake, you are likely to overreact. This not only causes more immediate harm than is necessary, but also risks escalating the situation.

2   Listen to yourself!

If someone's actions nonetheless give you a vaguely uncomfortable feeling, don't just ignore it. Trust your instincts – and react. Make clear that you are ready to defend your territory, but do so in a reasoned manner that makes further discussion possible.

3   The disarming defence: with a laugh and a wink

If someone defines you as loyal or generous or something equally praiseworthy, with the intention of limiting your freedom of response, thank them but also add that you only wish that what they say was true! Sadly, however, you are not as perfect as they seem to think! This is a neat and inoffensive way of putting the ball back in the other person's court.

4   Reframing self-definition

Brigit knew that as a project leader she should delegate more, because her desire to do everything herself often caused bottlenecks in the projects for which she was responsible. She had thought about the problem and discussed it with others, and had now come to the conclusion that this approach was a result of her sense of duty and responsibility. 'If I do things myself, I know they are done well. And if I closely monitor the remaining work my team are doing, that's only because I want to make sure my clients and stakeholders get the value they deserve.' You could hardly reproach her for feeling this way, especially when it was so obvious that she really meant it.

Her colleague Christine recognised that Brigit had painted herself into a corner with this reasoning, but cleverly found a way to get her out again. 'I saw how hard Brigit was working, driven on by her sense of responsibility. What she did was fantastic, but I also tried to make her see that being responsible involves much more than simply working your fingers to the bone. She also had a responsibility to the company to see that the members of her team could develop and grow. As a project leader, she was in a perfect position to do this, but only if she allowed her people to do some of the more complex and challenging tasks that lead to greater experience and self-confidence. Thankfully, I was able to persuade her that delegation – under her careful supervision – was the key.'

Reframing means that you accept and value the self-definition, but seek to give it a new and broader meaning. This almost always works, because you actually help to expand a part of the other person's territory (in Brigit's case, her work ethic) that means a lot to them.

5   Correct - but with a gentle touch

If someone tries to justify their undesirable behaviour by camouflaging it with good intentions, you can still value what they are doing, but perhaps add that while passion is silver, passion allied to control is golden.

GIVING TO RECEIVE

Do you remember the iconic opening scene of the Godfather epos?

With obvious pain and bitterness, a father tells Don Corleone how his daughter was molested and scarred for life by two young men who were tried for the crime but released the same day. Would Don Corleone now exact vengeance, killing the men on the father's behalf? Money was no object. The mafia boss could name his own price.

The Godfather refuses. Why should he do the man this favour, he asks, when he has never shown him any respect in the past? For money? He already has money. To accept more in these circumstances would simply reduce him to the level of an ordinary hired killer. No, Don Corleone wants more. Not money, but loyalty and subjugation. If the man is willing to kiss the Don's ring as a sign of his fealty, Corleone will arrange the hit. But he also makes clear that there is a price to pay: 'I will do what is necessary. Regard it as a gift to your daughter. But remember this: there may come a time, or there may not, that I will ask you for a favour in return. If or when that happens, I expect to be able to rely on you.'

In some ways (although the contexts are very different!), this scene is reminiscent of the Biblical precept: 'Give and it shall be given unto you' or in more modern parlance 'Give and you shall receive'. This is a basic rule for anyone seeking to make alliances or cement relationships. You give something to someone, something that is close to their heart, and they will no doubt willingly give you in return something that is close to your heart. Generosity breeds generosity.

The ancient Romans had a similar expression: *Do ut des*. Similar, but not identical. The phrase literally means 'I give so that you must give'. You might think that the two sayings amount to more or less the same thing, but you would be wrong. They reflect a very different dynamic in two key areas.

Firstly, there is a difference in intention. *Do ut des* is what the Godfather did: I make use of your weak position to strengthen my position. In this instance, 'giving' is an instrument to expand his power base, increase his territory. The effect on the other is compelling: he is in Don Corelone's debt and is obliged to do something in return. He can only redeem his debt by doing what the Godfather asks of him at the appropriate time. When this happens, he has no other choice but to comply. His autonomy is limited, his territory is reduced. This explains why giving is a guerrilla tactic that always has negative consequences somewhere further down the line.

This is very different from the dynamic that Byron Katie creates in her seminars. Katie is a woman who is able like no other to show people how they need to make a distinction between what happens to them in their life and how they interpret those (often dramatic) events. She explains how people construct 'stories' in response to events and how they often suffer more from the stories than from the events themselves. With this in mind, she then teaches people how they can detach the event from the story.[2]

Her students follow her courses for a couple of weeks, twelve hours a day, often in groups running into the hundreds. One of the continual tasks she sets them throughout the course is this: 'When you see something that you value in one of your fellow students, in what they do or how they are, write it down on a scrap of paper and drop it amongst their things, where, sooner or later, they are certain to find it.' There are three rules for this task: you must mean what you write; it must be specific rather than general; and, most importantly, you must find a way to slip your anonymous note into their things without them seeing.

This is not so very different from what happens in your family or in the circle of your closest friends, where care and concern for each other, rather than power, is the currency of exchange. This is an environment where giving is natural. So, too, is receiving. Both actions strengthen the bond and the common territory the participants share. Of course, even here guerrilla tactics occasionally occur: that's just the way we humans are. But if they are used and if they do cause discord, in this personal context something very different is given in return: we give forgiveness.

But that is not necessarily how things work in a professional context. If you can build up a reputation for authentic generosity among your stakeholders, their trust in you and their goodwill towards you will grow. You will read more about this later in the book. But in contrast to the private domain, interpersonal warmth is not an essential part of professional relationships. At best, it is a bonus. What is essential is a willingness to conduct transactions in a manner that is voluntary, transparent and regarded as fair by all concerned.

The condition for 'fairness' is that the things that are exchanged are roughly equivalent.

Imagine that you are the manager of a department store. You are responsible for maximising turnover. You have a good knowledge of your customer population and you want to be given room to adjust your assortment as you see fit and to launch commercial actions of your own. Your regional manager is responsible for the results of a group of stores and must ensure not only that the deals made with the company's various suppliers are respected, but also that commercial actions must be uniform across all stores.

So how can you, as the store manager, make a deal with the regional manager? You might, for example, agree on a list of products from the company's assortment over which you are free to make decisions; also that you will submit an extra monthly report with a profit and loss analysis of the assortment decisions you have taken; and that you will only launch local commercial initiatives that supplement the company-wide initiatives, and only after you have first consulted the regional manager.

In this way, both you and the regional manager have agreed to surrender territory: you by the need to submit an extra report and to ask for prior permission; your manager by giving up some of his control over your actions. In exchange for this, you hope to reap a common reward: better overall results.

The process that led to this redistribution of territory was transparent and not motivated by the wish of either party to try and influence or outsmart the other with clever tricks. When there is transparency of this kind, there is little or no residual ill-feeling. When guerrilla tactics are used, there is always residual ill-feeling.

In this context, flattery is an interesting variant of the guerrilla technique (see chapter 5). In territorial terms, it works as follows. Without damaging his own interests, the flatterer voluntarily gives away a piece of his territory ('That is something you are so much better at than I am'). Once it is clear that the flattered party is enjoying the benefits of this 'gift', something is taken back from his territory in the form of a 'favour' asked for by the flatterer.

In essence, this mechanism is the opposite of bluffing. Bluffing amounts to saying that a piece of territory is yours when you don't yet own it. Because bluff and flattery broadly belong to the same 'family', people who are prepared to bluff also tend to be more susceptible to flattery. Manipulators can see this a mile off and can exploit it expertly as a weapon, sometimes through a subtly disguised request for advice.

If you are asked to give advice with regard to a territory about which you know very little, the alarm bells should immediately start sounding in your head. That being said, this is not always an easy tactic to detect, because a number of things are all happening at the same time: your ego is being massaged, you are being defined ('People say you are the expert on this'), and the approach might indeed by a sign of genuine appreciation (and who could take exception to that?).

There is one final characteristic of this guerrilla tactic that it is important to note: the bigger the gift you receive from the other, the harder it will be to prevent part of your territory from being occupied as 'compensation' at a later stage. Hopefully for you, the exploitation will not be as flagrant as in the case of Sophie and Carl.

On the day when they moved into their new house, the young couple were surprised to see a large delivery van standing outside their front door. It was there to deliver a brand-new three piece suite, which Sophie's mother had chosen for them as a house-warming present. And it wasn't exactly the kind of suite you find on a second-hand site. More the kind of thing you buy in Harrods or Maceys. This 'gift' had a number of consequences:

1   The parents (in-law) had immediately and very visibly annexed a large part of the house to their territory.
2   Sophie and Carl were furious and had a huge row about her mother's interference.
3   Sophie was obliged to make an enthusiastic 'thank-you' telephone call to her mother: 'You really shouldn't have!' (meaning 'I really wish you hadn't!').
4   The couple were forced to live for at least the next ten years with a suite that was not of their choosing. And to add insult to injury, they had to put up with comments during every parental visit about how wonderful it looked in their home!

If people try to use this 'give to receive' tactic against you, there are a number of things you can do:

1   You can politely refuse the gift and retain your autonomy, although the giver is likely to feel snubbed and you can assume that he will hold it against you.
2   You can accept the gift but be extra alert for the moment when the compensatory favour is asked. You need to be especially on your guard when you feel flattered by a request for advice.
3   You can do what Eric did in Singapore. He and his family were invited to a fancy restaurant by a client to celebrate the birthday of Eric's daughter, Lilly. It was not possible to refuse this kind invitation without offence and so Eric agreed to go. And it was all very pleasant: excellent food, enjoyable conversation, good atmosphere, great view, etc. In fact, everything was going swimmingly... until dessert. This was the moment when the client produced the 'present' he had brought for Lilly: a huge pile of bank notes, which he handed over with a big smile and the comment: 'Buy yourself something nice!' Eric's dilemma was clear. He could either let himself be bribed in this manner or he could refuse the money but risk insulting – and therefore losing – this important customer. Fortunately, Eric has always been able to think quickly on his feet. He thanked the man effusively for his generosity towards Lilly and said that he was sure his daughter would use the money to do what she most enjoyed doing: helping others less fortunate than herself. In fact, Eric was certain that she would want to donate it to the local orphanage in the street where they lived. Honour satisfied on both sides.

3   BLITZKRIEG AND INFILTRATION

A local committee had been trying for 20 years to do something to prevent traffic from taking shortcuts through their streets. There had been hours and hours of discussion with the local council, followed by promises and declarations of intent, but always with the caveat 'there are still a few things we need to investigate first'. At the end of the day, nothing actually happened to improve the situation on the ground. On the contrary, the traffic got heavier and heavier all the time, including big lorries that made the narrow streets more unsafe than ever.

Recently, however, it seemed as though a breakthrough might be possible. A perfect solution to the problem now exists in the form of smart cameras, which theoretically can meet all technical, legal and financial requirements. Encouraged, the action committee piled on the pressure, with black flag campaigns, flyers and a new website. They even set up a column alongside the busiest road, which showed the number of car passing in real time in big red numbers. The fact that this was a year in which local elections were scheduled to be held also helped to create a 'now or never' feeling amongst the campaigners. The committee entered into discussions with the current majority parties but also with the opposition (who, of course, all claimed to be on the side of the protesters, because they were only too happy to make things difficult for their political rivals). It was finally agreed to organise a joint discussion forum at which all the parties were represented, just before the crucial meeting of the town council that would finally decide what would be done.

The action committee was well prepared. They had put together a professional presentation, which explained the problem and clearly outlined the possible solutions. The last slide of the presentation asked three questions to which they wanted answers:

1 Do you recognised that there is a problem with through traffic taking shortcuts?
2 Do you agree to the installation of two smart cameras that will note the number plates of cars passing through the streets in question, so that they can be sanctioned?
3 Do you agree to order the cameras before the forthcoming elections?

On the same slide, they had also made a summary of the standpoints of the various political parties with regard to these questions: either green ticks for 'in favour' or red question marks for 'not yet known'. Not a bad idea. An even better idea when they decided without consulting those involved to put green ticks alongside the answers to questions 1 and 2 for the two majority parties in the current ruling coalition! The large screen at the front of the meeting hall showed it clearly: the partners in the coalition were in agreement with the protesters! This more or less presented the mayor with a fait accompli that left him little room for manoeuvre. He could not reclaim the territory that had been captured from him by the action group without seeming to go back on his word, which could be disastrous in the context of the approaching elections...

This is blitzkrieg: you create a fact that seriously limits the sphere of action – and therefore reduces the territory – of the other party. In this situation, the limiting effect was a particularly powerful one, because the meeting was held in public: the ruling coalition and opposition parties were all present, as were a number of interested residents. As a result, it was very hard for the coalition not to agree with the protesters, without seeming inconsistent and losing face.

This is also a tactic used at a different level by trade unions: first provoke an incident, then plan for strike action in response to that incident and only then sit down to negotiate with management. It even happens in international politics: pieces of land are seized without warning, retaliatory bombardments are carried out without prior consultation or discussion, and sometimes even physical walls are erected. These are all ways to create a new fact that unilaterally resets the agenda and automatically limits the autonomy of the other parties involved.

But look at this variant as well

Chantal is on the point of selling her thriving IT company to one of the sector's major players. The final meeting is planned for this afternoon, following which a declaration of intent will be signed. The directors of both companies are present, together with their lawyers. There are just a few final details to be negotiated and agreed. Or so everyone thought.

Just before the signing of the declaration, the CEO of the IT giant asks for a face-to-face meeting with Chantal in private. He now chooses this moment to introduce a new element into the discussion: would Chantal be prepared to surrender 50 percent of her bonus during the one-year transition period they had previously agreed?

Chantal is taken by surprise. She is not happy with the idea and offers some token resistance, but she wants the deal to go through and knows that everyone is sitting in the office next door, waiting for her and the big boss to reappear. Against her better judgement, she agrees to a 40 percent reduction and signs the declaration of intent. But she is not happy: not with herself, not with her legal team for failing to anticipate this move and not with the company's new owners, who she feels backed her into a corner. It was not exactly the ideal start to what was supposed to be an intense collaboration. And as later became apparent, this was not without repercussions.

On a smaller scale, you can see the same kind of thing in meetings, where someone might begin a consultation process by announcing out of the blue that four crucial questions first need to be answered before any move forward can be made. This immediately puts his agenda at the centre of the discussions, reducing the analyses and priorities of the others involved – if they accept the limitation he is trying to impose – to secondary importance.

Because this tactic is aggressive – it attempts to 'force' the other party to do something – it often encounters resistance. Sometimes immediately, but more frequently afterwards, when the initial feelings of surprise and dismay have died down. At the meeting with the traffic action group, the response of the majority coalition was vague and non-committal. But at the subsequent council meeting they were unwilling to go any further than to sign (yet another) declaration of intent, which also very pointedly referred to a number of reasons why the proposed solution might not work in practice. They felt that they had been unfairly put under pressure in the public arena and so they now responded 'behind closed doors' with one of their traditional delaying tactics. In this way, they regained the territory they had lost. But in the meantime, their confidence in the action group had been severely damaged, so that future negotiations would be even more difficult, with an escalation of the situation as the most likely result.

There are ways you can parry a blitzkrieg: by thoroughly preparing for the meeting, by agreeing an agenda (preferably a written one) in advance, and by having a clear picture in your head of the type of outcome (decision, exchange of ideas, notification of information, etc.) to which each point on that agenda should lead.

If someone launches a blitzkrieg against you, it is a good idea to openly praise what he is trying to achieve and to assure him that the points he raises will certainly receive the attention they deserve – but perhaps not right now. Would it not be better to look at these things in more depth at a later date, particularly as all the relevant factors might not yet have emerged?

When a blitzkrieg attack is combined with social pressure, as was the case with Chantal, the best way to respond is by making clear that this is not what had been previously agreed and that, consequently, it complicates matters in a potentially sensitive manner. All the more reason to postpone any hasty decision and to look at the points at issue again in a subsequent meeting. In this way, you not only protect your own territory, but also send out a warning signal to deter any future attacks.

There are many disadvantages to a blitzkrieg. It polarises, encourages aggressive behaviour and quickly leads to escalation, not necessarily about the merits of the case but about who controls which bits of territory. In other words, the focus switches to the marking and defending of territories, which soon monopolises everyone's attention and energy.

As if the blitzkrieg was not bad enough, there is another similar tactic that achieves the same effect but is even more dangerous, because it is harder to detect: this is anchoring.

You can see the prototype of this mechanism in the bartering process inherent in sales transactions. The higher the first price named by the seller, the higher the final price that will ultimately be agreed by the buyer. If you set a reference point (the first price), subsequent discussion will result in some kind of downwards adjustment, but this adjustment is not usually large. The buyer continues to think within the same general range that has been fixed by the opening offer. The territory in which he is free to determine what he is willing to pay has been significantly reduced.

Anchoring in many different domains has been studied extensively during the past 40 years and the results of this research suggest its effect is highly robust.[3] It derives its power from the fact that it remains under the radar of rational and critical thinking. It is an automatic process whose influence only becomes apparent much further down the line. In some ways, this makes it a fascinating phenomenon – as we shall shortly see.

Anchoring was first studied systematically by the subsequent winner of the Nobel Prize for Economics, Daniel Kahneman, working together with Amos Tversky.[4] One of their experiments was as follows.

The test subjects were asked to estimate the percentage of African countries currently sitting in the United Nations. Immediately before they made their prediction, the researchers spun a kind of 'wheel of fortune', which was marked with values between 1 and 100. The participants were then asked two questions: (1) Was their estimated percentage higher or lower than the value selected at random by the wheel? (2) What was their actual estimated percent-age expressed in figures?

The results showed a remarkable yet unmistakeable pattern: there was a strong correlation between the random figure on the wheel and the estimated percentages of African countries believed to be in the UN. A high figure on the wheel usually led to a correspondingly high estimate. A low figure led to a low estimate. Do these two different facets of the experiment really have anything to do with each other? No, of course they don't. Are people's minds influenced and their judgement affected by a random figure? You bet they are! Does this mean that the area (territory) within which you can reach your own conclusions based on your own thoughts has been significantly limited? What do you think?

The effect that anchoring has on our perception of the length of the Mississip-pi River, the amount of time it takes Mars to complete its orbit around the Sun and even the weight of Julius Caesar are all things that have been researched. Intriguing though the results of these projects were, they are hardly matters that will cause us to lose sleep at night. But some other examples from real life should, perhaps, give us more cause for concern.

In 2006, the message transmitted by the White House about the number of civilian deaths during the Iraq War was repetitive and very clear: 30,000. This was the figure given by President Bush. It was the figure given by General Casey, the officer commanding American troops in Iraq. It was the figure used in all official communiqués. As a result, it was the figure that became anchored in the heads of anyone interested in the consequences of the war. A critical citizen or a cynical journalist would probably be quick to realise that the government had much to gain by keeping the figure as low as possible and that consequently the 30,000 estimate should be taken with a very large pinch of salt. They might even have thought that the real figure might be as much as twice that amount. But they would almost certainly never have come close to assessing the true realities of the situation.

In the October 2006 edition of the prestigious *Lancet* magazine, researchers from the equally prestigious John Hopkins University published the results of their study into the actual number of civilian casualties. Backing up their claims with well-documented evidence, they concluded that the number of civilian deaths in the first three years of the conflict directly attributable to the invasion was not 30,000, but a staggering 654,965.[5] This figure is of such a different order, is so far removed from the range of 30,000 anchored by the White House, that for many people it is still difficult to accept, even though its source is unimpeachable.

But let's now take things a stage further. The Iraq example essentially relates to the effect of anchoring on ordinary citizens and journalists; in other words, people who are not specialists in the material concerned. This might lead to the conclusion that anchoring has a stronger effect in relation to the extent that the factual reality is not familiar or clear to those involved. And indeed, up to a point this is true – but not always, as a team of German researchers has been able to demonstrate.[6]

Their project investigated the following question: would a test population of court judges and public prosecutors with an average professional experience of 10 years be influenced by a set of seemingly irrelevant anchors when determining the level of punishment for convicted offenders? 'Hopefully not,' you might think. But you would be wrong.

To ensure that all decisions were based on reliable material, a series of case files were checked for completeness, accuracy and validity by an independent panel of legal experts before being submitted to the test group for judgement and sentencing recommendations.

One of the cases involved a rape. After reading through the full case file, the magistrates were given information about what a journalist – in other words, a non-specialist – had suggested in his paper might be an appropriate sentence for the perpetrator. Each magistrate was given a different figure: 5 years, 10 years, 15 years, etc. Half of these figures were near the maximum that the law allows in cases of this kind; the other half were closer to the legal minimum. None of the proposed sentences were documented or justified. There was just a figure.

The results showed that the sentences proposed by the judges and public prosecutors closely matched the opinion of the journalist. When the journalist suggested a heavy sentence, the magistrates also gave a heavy sentence. This was reversed when the journalist suggested a light sentence. Even though they had all viewed precisely the same case material, the average difference in sentencing was 50 percent.

In summary: even experienced professionals allow their judgement to be determined and their autonomy to be limited to a significant extent by a non-relevant source (in this case, a journalist) and by unfounded information generated by random factors (the journalist's opinion). Expertise and experience do little or nothing to limit this effect.

It is still not clear precisely how this mechanism works, but we can no longer doubt that it does work. The results of numerous studies are conclusive on this point. The simple truth is that we are no longer always the masters of our own thoughts.

How can you prevent this?

So what can you do to fend off this assault on your mental territory? The short answer is (sadly): not much. Being aware of it doesn't help. Neither does forcing yourself to make counter-arguments to whatever is suggested. The effect goes too deep for that. There are only two tactics that can really be of any use. The second is one that we will examine more fully later in the book: looking closely in advance at the reasons a stakeholder might have for adopting a certain position and creating enough distance to place that position in its proper context, so that you can defend yourself against its possible anchoring.[7]

The first tactic can be equally effective. When someone asks you to take a decision, ask them to explain not only on which working hypotheses their proposal is based, but also which other hypotheses they considered and rejected, and – equally important – why. This can be especially useful when you are under time pressure and are tempted to accept the first plausible suggestion put to you.

Blitzkrieg and anchoring are strategies that take you by surprise. They hit you like a bolt from the blue. With infiltration, the invasion of your territory is much more gradual. Angela was an agency worker employed in the training and development department of a metal company. In addition to training, her manager was also responsible for quality control. Because he had so much to do, he was happy to leave all his administrative tasks to Angela. She booked the rooms for the training, made the planning schedule for the trainers, finalised the budgets, contacted the necessary suppliers and processed the subsequent evaluations of the programmes, as well as taking on all the other little jobs that her manager found too tedious or too time consuming to complete himself.

In this way, Angela was slowly but surely able to extend her territory. Within a year she was drafting the agendas for evaluation meetings, making proposals to strategically re-orient the department, suggesting programmes that should be scrapped and others that should be added, etc. What's more, she did all this without much consultation with her boss. In effect, she was now running the department, so that her position became ever stronger. In fact, she was unmissable. In the beginning, her manager had been happy for her to take all the routine tasks out of his hands. But now he was increasingly reliant on her, to the extent that she was now calling most of the shots.

As in Angela's case, infiltration often starts with the best of intentions: the desire to work hard and make yourself as useful as possible. Precisely for this reason, it is often difficult to reverse infiltration once it has taken root. It feels unfair and ungrateful. That being the case, prevention is once again better than cure. Consider taking the following steps:

1 Write out job descriptions and job expectations in advance on paper. Agree a timetable for evaluation and possible amendment. In this way, you can keep all the strings in your own hand.
2 Assess your own position critically. Only hand over tasks (territory) if they will give you extra energy to tackle more important priorities. Never surrender tasks simply because you find them tedious or because you can't be bothered to make the effort necessary to master them.
3 Always make sure you have a back-up. Avoid concentrating key competencies in a single person, on whom you will eventually become dependent.

4 · RIDICULE

Ridicule is not really a guerrilla tactic; it is more like a bomb thrown openly into the middle of someone else's territory, often with devastating consequences.

Ridicule can sometimes seem like a form of humour, but there is nothing funny about it at all.

Humour is a bridge-builder that helps to reduce conflict; ridicule is a bridge-burner that intensifies conflict. The fact that ridicule can sometimes provoke (bitter) laughter is nothing more than a smoke screen behind which the ridiculer attempts to hide, so that he can use it to deflect attention from what he is trying to achieve ('Surely we're still allowed to have a laugh about things every now and then?').

In chapter 1, we saw how your psychological territory is determined to a large degree by the extent to which people take you seriously; the extent to which you can attract and keep their attention; and, consequently, the extent to which you exercise influence on their feelings and thoughts.

Ridicule – if you accept it – removes your right to have a say. Ridicule is destructive. It reduces you to the level of an imbecile and makes you socially ineffectual. The damage caused by ridicule is huge and often difficult to repair, especially if self-confidence and self-esteem are not your strongest points. Anyone who has ever been bullied knows exactly how this feels and what it can do to a person. The effect is comparable with being completely ignored, because this also reduces you to the status of an 'irrelevancy'.

That being said, ridicule takes things a stage further than simply ignoring someone. Ridicule is highly visible and, once released, has a tendency to live a life of its own. The witnesses to ridicule are frequently inclined to tell what they have seen to others – often because it makes such a 'juicy' story – so that the reputational damage to the victim gets bigger and bigger with each exaggerated account.

In a professional environment, teams and individuals are nearly always reliant on the goodwill of others to achieve their objectives. That is the core argument of this book. As a result, using ridicule as a weapon to conquer territory is nearly always a bad idea, and this for two main reasons.

Because ridicule is equivalent to a full-scale bombardment of someone's territory, it always leads to polarisation. If you make a fool of someone in public, they will never forgive you. Never. Not even if the contact is a one-off and you don't expect to have any further dealings with them in the future. The world is smaller than we think, and organisations smaller still. Sooner or later, your paths will probably cross again – especially if the person you ridiculed is actively looking for an opportunity to exact revenge.

But there is more to it than that. People not only talk about the ridicule they have seen; they also talk about the ridiculers. Almost overnight, everyone knows who they are and there is a growing reluctance to work with them. If they can hurt others with their ridicule, how can we be sure they won't do the same to us? In short, the ridiculers effectively shoot themselves in the foot: they also suffer significant reputational damage as a result of their ridicule.

If you are made the subject of ridicule, you must defend yourself. If you want to avoid being seen by others as a helpless victim, you need to do more than stand there blushing and stammering with embarrassment. If you don't, you will simply encourage the ridiculer to use the same tactic again and again, until you eventually give up the fight and surrender your entire territory. But defending yourself means more than simply reacting defensively, since this would mean playing along with the ridiculer's game – which is always a dangerous tactic. No, your response must be more positive and here are a few options worth considering:

1   Defend yourself positively and with confidence

The ridiculer is probably expecting you to freeze under his scorn. Don't give him this satisfaction. Retain eye contact with your attacker, smile at his 'joke' and instantly return to the essence of the matter you were discussing. This sends a powerful signal to the ridiculer and to any others who may be watching.

In all cases of aggression – and ridicule is a form of aggression – the origin is the aggressor's own fear. The more he feels that his own territory is under threat, the harder he will lash out in defence. By making this clear – 'You must really be feeling nervous to reduce yourself to the level of this kind of childish mockery' – you can take the sting out of his ridicule.

3   Counter ridicule with ridicule

This requires a degree of mental and verbal agility, something for which British politicians down the centuries have been famed. The number of brilliant examples is legion.

Benjamin Disraeli was twice a Conservative prime minister of his country. He was the first Jewish premier of Great Britain and in addition to being a politician was also a writer of some repute. He had a mastery of the English language that was second to none and he used words both to amuse his friends and as weapons to wound his political opponents. The greatest of these was the Liberal William Gladstone, who was also prime minister on more than one occasion. During one fierce debate tradition says that Gladstone predicted that Disraeli would either die of syphilis or on the gallows. To which Disraeli replied: 'That depends, my dear Gladstone, on whether I embrace your politics or your mistress.' Ouch!

Another famous writer-politician was Winston Churchill, winner of the Nobel Prize for Literature in 1935. Like Disraeli, he was famed and feared for the sharpness of his tongue, and his exchanges with the equally eloquent playwright George Bernard Shaw are legendary.

Shaw: 'I am enclosing two tickets to the first night of my new play; bring a friend... if you have one.'

Churchill: 'Cannot possible attend first night; will attend second... if there is one.'

As these examples show, disarming the power of ridicule with counter-ridicule can be highly effective, but it must be repeated that this requires both quick wits and great verbal dexterity, which often only come with many years of practice and experience.

What's more, although this tactic is fine, even amusing, it should only be used to a point. As long as everyone involved accepts that it is just verbal sword play, no real harm is done. But if the participants insist on continuing to try and outdo each other in terms of rhetorical wizardry, this can only lead to an increase in the polarisation that was initiated by the first ridiculer. When this happens, the situation soon degenerates into 'an eye for an eye' confrontation, which can only have one outcome: before long, everyone is blind...

4   Pre-empt ridicule by using self-ridicule

During a furious debate in the Flemish Parliament, the Minister for the Budget was under heavy fire from the opposition benches. In the heat of moment, he shouted at his opponents: 'Of course I can count! 72 million and 35 million make a total of 117 million. That is what I am proposing. For anyone who can count,' [and, let's be honest, if counting belongs to anyone's territory, it should be the Minister for the Budget's!] 35 and 72 still add up to 117.' The chamber dissolved into laughter on all sides. You could see Minster Muyters mentally counting on his fingers until he finally realised his mistake: his arithmetic was out by 10: 72 and 35 make 107, not 117! It was only then that the minister grinned at his own stupid error – and that was his salvation. This kind of open and honest reaction was much better than simply trying to ignore the matter or, worse still, behaving defensively. In these latter two cases, he would have shown himself to be personally vulnerable, so that the opposition, sensing blood, would have torn him apart with ridicule. But not now. True, he had to put up with a good deal of teasing in the months ahead, but teasing is more an expression of camaraderie than aggression. Muyters' territory remained intact.

Were there any lessons that Julian could learn from this? His Belgian company had recently taken over another company in the same sector, but in a much larger neighbouring country. Julian's company already had a presence there, but on a much smaller scale than the factory that had now been bought. Not surprisingly, the people in the factory were suspicious of the newcomers and worried about what the future might bring: 'Who the hell do they think they are? A minor player from a midget country with only a fraction of our market knowledge! Well, they'd better not think they can come in here and start laying down the law about what we can and can't do!'

Julian was tasked with the integration of both companies. He was fully aware of the underlying mistrust and the scarcely concealed hostility. It was therefore with some trepidation that he set off to attend his first meeting with the local directors.

During the informal chat before the meeting, Julian told anyone who was prepared to listen what had happened to him earlier that same morning. He had arrived the day before and parked his car on the main square in the city centre, not far from the sea.

When he returned this morning, he immediately saw that all the other cars had disappeared. There was only one car left standing – and that was his! When he moved closer, he could soon see why: his car was almost completely covered with... bird shit! Julian continued: 'The locals must have killed themselves laughing. They know exactly where they can leave their cars and when. And they also know that the birds only come out at night, when the city has quieted down. But here was this stupid outsider with his foreign number plates who had no idea about any of this. They must have thought: "He'll soon learn his lesson" – and they were right!'

Julian had not made this story up, but by telling it the way he did he showed that he knew his place, that he had respect for local knowledge and experience, and that he had no intention of trying to take their territory by storm. Smart. Very smart.

Self-ridicule can help you to avoid the more savage ridicule of others, because it implies that you are somehow above personal attacks. In fact, you show that poking fun at each other is fine and can even be seen as a form of appreciation. It removes the fuse from the powder keg and, at the risk of mixing metaphors, takes the wind out of the sails of would-be ridiculers.

That is the paradoxical thing about self-ridicule. Instead of reducing your reputation and credibility, it actually increases them. At least in our culture.

5   Know where you are vulnerable

We are all familiar with the 'hook and eye' system. We have all used it to hang things on our walls. And we all know that it is only possible to do this if there is an eye into which the hook can fit. And the same is true in human terms. Someone can only hurt you with his ridicule, if somewhere within you there is an 'eye' waiting to be hooked. This 'eye' is the place where it is possible to touch you emotionally; to cause you pain about something that is important to you. If you don't care about the way you look, people who poke fun at your appearance – insulting remarks about your height, hair colour, weight, clothes, etc. – will be unable to harm you. But it is different when these attacks focus on things that mean a lot you – family, relationships, your past achievements, etc. – things that are integral to who you are. That is much harder to take and much harder to combat.

If you highly value your professionalism and someone suggests that you are nothing more than a charlatan; if you are proud of your broad-mindedness and someone suggests that you are stupid and short-sighted; if you regard yourself as an independent spirit and someone says that you are a naive boot-licker; these are all areas where you are vulnerable to ridicule in a manner that will hit you hard.

In order to identify and map out these areas of vulnerability, it goes without saying that you need to ask yourself frankly and honestly about the things that you are secretly proud or ashamed of. Because these are the things that will most affect you if people start to mock them.

You can do this by asking yourself two crucial questions: (1) How would I like people to talk about me? (2) What subjects can people use to irritate me easily? Both questions give you information about the things that mean a lot to you. The first question does that directly; the second question does it indirectly. The first tells you about who you really want to be; the second tells you about who you definitely do not want to be. By turning the answers to this second question on their head, you can also discover more about the most important things in your life. That being said, there is also another way in which these two lists are closely related to each other.

We have all met the Anne's of this world. This particular Anne was an IT specialist in her company and was proud of the thoroughness of her work. She hated shortcuts and temporary solutions and detested the meaningless slogan-like language used by many of her colleagues in meetings. One day, however, she was put under huge pressure by her managers to come up with a rapid solution for the revision of the company's system for stock monitoring. They didn't care how she did it, as long as it was fast and cheap. Anne was not happy and tried to dig in her heels: 'Look, what you ask is simply not possible without reconfigurating the entire stock system. Let me explain...' But the management response was uncompromising: 'Listen, Anne, we're not interested. Just stop moaning and get on with it. You've already wasted enough time.'

But Anne wouldn't listen. She kept harping on about how the system worked, how it should work and how complex it all was, but all to no avail. Her bosses were forced to remind her time and again who was the customer and who was the provider in this situation. In the end, she caved in and gave them the kind of 'no questions asked' solution they were demanding.

Not surprisingly, the problems with her new application started almost from the very first day. She was soon called before the IT management team to justify what she had done, where she was introduced with the words: 'Here is Miss Quick-fix with her magic wand, who has single-handedly managed to ruin the reputation of our department overnight...' These hurtful words cut Anne to the quick. She left the company soon after.

How does this mechanism work?

If you have an idea that means a great deal to you and if you want others to accept that idea, your strongest reflex will probably be to use all your powers to achieve that objective. These powers might include your rationality, your enthusiasm, your ability to persuade or any of a wide range of other commendable personal qualities.

In most cases you will achieve your objective, not in the least because your personal method of approach is one that suits you well and you have developed the skills that allow you to show your strengths to the best advantage. On the occasions when it looks like you are failing to achieve your objective, you effectively have one of two choices. The first option is to change your tactics (and in this book you will find a wide selection of options). If you make this choice, there are not too many things that can go wrong. You look at what your new approach has to offer and continue to change gear as often as is necessary, until you eventually arrive at the place where you want to be, bearing in mind the possibility that somewhere along the way you might exchange your original idea for a better one, based on new insights gleaned from consultation with your stakeholders.

Things are more difficult if, like Anne, you decide to stick to your guns. You are still convinced that your original approach was the right one and so you persist with it ad infinitum, although possibly with a slightly different emphasis here and there. Unfortunately, in this situation your enthusiasm will be seen as stubbornness and your rationality as lecturing. To make matters worse, your message is now often charged with negative emotion, frequently derived from your own irritation and impatience.

We all know that if you transmit a message with an emotional charge it is almost certain that people will respond with equal emotion. They will look less at the content of your message and more at the way the message was delivered. As a result, the chance that your message will land where you want it to land is significantly reduced. In these circumstances, don't be surprised if your emotions rise still further, with a correspondingly negative impact on your effectiveness, in a process that is repeated until you eventually reach the limit of what you can accept.

At this point, there is a danger that after some a time your reaction will switch to the very opposite of the things you originally regarded as your strengths. Your rationality will be transformed into condescending aggression and your enthusiasm will become passive indifference – and it is precisely on these points that you will be most savagely ridiculed by those who do not agree with you. This will hurt you deeply, so that the possibility that you surrender your territory completely without any further fight is a very real one.

That is the paradox of this mechanism: your greatest strengths (as you see them) are also your greatest weaknesses. Once again, the universal law of symmetry is at play: the greater the positive impulse, the greater your potential vulnerability. If you can recognise this mechanism at work in yourself and are able to give it a place, you will not only make yourself less vulnerable but will also be able to respond more quickly and restore your personal balance on those occasions when the mechanism has you in its grip. Why? Because you understand what is happening and can adjust accordingly, but without surrendering your fundamental ideas or your territory.

TAKE AWAY

1   Remind your stakeholder how constructively you have worked together in the past.

2   State your desire to reach workable and sustainable solutions.

3   Nuance the praise you receive from stakeholders.

4   If you want to achieve a change to more desirable behaviour in a stakeholder, first establish the positive intention of the person concerned to do what he currently does. Regard the desired new behaviour as a further expression of that positive intention.

5   Build up a reputation for generosity by giving attention, information and time to (potential) stakeholders, without expecting anything from them in return.

6   Be on your guard against large and unsolicited 'presents'.

7   Never present stakeholders with a fait accompli – and never do it at all in the public arena.

8   If you are given advice, always check if there is a good reason not to follow it.

9   Ask yourself what intention the giver of the advice had in giving you this advice. What purpose does it serve for him?

10 Answer ridicule with a smile.

11 Clearly and explicitly define the boundaries of roles and competencies.

12 Ensure that crucial competencies are never concentrated in a single person.

13 Be self-effacing during contact with stakeholders – and certainly if there is a chance that you might come across to them as threatening.

14 Map out the territory in which you are personally vulnerable and can be hurt by others. Be as objective as possible.

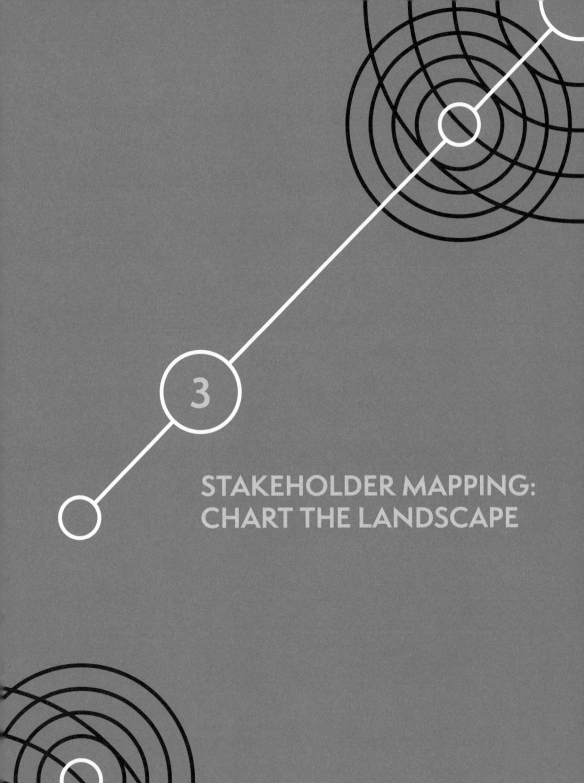

3

STAKEHOLDER MAPPING: CHART THE LANDSCAPE

To successfully complete your projects, you are to a significant degree dependent on others. These 'others' can be individuals or groups. The more complex your project, the greater the role these dependencies will play. We call the people on who we are dependent 'stakeholders'. Within the context of this book, they have two key characteristics:

1   A stakeholder has an impact on the success or failure of your project

A stakeholder can make 'go/no go' decisions, can speed up or slow down processes, can remove obstacles, can improve content quality, can give the project a voice to the outside world and can ensure that the result of your work is implemented – or not.

2   You can exercise influence directly or indirectly on stakeholders

In projects with a broad scope, forces are often at play over which you have no direct control, but which can nonetheless be decisive for making your project viable, both in the short and long term. Factors of this kind include market conditions, technological evolutions, legislation and other regulations, but influence can also be exerted by groups – for example, customers or citizens – who only impact on the chain at a point beyond the immediate scope of your project. Some of these factors you can attempt to anticipate; others you cannot. For this reason, and because you need to be selective in the use of your available time, energy and resources, it is advisable to take no account of these factors and groups. Not because they are unimportant in the context of the bigger picture, but simply because they are beyond your sphere of influence.

In contrast, your stakeholders can be influenced. To be successful, you need to carefully map them out, including their various positions within your project. You will need to know and understand their various interests and agendas and must find ways that will allow your project to create added value for each of them. In territorial terms: you need to align everyone's different wishes in order to create a common territory that is greater than the sum of the individual parts. How you can achieve this is something you will discover in the remaining pages of this book. But this is how you start.

Step 1 Identify your stakeholders

It is useful to start by making a full summary of all your stakeholders. This means everyone who can play a role at some point within the full life cycle of the project. There is nothing more annoying than to forget someone who then suddenly appears on the scene at a moment when you were least expecting it. It can be especially annoying if this person can potentially have a significant impact and you have failed to previously involve or even inform him.

Because completeness is crucial, it is a good idea to ask one of your managers or colleagues to draw up his own list, which you can then compare with yours. You can use the following scheme as a starting point.

What do you need them for?	When do you need them?	On whom should you focus?
Approval	For intermediary and final decisions	The commissioning client and his management
Input	Continuously	Experts who have an impact on the implementation
Manpower and resources	Continuously	The line managers of the members of your project team.
Acceptance of the end result	Periodically, particularly during the later stages	(A selection of) those who will be affected by the results of your project or who represent this group
High quality work	Continually	Your team as a whole and all members separately

Depending on the scope of your project, all or only some of these categories will be important. Ignore the categories that are not relevant in your case.

The one category that you can never ignore is your project team. They are probably your most important success factor. We often regard their contribution as being so self-evident that we lose sight of them as crucial players.

Your project team is very visible. This is often not the case for other stakeholders, even if they also play an important role. When you are under pressure to produce quick results, there is often a tendency to focus all your attention on the project itself and its internal processes. In these circumstances, it is often easy to overlook groups like the unions, sub-contractors, the press, consumer associations, local authorities, etc. Perhaps this is understandable. There is an old adage which says that when you need to choose between things that are urgent and and things that are important, you will generally choose what is urgent. And what are your most urgent priorities? Completing your project according to plan, respecting the budget, producing an end product that works, etc. And preferably getting it right the first time. But in projects with a sizeable scope, this is sometimes not enough – as the following example will show.

A financial institution wanted to develop a new product for a very specific group of customers: farmers. When the product was launched onto the market with much publicity, it was met with a storm of protest from... the farming associations. They were outraged, because they felt they were being condescended to, even discriminated against! Why did they need special banking arrangements, arrangements about which they had never been consulted? Were the banks trying to earn even more money from the decline of the farming industry? And what about the many farmers who were in such a perilous financial position that they could never afford the new product? Who would give them the cover they so desperately needed? This was not the reaction the financial institution had been expecting from its prospective new customers and the situation was made worse by the wide attention the matter received in the press.

Viewed objectively, these reactions were unnecessary and perhaps even unjustified. But that is not the point. The people for whom the product was intended felt that they were being presented with a fait accompli. As a result, they reacted with indignation. This could, of course, all have been avoided by involving the farming associations in the project from an early stage. Agreed, that might not have been as easy as it sounds. Once a consultation process of this kind is started, there is always a risk that information will be leaked prematurely, often to the benefit of rival companies who may wish to develop a similar idea.

There is also the inevitable pressure to produce results against tight deadlines; pressure which consumes so much of your team's energy that there is sometimes a tendency to ignore consultations that are seen as 'unnecessary' or 'time-consuming'. Such thinking is understandable but ultimately wrong. The effort (time, energy and money) needed to neutralise protest and re-launch your product in the market in a viable manner is often much greater than it would have been simply to involve the end users in the project from the beginning.

Step 2 Position your stakeholders in relation to your project

There is a variety of ways you can map out the positioning of your stakeholders. The following matrix is a synthesis of a number of these different models.[1] The matrix operates along two axes with a graded scale from 0 to 10.

The vertical axis is the IMPACT axis: to what extent does the stakeholder have an influence on the progress and outcome of your project? This influence can be either positive or negative.

The horizontal axis in the AGREEMENT axis: to what extent does the stakeholder agree with what you are doing? This can relate to both the objectives of the project and the methods you use of achieve those objectives.

When you have added each of your stakeholders to the matrix, they will be positioned in one of five sectors, but at different points within each sector. This makes it possible to approach each of them in a slightly different way later on in the project.

You should always carry out the mapping in the order outlined above: first scale in each stakeholder along both axes and only then consider the sector into which he falls. Do not take the sectors and their designated names as your starting point, since this risks losing important nuances in the positioning. Also remember to regularly update your mapping, so that it reflects the current situation during the different phases of the project.

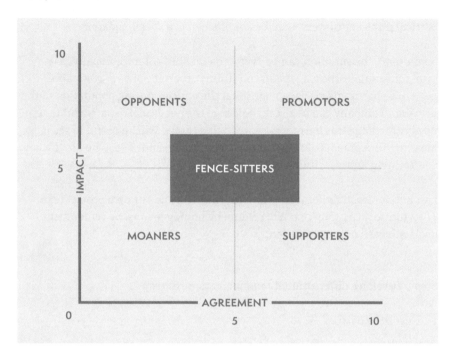

Step 3 Differentiate the stakeholder groups

There is a good chance that some of the stakeholders you have identified are individuals, whereas others are groups. Groups are seldom homogeneous. This means that approaching them as single unit is often unhelpful. Perhaps you have identified 'the directors' as a stakeholder. Whereas key decisions will be taken collectively by the board as a whole, the individual directors will not all be involved to the same extent and each will look at your proposals differently. For some, your project may be irrelevant; these you can safely leave alone. Instead, identify the directors who can be important for you and give them an individual place in the matrix.

The same applies to other groups, such as the unions. Like the directors, the unions will not form a homogeneous body. Each union has its own agenda, its own hierarchy, its own 'brand' and its own electors who believe in the brand. The union's militants will have a different impact than the formal representatives at company level, who in turn will have a different impact than the external union officials at regional or national level. Once again, it is necessary to distinguish between these different elements, so that each of them – and in particular the key players – can be approached in a specific manner.

Sometimes, the situation can be even broader still. After a company take-over, for example, the wages and conditions of service of both companies need to be harmonised. This means that the entire working population of the new joint-company can be a stakeholder of the personnel department that needs to arrange this harmonisation. In this case, it will be useful to see if meaningful segments of staff can be differentiated and, if so, who are the key determining figures within each segment.

Last but not least, remember to differentiate within your own project team. They, too, form a group that will seldom be homogeneous. So remember to deal with each of them differently.

Step 4 Develop a differentiated communication strategy

1   Check the basics

By definition, your project will result in a change of some kind. To make this change viable in the long run, you will need to satisfy a number of criteria:
- There will need to be a felt need for change.
- There will need to be a clear and shared vision about what the change must achieve and why.
- There will need to be sufficient capacity and resources to achieve the change and a differentiated plan for its implementation;
- There will need to be a systematic implementation trajectory, which is effectively carried out.

The importance of each of these components is reproduced in the schedule below.[2]

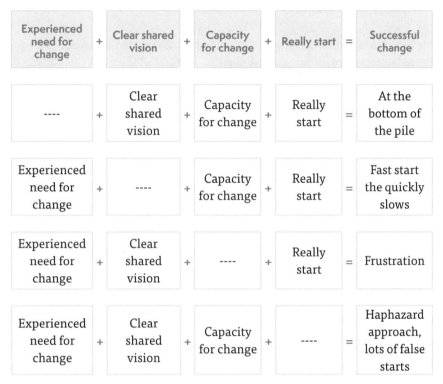

Experienced need for change	+	Clear shared vision	+	Capacity for change	+	Really start	=	Successful change
----	+	Clear shared vision	+	Capacity for change	+	Really start	=	At the bottom of the pile
Experienced need for change	+	----	+	Capacity for change	+	Really start	=	Fast start the quickly slows
Experienced need for change	+	Clear shared vision	+	----	+	Really start	=	Frustration
Experienced need for change	+	Clear shared vision	+	Capacity for change	+	----	=	Haphazard approach, lots of false starts

The need for change, the shared vision about the change outcome, and the plan that will lead from A to B must be clear to each stakeholder right from the very beginning and must be repeated regularly throughout the project. When the proposed change is far-reaching, it is important to do this in face-to-face meetings during which the stakeholders can have their say. This increases not only their understanding and their insight, but also their engagement. Later in the book, you can find many tips and tricks that will help you to accurately design and implement these processes.

2 Adjust your methods to the positioning of your stakeholders

We all know how under the pressure of time our thinking can sometimes become simplistically binary: cowboys and indians, for or against us, worth the effort or not. We invest in people who are on our side and leave the others to their own devices ('If they are sensible and take the trouble to think, they will see that it is smart to work with us, primarily because it is also in their own best interests'). This results in a 'one-size-fits-all' approach and an identical communication strategy.

Positioning your stakeholders in a matrix helps you to think and communicate in a more differentiated manner. In terms of the main categories, you can consider the following strategies.

PROMOTERS

Promoters have a significant impact and are on your side. Your most important consideration is to keep them that way. Don't assume that this will happen automatically without any effort on your part.

You can strengthen your alliances by taking the following actions:

- In addition to formal reporting moments, send them a short (never more than half a page) status update every two weeks: what has been completed, where are things falling behind schedule, how are you planning to make up the lost ground, etc. Check every couple of months or so to confirm whether or not the promoters still find these status updates useful.
- Warn promoters about potential threats and obstacles, how these can be overcome and what they can do to help. Once again: never more than half a page, unless they specifically ask for more information.
- Thank them regularly for their contribution.
- Ask for advice, preferably during face-to-face contact.

To know who your real Promoters are, it is sometimes useful to look further than what they say. For example, if a Promoter is quite high up in the hierarchy, expressing complete support for your project might be the only politically correct thing he can do. Try to find out via other channels what he really thinks.

You will get more valid information if you look at your Promoter's behavioural indicators: what does he actually do (as opposed to what he says)? The following list of indicators will offer a better picture of his real level of engagement. You know that a Promoter is paying more than mere lip service to your project when he/she:

- answers your mails;
- is present at meetings about your project;
- takes active part in these meetings with questions and suggestions;
- honours any agreements made;
- responds to your questions for input and advice;
- volunteers comment on the reports you send out;
- changes his/her agenda to devote time to your project;
- invites you to talk in his/her team about your project;
- talks to you informally about your project.

OPPONENTS

Opponents also have a significant impact but are not on your side. It probably won't be your favourite occupation, but you will need to invest time in them as well, since they have the ability to delay your project, starve it of resources, spread negative publicity about it, etc. They focus on what they see as the weaknesses and risks of your project. Sometimes they are even in a position to pull the plug.

When we encounter serious resistance or opposition, there is often a tendency to stick negative labels on the motives and reasons of our Opponents. We are so strongly convinced (for the right motives and reasons, of course) of our own good intentions, sense of responsibility and professional knowledge that we fall back on a position which effectively says that whoever is against us must either be pretty stupid or just bloody-minded.

Approaching an Opponent with this mindset will nearly always lead to a self-fulfilling prophecy. We either try to avoid them, which makes them feel even less involved with what we are doing and more inclined to follow their own agenda, or else we put them under pressure, which threatens their freedom of thought and action (their territory), so that we actually strengthen their resistance rather than lessen it.

Later in the book we will look in more detail about how you can best deal with resistance. The starting point should always be the working hypothesis that the Opponent, viewed from his perspective, has good reasons for his opposition to your proposals. Trying to meet this opposition head on is always counterproductive. You first need to explore it, to look at things from the other person's point of view, to try and understand his doubts and concerns, to follow and respect his reasoning. In this way, you open up the possibility to build a bridge between your respective positions, in the hope of being able to develop a common platform you can both support.

When faced with opposition, consider the following options:

- Arrange face-to-face discussions that will allow you to map out the Opponent's vision of your project (you can find a checklist in the following chapter).
- Summarise his arguments regularly to be sure that you have understood them properly and in full. Do not be afraid to say if this is not the case. In this way, you show that you really want to make sense of his logic.
- Deal first with the points of common concern, leaving points of difference until later in the discussion.
- Search for low-hanging fruit, first exploring solutions for easy-to-solve problems and again leaving the more difficult points of difference until later on.
- Ask what he suggests as the best way to collaborate and communicate, both in terms of content and form, and with a clear list of do's and don'ts. Keep strictly to whatever you agree.
- Explicitly express appreciation for his engagement.

FENCE-SITTERS

You are probably familiar with the expression that the only people waiting for change are babies with a wet nappy. It is hardly surprising then that whenever change comes on the agenda many people's first reaction is to be non-committal. Even after you have explained the need for change and how you plan to get there, most of them continue sitting on the fence: 'Let's just wait and see what happens.' And there is nothing wrong with that.

When these Fence-sitters are individual stakeholders who you really need to prompt into action, the following options may be useful:

- Ask them what, in their opinion, are the respective pros and cons of your project.
- If there are clear gaps in their knowledge, provide additional information about the 'why' and the 'how' of your project.

- Ask what could give them more confidence in your project and how this might be achieved in practical terms.
- Bring them into contact with people who have already committed to the project, so that the latter can talk about their initial reservations and how these were overcome.
- Keep them informed regularly but briefly about the progress of the project.

If your Fence-sitters are groups rather than individuals (and this applies equally to other stakeholders), it is better to approach their opinion leaders or meet with a representative sample: focus groups.

An opinion leader is someone from the target group who does not necessarily have a senior position in the hierarchy, but who nonetheless possesses considerable moral authority. This is the person to whom colleagues look for guidance at moments of uncertainty: whatever he/she says and/or does will usually be followed by the rest of the group. If you can identify these people in advance and get them on your side, you will have a serious lever to persuade others. How can you discover who these opinion leaders are? Just ask any group's first-line manager: he or she will be able to tell you immediately.[3]

It was decided in a large petro-chemical company that there was a need to introduce a new ERP system. As a result, many of the existing functions would be automated. People knew from their knowledge of comparable systems that this meant almost all the 'old' operational procedures with which everyone was familiar would be ditched. Since few of us change our old habits willingly, enthusiasm for the proposed new system was muted, to say the least. The key question for the management was therefore this: when the button launching the new system was pressed, how many people would they be able to get on board and how quickly? The company knew that the transition would not be straightforward. From one of their sister companies it was learnt that in a similar situation only 10 percent of the workforce had adjusted immediately to the new processes. Everyone else tried to hang on to the old way of doing things. With massive chaos as a result. This was something that no-one wanted to see repeated.

So what was the management's strategy? They identified the opinion leaders at various levels in the organisation and focused extra attention on them. They were invited to attend a consultation session in a hotel, where they were well looked after and, more importantly, fully briefed about the 'what', the 'why' and the 'how' of the proposed change. Most important of all, they were asked to suggest possible obstacles to the introduction of the new system and how its details might best be adjusted. The suggested amendments were implemented as far as possible and with a minimum of delay, and the company made sure that the opinion leaders were made aware of this. This gave these leaders the feeling that they also had some kind of grip, at least in part, on the situation, which was instrumental in helping to turn them into supporters of the plan. When the new system was launched, it was to these influencers, and not to their line managers, that people looked to see whether or not they should accept the change. As a result, the transition was remarkably smooth. The time and money invested by the management in preparation for this moment had been time and money well spent.

Focus groups give you the opportunity to test the opinion of large groups of people and possibly even to prompt them into action. How can you create a focus group? Simply ask all your managers to nominate two representatives from their team and bring them together regularly in an open forum. Depending on the numbers involved, it may be wiser to split them down into smaller groups. As a rule of thumb, never have more than ten people in a group.

If you want to obtain valid information, make sure that different hierarchical levels are not represented in the same group. Allow each group to be chaired by someone who is sufficiently far removed from the department or group concerned.

An essential part of the group process is the collection of information based on the questions listed above for individual Fence-sitters.

After each session, report the resultant findings to the entire group. If a number of focus groups are working in parallel, each group should report in turn to their rank and file. In this way, everyone has access to and control of any information that comes to light. As the project manager, you can be present at the focus group meetings, perhaps with one or two of your junior managers. Make sure that the following two things happen: (1) If there are points of concern to which you can respond immediately (either with an answer or with action), do so on the spot. In this way, the group members will see that you have de facto impact on the entire

process, which can only serve to increase their engagement. (2) If there are
questions to which you are not able to give a direct response, say that you
will look into the matter and give them an answer within an agreed period
of time. Even if you are eventually unable to give them the answer they
were hoping for, the fact that you have taken their question/proposal seriously and have tried to do something about it will be viewed as positive.[4]

MOANERS

Moaners – as the somewhat biased name suggests – are people who are
not particularly happy with your project but do not oppose it as such.
Moaners do not generally have much impact on what you are proposing,
so you do not need to invest a huge amount of energy to try and win them
around. You do, however, need to be careful that you do not provoke them
into something more than just moaning by saying uncomplimentary
things to them or about them. Not only directly, but also in the hearing of
third parties who might pass on your words. If you do make this mistake,
the message will quickly spread and before you know it their passive
moaning will have been converted into active opposition.

A large production company decided to launch a large-scale campaign
focused on a reduction of sick leave and the creation of a more stimulating
working environment. Considerable negotiation was necessary before the
management was able to win union acceptance for the campaign, albeit
without much enthusiasm. During a meeting of the campaign steering
committee, one group of manual workers was described as a 'bunch of old
whiners, for whom you can never do anything good'. Unfortunately, this
unwise comment soon found its way to the workfloor, where the reaction
was one of outrage. The unions felt that they had little choice other than
to stand shoulder to shoulder with their 'insulted' rank and file, and so
they removed their support for the campaign in protest. A Promoter had
been turned into an Opponent, simply because the Moaners had not been
treated with sufficient care and respect.

SUPPORTERS

Supporters can only be a source of joy to you, especially if they used to be
Fence-sitters or Moaners. Although they are not Promoters, don't lose
sight of the fact that they are often crucial for the success of your project,
above all during the implementation phase. They are the critical mass

that you need. Do not assume that their buy-in is necessarily permanent. Continue to keep them well informed and ensure that all the signs of their engagement and collaboration are both made visible and properly rewarded.

It is self-evident that most of your energy and attention will be focused on persons and groups in the upper half of the acceptance matrix. There are good and obvious reasons for this. These are the people who play a decisive role in the decision-making process at the key moments of your project. It is largely in their hands whether or not your project continues to move forward and, if so, to what extent it is rolled out in the breadth and depth. They are particular important in the early phases, when the project architecture and processes are being designed.

Of course, whether or not your project will achieve the results you envisaged and whether or not it is successfully implemented in the way you had planned is also dependent on a wide range of other factors and people. This is where the bottom half of the matrix comes into play. They can also make and break a project. For this reason alone, you need to keep them on your radar right from the very beginning.

Johnny Thijs was the CEO responsible for the transformation of the Belgian postal service, bpost. In order to comply with European legislation, he needed to achieve a significant increase in productivity (and later he also successfully launched the company onto the stock market). To make this possible, heavy investment and major process innovations were required, but equally important was a necessary change in the culture and mentality of the organisation. How was this achieved?

Thijs and the members of his executive committee entered into a personal dialogue about the new company strategy with all of bpost's employees. Not through video-conferencing or e-mail circulars, but face to face. With all of them. When groups of postmen and women arrived for work early in the morning at their local post offices, Johnny or one of the other senior managers would be there to talk with them, to explain what was planned, to ask about their concerns, to give them reassurance. If you realise that bpost had more than 30,000 employees at that time, you can imagine how frequently they had to do this. Sometimes these informal meetings were close to their homes; sometimes they were on the other side of the country. But at six o' clock each morning they were there, waiting for their people to arrive.

They did this at the start of the implementation process; they did it again two years later; and they did it a third time, two years after that.

Of course, these meetings also provided Thijs and the leadership team with a mine of useful information about what was really going on inside the organisation, information that the senior management team was able to use to their advantage to push the project through. But the decisive intervention was the original initiative to set up the interactive consultation process. This was a clear and tangible sign of how much importance and value the executive committee attached to the people on the workfloor (Supporters and Moaners) as the key factor in ensuring that the transformation could be completed successfully. The fact that this required a sustained physical effort from the senior management over a long period showed that they meant it.

Step 5 Decide which migrations are possible

You have now positioned your stakeholders on your acceptance matrix. This reflects the position as you see it today and it allows you to analyse in which direction you need to try and move them in the future – not only between categories but also within each category. By giving each stakeholder a score between 0 and 10 on both axes, you now have a series of points which helps you to assess what migrations might be possible and also gives you a good idea about what kind of approach you need to make this happen in each case. Here are some general guidelines that you should also bear in mind:

1   It is not necessary for everyone to be a Promoter or a Supporter before you begin with the project's implementation. It often happens that people only come around once the implementation has started and they can see the benefits it brings (or are at least persuaded that the disadvantages they feared can be successfully dealt with). Begin by trying to achieve a number of quick, small successes, to which you can give maximum publicity.

2   Opponents will never become Promoters in a single step, so don't waste your time and energy trying to bring this about. It will often be the case that Opponents have started their opposition openly and that this also

contributes to their social status in some quarters. To suddenly become a Promoter overnight would involve a serious loss of face, which is something they could not possibly contemplate. With this in mind, make sure you give Opponents sufficient space to first become Moaners or Fence-sitters. If they reach the point where they are prepared to give you the benefit of the doubt, this is more than sufficient for your purposes, even if they continue in public to air their scepticism about the project's value and likelihood of success.

3   You will find it easier to persuade Opponents and Moaners to migrate if you recognise their right to exist. For this reason, it is a good idea to mention their comments in the reports of meetings, even if they are only a small minority. In this way, you show them respect, which is the best way to create goodwill in return.

4   The initial matrix charts the situation as it is today, before your project starts. Once the project is underway, this situation will evolve. So will the attitudes and influence of your stakeholders. Some people who have relatively little impact during the development phase may have a huge impact during the implementation phase. Try to anticipate this change.

With this in mind, prepare a second matrix which maps out the situation as you expect it to be at the start of the implementation phase. It is already worth asking the stakeholders whose influence will increase during this phase precisely what this will involve. It also pays to keep them in the loop by providing them with frequent but short summaries of progress, even for the earlier processes in which they are less directly involved. This helps to secure their continued engagement.

This is a task that you should repeat for each phase of your planning. Give each stakeholder a new position on each new chart. Is your set of stakeholders complete? Should anyone be added? Should anyone be removed? On which stakeholders should you focus attention during the next phase? Make sure that no-one is overlooked – which can easily happen in a rapidly changing organisational environment.

5   By placing your stakeholders on the matrix one by one, it may seem as if
    they are wholly independent of each other. Of course, the reality is very
    different. Many of them are closely inter-related. If you focus on your
    Promoters, it is worth asking yourself what impact they might be able to
    have on the stakeholders in other sectors. If feasible, do not hesitate to
    use them as ambassadors for your project. They may be able to persuade
    others to act more easily than you can. Why do you think they are called
    Promoters?

Additional comment

'It's impossible to do anything with that union rep,' sighed the people in the
HR department. 'He just doesn't listen to a word you say!' The man was indeed extremely difficult: dominant, rude and unreasonable, so much so that
he single-handedly threatened to jeopardise meaningful dialogue between
employer and employees. Many attempts had been made to improve the
situation but all of them had failed. As a result, the relationship between the
management and the workforce was at an all-time low.

It took a long while before a solution was finally found, in the shape of an
external union official, who occupied a higher position in the union hierarchy
than the internal troublemaker. The official could see that the interests of the
staff – his members – were best served by healthy collaboration with the management. More importantly, he was someone that the firebrand was prepared
to listen to. Problem solved. Sometimes – as in this case – you can only nudge
your stakeholders into more positive action by searching for ambassadors
outside the organisation with whom you can build up a constructive relationship.

TAKE AWAY

1. Focus your efforts on the stakeholders who you can influence directly or indirectly.
2. Pamper your Promoters, Supporters and, above all, your project team.
3. Identify opinion leaders and use them as levers.
4. Do the same with the Promoters who may be able to influence the stakeholders you have positioned in other segments.
5. Value the right to exist of Opponents and Moaners. If, after a time, they are prepared to give you the benefit of the doubt, so that they perhaps become Fence-sitters, this is all you need.
6. Regularly update your stakeholder analysis.
7. Find ways to involve all stakeholders in your project right from the start, even if some of them only become important later on in the process.

4

INVEST IN THE CREATION OF COMMON TERRITORIES AND PARTNERSHIPS

You have mapped out the playing field. You know who will help to determine your success and you know the extent to which they are currently on board (or not). Depending on their position, you want some of them to stop being merely passive spectators of your project and instead become its active supporters. For others, you hope to see their existing support raised to a higher level, while for some it will be sufficient if they just cease to be actively hostile towards you and your team. In each of these instances, you want to see people move to a different position from the one they now occupy. To achieve this, you can either pray to the gods for divine intervention, trusting that somehow things will eventually turn out for the best, or else you can actually take concrete measures to try and make it happen. In other words, you need to do things that will gradually push your stakeholders in the direction you want. You will only be able to do this if you respect their individual territories. But even then, you will still need to be highly skilled in the subtle art of influencing.

1   INFLUENCE IN THE WORKPLACE

Let's be clear on this: without you ever knowing it (and perhaps it is better that way), you have no idea as a consumer just how often and how intensively you are subjected to external influencing. This is the life's work of whole armies of marketeers and trainers in sales techniques. Their influence is huge, all the more so because it takes place largely through unseen channels, using techniques that have been worked out to the minutest detail in order to maximise their considerable efficiency. We buy their products without realising that it is they who have made the choice, not us. It is not without good reason that in quite a few countries there is legislation that gives you 14 days after you have signed an order form to change your mind, by which time you will have possibly come to your senses. In some ways, there is nothing wrong with all this: after all, it helps to oil the wheels of our economy. And it certainly does no harm for the salespeople, who rake in huge bonuses, nor for the shareholders, who rake in even bigger dividends. But what about us, the poor old consumers? Are there any benefits for us? We end up with our products, of course, and a prosperous economy generally works in all our favours. Even so, these are at best pleasing side effects. Consumer influencing exists first and foremost for the benefit of the makers and sellers, not for the benefit of the buyers and users. That is just how things work in the crazy world of consumerism.

If you are thinking of using these same kinds of influencing techniques in a professional context, you would be well advised to think carefully about what you are planning. A working environment is typified by a number of characteristics which mean that you cannot use just any old techniques. Some methods will be deemed acceptable; others are a definite no-no.

Relationships between colleagues are frequently of long standing and you are often dependent on each other in a number of different ways. If, in such a context, you only think about your own interests (and your bonus) and use manipulative techniques to achieve them, you are taking a big risk – especially if in doing so you damage the interests of others around you. If these others catch on to what you are doing, there is a danger that you will lose your credibility overnight. Before you know it, people will be talking about your reputation as someone not to be trusted, which means that you can kiss goodbye to any hopes of influencing them again in the future. You tried to be clever, but all you managed was to shoot yourself in the foot. And it serves you right, because you attempted to impinge on the personal territory of your colleagues without their permission. In work terms, this is the equivalent of breaking into someone's home. The victims will not only increase the security of their own property, but will also warn people in the neighbourhood to be on their guard against thieves, so that they too can strengthen their territorial defences.

The purpose of sustainable influencing will always be to develop a mutually beneficial partnership, a partnership that makes everyone better off and respects everyone's territory. Or that, at least, is the principle – and it sounds simple. In practice, of course, it is a little more complex.

Consider, for example, the case of Brian. He is a customer service agent working in an airport and has been briefed to deal with a group of American students who have missed their connecting flight to Athens. Their incoming plane from the States was late arriving in Brussels, so that they can now only leave in three hours' time.

Brian wants to talk with the group leader about the situation. He soon finds her: a young woman in her early twenties with a big pile of papers in her hand and a harassed look on her face that seems to say: 'How can they do this to us!' She tries to explain just how big a mess they are in. Brian tries to make her see that it is not such a problem, after all.

'I have already arranged everything with your travel agent in Athens. There will be somebody there to meet your group and drive you to the hotel. Your flight tickets have also been re-booked and in another three hours you will be out of here.' You can almost hear him thinking: 'Another case solved, quick and easy. Who says that experience doesn't pay?'

But the group leader is far from convinced. 'What do you mean, a three hour wait? That will ruin our entire stay in Athens. There is a boat waiting for us and everything! This is never going to work out!' As she speaks, her voice gets louder and louder, and she finds increasing support from the equally unhappy students who are listening to the conversation.

'No, no,' says Brian. 'I've just told you: everything has been arranged. You will hardly notice the difference. Even so, I think it's a good idea if you head off now to the check-in desk to change your tickets. That can sometimes take a bit of time.' Adding silently to himself: 'It's not as if I have haven't got other things to do than look after you lot!'

But the young woman is not having any of it. 'Hey, buster, you don't get away with it that easy. Don't you realise that we are just a bunch of poor students who have saved up thousands of dollars to pay for this journey of a lifetime? And now you tell us we are going to miss out on our visit to the Parthenon, not to mention the archaeological museum and the flea market!' Her face begins to colour red with anger and you can hear the gradual change in her voice from victim to judge, jury and executioner.

'I don't believe it,' says Brian to himself. 'Some people are never satisfied.' Even so, he decides to pull out another surprise from his professional box of tricks. 'Look, I'm more than happy to offer you complementary drinks while you wait...'

'A drink is not the same as the Parthenon!' she shouts, so that the entire departure terminal can hear. 'The president was right: this place really is a hellhole. I hope that I never have to come here again!' And with that, the entire group stormed off, leaving a bemused Brian behind them.

'What a lot of fuss about a measly three-hour wait. And poor students? Don't give me that. I bet their rich parents paid for the lot. Who is she trying to kid?'

End of story.

But not a happy ending. Both sides aggrieved. Both sides feeling they have been hard done by. Bad luck for the students. But also bad luck for Brian. He used a great deal of energy and skill to find and organise the best possible solution, but in the end all he got for his troubles was a verbal blasting. All his efforts to help were simply ignored. What a shame! Doubly so, because Brian's job (of course) consists of two separate elements: he is certainly there to solve people's problems, but he is also there take care of the PR for his company. And as far as this latter aspect is concerned, he failed totally.

If you look at this dialogue again, you can see that it began to go wrong from the point where the group leader said 'This is a big problem' and Brian replied 'No it isn't. I've already solved it.' From then on, the protagonists moved further and further away from each other, as a result of which their arguments became increasingly irrational and their behaviour increasingly hostile.

Curiously enough, the original impetus for developing the theme on which this book is based was also related to an airport situation. Several years ago, I was approached by a telecom company with the following problem: 'We have excellent engineers who have a high level of expertise and are highly inventive, but what they lack is the ability to sell their ideas effectively within the organisation.' The importance of this request for the company was immediately obvious: if you can't sell good ideas, you might as well not have them in the first place. In fact, you are better off without them, because an idea that you know is valuable but is nonetheless not accepted, ultimately leads to disillusion and cynicism. This is not only harmful to the motivation and job satisfaction of the experts, but is also a terrible waste of knowledge and expertise. To avoid this, it helps to have greater insight into the ways in which you can have more impact on others. The objective remains the same: to let these others also benefit from your good ideas. Or to express it in slightly different terms: to enrich their territory by allowing them access to a little piece of yours, so that they are prepared to put their shoulder behind your project, because it has also become (in part, at least) their project.

The key is a formula that you have already seen in various variants in this book:

Impact = Quality x Acceptance

Or: the impact that you have is a function of the internal quality of your idea multiplied by the level of acceptance.

Particularly in an expertise-driven environment, you can assume that this formula is (or at least should be, so they believe) slightly different; namely, I = Q. This is the pious and optimistic view that ideas should be judged on their merits. If an idea is brilliant, it should automatically be accepted for that reason alone. Sounds sensible? If that's what you really believe, dream on!

That being said, we need to be clear on one point: the Q in the equation nonetheless continues to plays an important role. Many people try to sell hot air and some even do it successfully. But hot air is still hot air, and even if the initial willingness to buy it (= acceptance) is great, it will have no lasting impact when people finally see that there is nothing more to it. The quality of an idea therefore continues to be a key factor, but it is not enough by itself to have an impact.

At the end of the day, this Q element of the equation is almost never a problem in terms of impact. People are generally smart enough and have expertise enough – certainly in a professional context – to come up with an idea that is sound. The real secret to impact is tied up in the A element. What can you do to get your idea accepted, so that it can be developed properly and valued in the way it deserves? How can you persuade others that, in addition to being a good idea, your project is also in their own best interests, so that it makes perfect sense for them to support it?

Theoretically, it is not so complex. People usually say 'yes' to ideas or proposals that work to their benefit in areas that are important to them; in other words, in areas that allow them to add to or better manage their territory. This means that the pathway to success is deceptively straightforward: first find out what is important for each of your stakeholders and then find a way that your project can contribute towards those priorities. Put simply (and perhaps a touch disrespectfully): influence is easy if you can hitch your wagon to someone else's train. It is a transaction between different territories. I ask you to help me to better manage my territory, and in return in will give you access to part of my territory in a manner that will help you to expand yours.

So the first question you need to ask is this: what is their 'train'? What can prompt my stakeholders into action? To answer this, you first need to become more deeply acquainted with their reality.

2 UNDERSTANDING THE TERRITORY OF YOUR STAKEHOLDERS

To find out what things matter for your stakeholders, you need to map out two separate territories. The first is task-oriented; the second is emotional. As far as the task territory is concerned, you want to know as precisely as possible how each of them relates to your project. For the emotional aspect, you need to explore which non-rational elements will help to determine whether or not your stakeholders are willing to back your plans.

Step 1 Explore the perspective from which your stakeholders relate to your projects

Below you can find a questionnaire to map out how your stakeholders view your project. Use these questions as a source of inspiration. Not all questions will be relevant for every stakeholder. But for your key stakeholders, those who have the greatest impact on your projects, you really need to answer them all. It is sensible not to make too many assumptions about what they think. Ask them face to face.

CHECKLIST to explore your stakeholder's view of your project

1 What for you is the importance of this project and why is it important?
2 For who else is the project important and why?
3 How will you measure the success of the project? What needs to happen for you to be satisfied with the result?
4 If you need answers to two essential questions, what would those questions be and why?
5 For which other domains will the project have consequences? What consequences? Who are the owners of these domains?
6 Which approaches/solutions for the theme of my project have been considered or tested out in the past and were ultimately not selected or accepted, or did not work? Why exactly?
7 Which ideas were accepted but not implemented? Why not?
8 Which comparable projects have been successful in the past? What were the reasons for this success?

9   What kinds of solutions have not yet been considered? Which questions have not yet been asked?

10 Which boundaries (times, resources, legislation, etc.) need to be respected and why?

11 With which (generic) conditions must each and every solution comply and why?

12 Who stands to benefit from this project? What will those benefits be?

13 Who stands to lose out from this project? How exactly will they lose out?

14 Who, in your opinion, are the key stakeholders and how do they relate to each other?

15 Who takes the final decision?

16 Which persons or other parties need to be involved in the project and at which times?

17 What things do you want to see happen in our mutual collaboration? What do you not want to see happen? Why not? How can we best monitor this?

You will probably have noticed that some of the questions are fairly probing, even intrusive. There is a danger that this might initially startle some of your stakeholders, so that they are less inclined to give you the information you need. Or that they will only say what is socially desirable, which is not likely to be of much help to you. To avoid this, there are two things you can do.

The first is something that you must always do as a matter of course: explain and justify the need for the conversation. Whichever way you look at it, you are asking your conversation partner to invest time and share information. For him, these are costs. It is only reasonable that he should know in return what is in it for him. It is therefore important when planning the conversation to make clear right from the very start that you want to know his opinion about a number of the project's crucial aspects, so that you can be sure that his perspective is taken properly into account and that the project can be completed as efficiently and productively as possible. Do this always.

The second thing you can do is to consider using a technique known as 'softening'. If you want to ask a question that seems blunt, you can introduce it by saying: 'This next question might seem a bit frank, so I apologise in advance...' By making this clear, your conversation partner no longer needs to think about it himself and so you effectively anticipate and disarm his potentially defensive reaction. Avoid, however, turning this tactic into a trademark: if you overuse it (like any technique), it will often be interpreted as a sign of weakness, so that you will be taken less seriously and will receive less of the information you need.

When looking at the questionnaire, it may also have struck you that some of the questions are less evident than others. For example: who might lose out from this project and how? The effect of this kind of question is double. You get information about the balance of power within the context where your project takes place and this allows you to anticipate possible resistance. Almost as important, however, it shows to your conversation partner that you know that your project is not all plain sailing and that in practice it may be less straightforward than you think. In this way, you show that you have insight and appreciation for the complexity of the situation, which increases the likelihood that you will be seen as a valuable conversation (and later sparring) partner. In other words, you not only get information, but also actively build up a relationship and enhance your credibility.

What these conversations will give you is a good understanding of what is important for each of your (key) stakeholders: their concerns, aspirations and ideas. Of course, your first priority is to acquire valid and reliable information. Whether or not you get this will depend in part on the willingness of your conversation partner to give it. But there is an even more important factor: you. In particular, your ability to listen. Being a good listener is not as easy as it might sound.

Are you one? Here is a little test that will help you to find out. Take a piece of paper and note down your answers to the following four questions.

1 What associations spring into your mind when you hear the word 'school'?
2 What memories are attached to each of those associations? Use keywords to describe them.
3 What feelings are attached to those memories?
4 Why do all these things together have meaning for you?

Now ask two of your family or friends to answer the same questions. When they have done so, sit down and compare your answers. You should each read out in turn what you have written. All that the two listeners can do is ask for further clarification. There is to be no discussion and no conversation. Just listen and clarify. Now we come to the crux of the matter: listen to each other and try to identify what is different from what you had written down in your answers. Do not try and find common denominators, only the points of difference. That is why it is so important not to enter into discussion.

At first, you will probably be amazed by the number of differences you hear and just how big they are. But this is not really so surprising: we each occupy our own different experience world, which we use to give meaning to words and concepts. If you fail to understand this, you risk missing much of the important information your stakeholders can offer. You will hear them talk of concepts that you think you understand, whereas in reality what you understand is your *own* conceptualisation of those concepts. The chances that you both view the same concept in exactly the same way is statistically very small. You can guard against this distortion by making systematic use of the following two questions: (1) Can you give me an example of what you are thinking? (2) When you say x, what do you mean and what do you not mean?

Additional comment 1

When compiling your summary of stakeholders, you will come across some individuals and groups who are key to your project, but to whom you have no direct access.

For a major IT project in a large bank the CEO was unquestionably a key figure. Steven was the project leader. He knew it was not realistic to expect that he could arrange to see the big boss at short notice. This means that he needed to rely on information obtained through his immediate boss, the CIO. In other words, Steven's information about the CEO was all indirect. Information of this kind is nearly always subject to distortion. It is filtered and interpreted by the person who passes the information on. In this particular case, there was nothing Steven could do to avoid it. But he tried to protect himself against the effects of the distortion by regularly testing the CIO's story with questions like: How did you reach that conclusion? Did you actually hear him say that in a meeting?

Additional comment 2

Interviews based on the checklist are never neutral. They are always about more than the straightforward exchange of information. You are also working towards the building up of a relationship. At the same time, you are also inevitably creating expectations in your conversation partner. By asking your stakeholders for their opinions, you implicitly give them the impression that they have co-ownership over your territory (your project). Of course, this is part of your intention: you want their opinions because you want to be able to take account of them. That being said, it is important to make clear to your conversation partner the limitations of his intrusion into and his influence on your territory. You can best do this by clearly setting out at the start of your conversation the exact scope of the project. Explain what is possible, what is not possible and why. You need to carefully manage stakeholder expectations right from the very beginning.

If, during your conversation, the stakeholder expresses wishes that give you serious pause for thought (and perhaps even raised eyebrows), don't simply let the matter drop. Ask further questions that will allow you to better understand his or her perspective. Do not immediately say that you think something is unrealistic, because this is likely to lead directly to a discussion that may jeopardise the rest of the conversation. Wait until the end and only then return to any points of contention. Say what your reservations are and why this is so, and agree when you will get back to them on the matter.

Step 2 Using the perspective of your stakeholders as a springboard

Let's return to the adage we mentioned above: influencing and steering is relatively easy if you can hitch your wagon to someone else's train. But before this can work, two conditions must apply: you must know what is important for your stakeholder and your stakeholder must know that you know.

This latter aspect is less evident for introverts than for extroverts. If you are more of an introvert type, you will probably be a good listener and pick up what the other person is trying to say, but you will probably be less inclined to repeat it back to him. Why should you? You already know what he means. Unfortunately, this makes communication more difficult, especially if your conversation partner is an extrovert, because that is the 'problem' with extroverts: they only know something if they have heard it from someone else. This underlines the importance of summarising and repetition, something you should have learned during your very first lesson in communication training: don't just check that you have understood something correctly, but *show* that you have understood it correctly.

More important still is what you do with the information you have obtained throughout the course of your project. Whenever you develop a new element or send a status report, link this explicitly to the things your stakeholders told you during your initial interview with them. This will cost you extra time, because in essence it means that in part you are personalising the reports. Even so, it is well worth the effort. Why? Because it means that time after time your stakeholders will be provided with concrete evidence that you are taking account of the things that are important to them. In this way, you can build up a good partnership, all the more so since it is a partnership that has benefits in both directions. Do you remember what we said earlier about the strength of the natural human desire to be internally consistent? By repeatedly reminding your partners of what they said in the past, you will reduce the risk of capricious behaviour. They will want to be consistent with themselves. And this means that they will be consistent with you as well.

Additional comment

It hardly needs to be said that every work environment is dynamic. The business context and the relationships within it are constantly changing, so that priorities are also subject to change. Do not automatically assume that what you heard during your initial stakeholder interviews will still be valid in the same manner and to the same extent six months further down the line. For this reason, it is a good idea to periodically check with your key stakeholders that their priorities and expectations remain unaltered. Wherever possible, take account of any changes you identify.

As we have just mentioned, people have a strong desire to be internally consistent. This can be both a blessing and a curse. The blessing: it protects you from unpredictable behaviour. The curse: there are sometimes good reasons for wanting that behaviour to change. It is often the case, that people – and especially people high up in an organisation – like to comply with an unspoken stereotypical image which says the constancy is one of the pillars of good leadership. Viewed from this perspective, a change of course is equivalent to saying that you got things wrong in the past. And some people might be too embarrassed (or proud) to admit this openly – for example, in the conversation you have with them to revalidate their opinions about your project.

If this is a problem with one of your stakeholders, there is a good chance that he will only repeat what he said to you during your initial conversation, even if his opinions have altered in the meantime. Unfortunately, this means that there is also a good chance that at some point later on he will nevertheless begin to adopt a different position towards your project. This can only lead to a lack of clarity and unnecessary delay.

You can avoid this by clearly reframing your revalidation conversation before you start. For example, you might say something like: 'We both realise that business contexts are dynamic, so that priorities are constantly changing. For this reason, I thought it would be useful to have a further chat with you, just to make sure that in this rapidly changing context we are still on the same wave length as far as your own priorities and expectations are concerned...'

Step 3 Respect the non-rational logic of your stakeholders (as if logic and rationality are not difficult enough as it is!)

Imagine the following. We are in the United States. A group of researchers[1] brings together two groups of test subjects. One group consists of fervent supporters of the death penalty; the other of fervent opponents. Both groups are given the same information: two reports about the effect of the death penalty on the incidence of major crime. These reports are entirely fictional, but the test subjects don't know that.

The conclusion of the first report reads as follows: 'Palmer and Crandall [the fictitious names of the researchers] compared murder statistics in ten pairs of neighbouring states that each have different legislation relating to the death penalty. In eight of the ten pairs there were more murders in the states where the death penalty is in force.' This conclusion is clear: the death penalty does not work as a deterrent.

The conclusion of the second report was very different: 'Kroner and Phillips compared murder statistics for the year before and the year after the introduction of the death penalty in fourteen different states. In eleven states there were *fewer murders* after the introduction of the death penalty.' Once again, the conclusion is clear: the death penalty is a very effective deterrent.

Hmm.

In addition to these conclusions, the test subjects also read the full texts of both reports. Although both were completely fake, they were carefully prepared by specialists, so that in terms of their scientific methodology they were comparable. All necessary details were given: how the study was set up, where the data was obtained, what analysis methods were used, etc. The same (contradictory) information was again given to both groups, but now with more extensive background information. At the end of their reading, the test subjects were asked two questions:

1   If you compare these two reports in terms of their technical quality, which of the two is better?
2   Now that you have read both reports, has this influenced your opinion about the death penalty?

The answer to the first question is not difficult to guess: the report that matched the opinion of the test subjects was deemed by them to be technically the best report. This was the same for both the supporters and the opponents of the death penalty. Both groups were affected by so called 'confirmation bias'.

This means that we seek out and believe information that agrees with the opinions we hold in advance about a particular subject. If we are subsequently confronted with facts and figures that do not support our opinion, we tend to cast doubt on their validity by branding them as 'fake news'. In this case, people claimed that faulty methodology had led to faulty conclusions. As a result, these conclusions could be safely ignored.

The answer to the second question was more surprising. Did you think that reading contradictory information would have no impact on the test subjects' opinions? You did? Well, you would be wrong. Most people's opinions were changed and changed quite clearly, but often not in the direction you would expect: in both groups, people now believed in their original opinion about the death penalty much more firmly than ever before!

So how does this process work? If I believe in something and am confronted with information that casts doubt on that belief, then I am more likely to dig in my heels and persist in my opinion or even intensify it, rather than 'give in' and say that I was mistaken. Why? Because to concede that I was wrong would destroy my internal consistency. It would take away my feeling of certainty – and that I cannot allow. This presents experts and all other proponents of rationality with something of a problem. What more can you do to convince people than to show them reliable facts and figures? Clearly, the situation is more complex than it might seem at first glance. Fortunately, it is also predictable – and therefore manageable. More on that later.

Let's now take another brief detour into the world of science, but this time without deliberate trickery and deception. In 2005, Robin Warren and Barry Marshall were awarded the Nobel Prize for Medicine. Their discovery: that gastritis and stomach ulcers were not caused by stress or bad dietary habits but by a bacteria, which could therefore be successfully combated with anti-biotics. Perhaps this doesn't sound like much, but before their breakthrough it was difficult to treat these conditions effectively, which caused suffering to hundreds of thousands of people and often led to severe internal bleeding and death.

After receiving the award at the presentation ceremony in Stockholm, it is customary for one of the winners to give an acceptance speech. This was done by Marshall. Amongst other things, he went on at some length to point out how their path to the Nobel Prize had been a long a difficult one. One of the main problems had been the objections they had encountered from their colleagues in the medical profession. A list of these objections is given below, but when you read them bear in mind that they were all put forward by some of the most eminent professionals in the world of internal medicine. In other words, we are not talking about some hack journalist or a barrack-room lawyer. No, we are talking about the best in the business – and that is what makes their interventions so fascinating.

The objections put forward (sometimes with a little more background information) included the following:

1   'The data cannot be correct, because the stomach is sterile.'

2   'The research must be faulty, because bacteria could never survive in an environment as acidic as the stomach.'

3   'The findings have never been reproduced' (which was simply not true).

4   If you are a scientist who has made a discovery, you want to have your research results published in a scientific journal – preferably in a journal with an outstanding reputation. In the medical field, this means, amongst others, The Lancet. One of the ways that a journal like *The Lancet* can safeguard its reputation is by conducting a peer review. This means that

when an article is submitted for publication, it is first shared with a panel of experts in the field for critical analysis and comment. These comments are then passed back to the original authors, who are asked to rework their article accordingly. Warren and Marshall submitted their research results to The Lancet in the usual manner but, unusually, the journal could find no experts willing to take part in the peer review: apparently, they all thought that the research's conclusions were so ridiculous that nobody wanted to be associated with them, not even from a critical perspective and even though the names of the reviewers are supposedly kept secret ('But what happens if my name leaks out!').

5   If, as a researcher, you believe that you have discovered the cause of a disease, you need to go through a number of strict procedures to prove that there is a real and causal connection between the supposed pathogen and the disease itself. This often involves tests on animals. However, Warren and Marshall had been unable to find any animal model in which the required causal link could be established with certainty. In desperation to prove their point, Marshall drank a solution containing millions of bacteria and became gravely ill, but at least he had shown that there was indeed a causal connection – or so he thought. When he and Warren attempted to report on this experiment during scientific congresses, their professional colleagues simply laughed at them, claiming the 'experiment' was nothing more than an unreliable gimmick: 'A nice try, but complete nonsense, of course.'

6   Some of the disbelieving reactions were almost ludicrous in their absurdity (remember: we are talking here about top scientists). One bacteriologist even asked: 'Where do these researchers come from? Australia? Well, that explains everything, doesn't it?' Not exactly what you would call a penetrating scientific argument.

There were two important factors that eventually led to Warren and Marshall receiving due recognition and their Nobel Prize:

1   A celebrated British professor had carried out the same experiments and come to exactly the same conclusions, which he reported to a congress in Brussels.
2   The American tabloids picked up the story about Marshall drinking his potentially life-threatening bacterial cocktail. Of course, this is the kind of story the tabloids love! What's more, hundreds of Americans

had subsequently written to Warren and Marshall, asking them to send
a supply of the relevant antibiotics for themselves or members of their
family. When all these people were soon cured, the proof for Warren and
Marshall's claims was clear for all to see.

The story of Warren and Marshall is by no means an isolated one. A Spanish
professor at the University of Madrid has documented how 24 subsequent
winners of the Nobel Prize were initially laughed out of court by the scientific
community.[2] It goes without saying that the world's leading scientists are not
stupid. So how can we explain this seemingly shortsighted behaviour on their
part?

The discoveries that lead to the award of the Nobel Prize are often ground-
breaking, in the sense that they cause us to reassess and even cast doubt on
what we have known in the past. These discoveries explore new territory,
which almost by definition involves a degree of uncertainty. Evolution has
taught us that the avoidance of uncertainty is one of mankind's most fundamental survival mechanisms. Unless there is absolutely no alternative, we
cling on to the things we know.[3]

But there is more to it than that. If I know that I am a top expert in my field
and if I am presented with new information that does not agree with what I
have known to be true throughout my career, this implicitly calls into question my status as an expert. How can I be such a top expert (my identity as a
scientist) if there is something of this magnitude I do not know? Not unsurprisingly, many experts solve this contradiction by convincing themselves
and anyone else who will listen that the new information must be fake news.
A person's sense of identity (scientist or not) is an essential characteristic of
his or her personal territory – which means that it will be defended with man
and might against possible invaders.

So let's now return to your stakeholders and how you can engage them in
your thinking about your project. As this previous section demonstrates, you
need to recognise that these stakeholders are not simply waiting for you to
come along with your bright new ideas, especially if they do not coincide with
their own. Fortunately, the resistance that you are likely to encounter follows
certain 'laws', which makes the situation capable of solution. Let me explain.

In communication theory, reference is sometimes made to an anchor point.
This is something that I know and believe about a certain subject at a certain

moment in time. I can easily integrate new material about this topic, providing it is positioned reasonably close to my anchor point. To use the jargon, there is a latitude of acceptance around my anchor point, in which I can absorb and appropriate new things. In contrast, information that is too distant from my anchor point in terms of content or nature is rejected and ends up in what is known as the latitude of rejection. The more emotionally I am committed to the subject, the bigger the latitude of rejection.

Joe is a good friend. He comes from a family of four children and his favourite sibling is his sister Michelle. One of the reasons they get on so well is because they can have endless arguments about anything and everything, at the end of which they always agree to disagree. Neither of them is ever able to persuade the other, but that is not the point. They argue and debate simply for the sheer pleasure of it. No subject is taboo. They enjoy discussing them all – except for one. If Joe dares to suggest anything that seems like criticism of the way Michelle brings up her family, suddenly the argument is in deadly earnest. If Joe keeps pushing, he knows that Michelle will erupt like a volcano. So why is Michelle so touchy on this particular subject? It is because she identifies so strongly with her role as a mother. This means that, for her, criticism of that role is the same as criticism of her person. On this subject, her latitude of rejection is very wide because she is emotionally committed at a personal level: her identity and therefore her personal territory is under threat.

It is the same with stakeholders. The more a stakeholder is emotionally committed to a particular subject – for example, because it is his personal brainchild or the source of much of his prestige – the more sensitive he will be to proposals that fail to match his own opinions on that subject. Exploring personal commitment and therefore people's personal territory is an integral and not always easy part of the general exploration of the playing field in which your stakeholders operate. Why not easy? Because it is difficult to deal with these matters in the context of an interview. Very few conversation partners will be willing to say that they are emotionally connected to this or that subject. But the people in their environment will know when this is the case. So ask them instead.

The most valid information that you can gain from your stakeholder himself is usually obtained from observing him in meetings and from informal contacts of one form or another. Take note of the subjects he talks about and the things he is passionately for or against. If you want to persuade him to new insights on these matters, you will only be able to do so one step at a time, and only by asking him questions rather than confronting him with facts. Make sure that these questions are always in the conditional tense: 'Would one way of looking at this perhaps be...?' Do not expect that you will get an immediate and whole-hearted 'yes!' in response. Simply leave the seeds you have planted to do their work: in due course they will bring him to new insights that are more in keeping with what can be useful to you – and him. Patience – even though it is a virtue that few of us possess in sufficient abundance – can work wonders.

Be aware, however, that in addition to personal commitment to a subject other emotional mechanisms may also be at play. What's more, their effect is often stronger than the effect of rational mechanisms, so that they can be a powerful influence in deciding what a person thinks and does, mainly because they are a more integral part of their personal or social territory, or sometimes both.

One of these emotional mechanisms is the need people have to score. This means that it is useful for you to know with whom your stakeholder wants to score and how this can be done. Do not simply assume that it will be his or her boss. This was certainly not the case for Emily, a researcher in a pharmaceutical company. Of course, she was pleased that her line manager also appreciated her work, but she was more keen to impress the university research group she had worked with during her doctoral studies. If she thought that her reputation at the university might be damaged if she were to take part in your project, then that would be reason enough for her not to co-operate.

Personal connectedness with a point of view for which your stakeholder has broken a lance in the past or the defence of the results on which his reputation in the organisation is based can be equally important non-rational drivers for determining his attitude towards your project. The need to score with his grassroots supporters may be another. Some of these drivers might also help to explain some of his odd or even unpleasant reactions to your proposals. We all know what these drivers are because we have all had contact with them at one time or another: internal rivalry, jockeying for position, personal loyalty, etc. These things can express themselves in some curious ways.

Barry and Carla were two line managers who both had their eye on the job of their boss, Patrick, who was their head of department. Ron was one of the team reporting to Barry. In a meeting with Barry and Carla, Ron was heavily criticised by Carla. To his amazement and dismay, Barry backed Carla up. Perhaps understandably, Ron felt badly let down: his own team leader had failed to defend him.

What had happened? Barry had immediately seen that Carla's criticism was justified and that she would be only too happy to make this clear (with the necessary exaggeration) to Patrick. This meant that if Barry supported Ron, he would share in his boss's anger. As a result, he decided to chicken out and save his own skin. Not nice for Ron, but perhaps understandable from Barry's point of view in the context of his rivalry with Carla.

After the meeting, Barry at least had the guts to apologise to Ron and to explain why he acted as he did. They also agreed what they could do to avoid any repetition in the future. Both of them knew that Carla had played dirty and they were both ready to get their revenge when an opportunity arose in the future.

We will examine the dynamics of positioning more closely in chapter 7 (about the nature of power). This is a world of its own! But before we end this section, perhaps it might be useful to look at a few of the other ways in which power can influence behaviour, often in the strangest manner and often involving some of your most senior stakeholders.

Kenny was implementing a major project for Laura, his director. He made sure that she was kept well informed about progress and tested out every step with her before moving on. He had learned to live with the fact that, although at a personal level his working relationship with Laura was good, she was constantly hyper-critical of his work in large-scale meetings, where the company's other project managers were also present.

The first few times she did this, he almost fell of his chair in amazement. She had never said any of these things to him in their one-to-one work meetings! Talk about inconsistent! Later, he came to realise that within the specific context of these larger meetings Laura needed to position herself as a demanding boss in front of her own superiors. Once he understood what was going on, Kenny decided to just grin and bear it. He was prepared not to let it affect their successful working relationship.

The final mechanism is different again. Some years ago, Robin was recruited to the electricity company where they both work by Phil, who was then a middle manager. Now a senior executive, Phil has ensured in more recent times that Robin has more than once received promotion. Not surprisingly, this has created a strong bond of loyalty between Robin and Phil. This also means that if Robin is now one of your key stakeholders, you can be fairly certain that he will do nothing that might harm the interests of Phil.

The existence of non-rational motives of this kind among your stakeholders certainly does nothing to make your project puzzle any easier. It would, of course, be much simpler if everyone were to behave in a rational manner. But that is not going to happen. That being said, every cloud has a silver lining. If you take the trouble to explore and decode these non-rational motives, it can yield you a double advantage: (1) once you are aware of them, you can base your approach on more elements of the situation; (2) it also allows you to better place and interpret some of the more bizarre reactions of your stakeholders (without taking these reactions personally and building up frustrations that can only lead to loss of energy as a result).

Additional comment

Being subject to non-rational motives is not exclusively the preserve of stakeholders. You may be subject to them yourself! Some of them you might easily overlook, but it is important to try and be aware of them, since they can have an important effect on what you can achieve (or not) in your relationships with your stakeholders. Here are some examples.

Nobody likes to feel uncertain. Even so, it is important to respect your uncertainty and deal with it realistically. There can be many reasons for feeling uncertain, not all of them rational, and there are many situations in which it can play a role.

For example, when you are exploring what your stakeholders expect of your project, it is inevitable that you will have to disappoint some of them. It is never pleasant having to try and sell a 'no'. But if you fail to do so, you risk getting yourself into deeper and deeper trouble. Of course, you will find it easier to correct expectations or even go against them if you know that your back is covered. So speak with your manager before you start your stakeholder conversations. Where is he prepared to support you, where does he advise caution? This will reduce your uncertainty and increase the likelihood that your 'expectation management' is completed correctly and successfully.

When you run through your list of stakeholders, you will notice that you have more affinity with some than with others. This might be because you share a common field of expertise (jurists understand jurists) or it might simply be a matter of personal preference. You just like some people and dislike others. Fact of life.

These likes and dislikes will certainly help to determine where you position certain stakeholders on your acceptance matrix. It is self-evident that you will prefer to have contact with Promoters rather than Opponents. That, too, is a fact of life.

That being said, you need to try and manage these personal preferences. If you don't, it will almost certainly lead to preferential treatment for the people you like the most. At one level, there is nothing wrong with this – it is a natural reaction – but it often means that you will invest less energy in others, so that you find it harder to get them on board. As far as possible, make an effort be even-handed in your approach to everyone.

3   ZOOMING IN: SKILLS TO GET INSIGHT AND FEELING FOR THE TERRITORY OF YOUR STAKEHOLDERS

You have already read a lot about the most obvious route: ask your stakeholders what is important to them and keep on asking until you have understood fully. If you really have no access to them (but don't assume this too quickly), ask people who do have that access, again persisting with your asking until you are sure that you are not being given filtered information.

So questioning is always your first choice, but be aware that it does have its limitations. For example, don't expect that you will get too much information about some of the things that can have an influence on your project but which are not easy or politically correct to talk about in the context of an interview. You are never going to hear a factory manager say: 'Of course, safety is not our highest priority. Production always comes first. If we can produce things in a safe way, so much the better, but in the grand scheme of things safety only comes in third or fourth place.' Nor is anyone ever likely to admit: 'My main priority this year is whatever is good from my bonus. And if 40 percent of my bonus is based on accident figures, then that means it's going to be Safety First.'

Of course, this is an exaggerated example, but it is not meant to be cynical. It is simply another one of those awkward facts of life. This is often the way that people think, but are not allowed to talk. If you are morally outraged when you read such things, this does credit to your standard of professional ethics, but it doesn't really help you much when confronted with situations of this kind in the real world. The message is clear: if you want to get information about what really matters for your stakeholders, you cannot simply rely on what they tell you, because that will almost certainly not be the full story. You need additional channels of information.

The first of these channels is observation, observation of what your stake-holders say and do. Informal conversations can be a goldmine of information in this respect, especially when your conversation partner talks about others (positively or negatively) in an unguarded moment.

To give you an idea of what I mean, imagine the following. You are taking part in a training programme. Your fellow trainees are people you have not pre-viously met, but that doesn't matter: at the start of the course there is always the customary introduction round. The trainer has divided you up into pairs and has given you the following task: 'Interview each other and make notes, so that you can introduce your partner to the entire group.' Your questions might include:

1 Who is a leadership figure you have met who has inspired you? Why was that exactly?
2 Who is someone you have met who you did not experience as being a good leader. Again, why was that?
3 What are the situations as a leader yourself that you find hardest to deal with? What makes these situations so difficult?

If you ask someone these questions, you get information at two levels. The first level is a content level. Your conversation partner tells you something about others, about himself and about situations.

The second level is less obvious but all the more fascinating. In order to an-swer your questions, your conversation partner has had to make choices. This almost never happens consciously, but is nearly always implicit. Of all the many hundreds of leadership figures he has ever met (in his family, at school, at work, in his sports club, etc.), he has chosen just two. Out of all the many experiences he has had with them, he has again selected just two. And it is the same when talking about himself as a leader. This selection is not made at random, like throwing a dice.

The people and experiences are chosen because for one reason or another they are relevant and have a special meaning. This always happens in this manner, because experiences are measured against the criteria that are important for a person.

This is how you obtain the second level of information you need. By getting him to talk about other people, your stakeholder will also give you insights into what he regards as the most important things (both positively and negatively) when assessing these others, the things that are important enough for him to mention almost without needing to think. Here is an example.

One of the leaders for whom your conversation partner has a high regard is Robert. Robert is intellectually very sharp, allowing him to instantly get to the heart of the matter but in a reasoned and reasonable manner, which makes it easy to accept his analyses. Your partner's memories of Francis are less fond. Again, intellectually brilliant, but bad tempered and aggressive in discussion, and not afraid to openly criticise his staff in front of others.

The situations your conversation partner finds difficult in terms of his own leadership are also connected to moments when there is a need to correct or criticise staff, and in particular to find a way to do this that is effective but without hurting or harming the people involved.

If you put all this information in a row, it should give you a pretty good idea about the value priorities of your conversation partner: in this case, intellectual sharpness combined with integrity and a connectedness with his environment and with those around him. If you need to work further with him in the future, these are the things you will need to respect and make reference to.

So how can you apply all this to your stakeholders? During informal conversations – together in the lift, during the five minutes before the meeting starts, over lunch, at the coffee machine, in the car on the way to a client – you will have access to a treasure trove of information that is hardly filtered at all, precisely because the setting is so informal and because you are not talking specifically about your project, but about other events and people both inside and outside your organisation.

You, too, should also try to enjoy the relaxed atmosphere of these informal moments, but at the same time your antennae must be finely tuned to pick up the nuances in everything your stakeholder says. Which issues are important enough for him to mention, often more than once? Which common themes run through his assessments of different people and situations? What does this say about the things that are important to him? What are the matters that he is most sensitive about? File all these things away in your mental hard drive. This will allow you to better 'read' his behaviour in more formal settings. It will also make clear the subjects for which you can appeal to him for support with the greatest likelihood of a positive response, because you will be speaking the same language, while also demonstrating your respect for his personal territory (in this case, his values).

In addition to listening out for these implicitly expressed values, you can use a second route to find out more about what your stakeholders really think: it is called 'perspective taking'. Perhaps you can start by testing yourself in this manner?[4] It works like this. Below you will find a number of statements to which you need to give a score: 1 if you think the statement applies to you fully, 5 if it doesn't apply to you at all, and 2, 3 or 4 if its applicability is somewhere in between.

1	I often feel concerned and have pity for people who are less fortunate than I am.	
2	I can easily see things from the standpoint of other people.	
3	When other people have a problem, I feel a personal responsibility to try and help them.	
4	When there is a dispute, I try to take account of everyone's opinion before taking a decision.	
5	If someone is being misused, I want to protect the person concerned.	
6	I try to better understand my friends by looking at problems from their perspective.	

7	I am easily moved by the disappointments of others.	
8	Even though I am certain I am right, I always listen carefully to the arguments of others.	
9	If I see that someone is being treated unfairly, I usually feel sorry for that person.	
10	I often feel emotionally affected by the things that happen around me.	
11	I believe that there are two sides to every argument and I try to take account of both of them.	
12	I would describe myself as a fairly sensitive person.	
13	If I am angry with someone, I try to put myself in the other person's shoes.	
14	Before I criticise someone, I always try to imagine what it would feel like to be in their place.	

You score your answers as follows:

Count up your scores for questions 1, 3, 5, 7, 9, 10 and 11, noting the total in the box alongside.	

Count up your scores for questions 2, 4, 6, 8, 11, 13 and 14, again noting the total in the box alongside.	

This questionnaire assesses two different aspects of empathy. The first score relates to the emotional component of empathy: feeling what the other feels. The second score relates to the rational component of empathy: thinking how the other thinks. It is this latter aspect that we know as perspective taking. In practice, of course, people make use of both components, but which one they feel most comfortable using (and therefore use most often) varies from person to person, depending on their character and experience. Your scores in the test will show which of the two components best matches your own personality. In America, they have compiled batteries of statistics based on the results of this questionnaire and some of the conclusions make interesting reading. For example, women score better than men for both the emotional and the rational component. This might suggest that women are more inclined to take notice of and show more interest in others than men. So much for male pride!

Research has also been carried out by MBA students into the effect of the respective use of the emotional versus the rational component of empathy in a business context.[5]

In a simulation, the test subjects were asked to engage with the owner of a petrol station whose business they wished to buy. The roles of the buyers were played by fellow students, who were divided up into three groups, each with a different set of starting instructions.

For the emotional empathy group, the instruction was: 'Try to understand the owner's feelings. How would you feel in his position?'

For the rational, perspective taking group: 'Try to understand what the owner is thinking. What are his objectives and interests? What would you be thinking in his position?'

There was also a control group with a neutral instruction: 'Focus on your role and get the best possible agreement.'

If you compare the results of the three groups and take as your criteria the extent to which the negotiations led to a solution that was satisfactory for both parties, the perspective taking (rational) approach scored noticeably better than the emotional and neutral approaches (between which there was little or no difference).

If, however, you ask the owner how satisfied he was with the manner in which he was approached, this time the emotional approach scores better than the rational and neutral approaches, although the level of difference is not significant (which means it might just have been a matter of chance).

What does this show? It suggests that in a business context it is always worthwhile sitting behind your desk and thinking carefully about the objectives and interests of your stakeholders. Other research has also shown that a rational approach towards the things that are important to others often leads to a better balance between these interests and your own[6] and to more creative solutions in negotiating situations,[7] as well as making you better positioned to receive concessions[8] and better protecting you against the first offer of your negotiating partner.[9] This last point is particularly important, because good negotiators know that the first offer sets the tone for the rest of the discussion.

Perhaps a liitle more strangely, there is also a significant correlation between perspective taking and a high sense of self-esteem.[10] If you are confident in your own strengths and abilities, it is less threatening to explore the feelings and opinions of others in depth, even if they are your opponents. Do you remember the experiment with the supporters and opponents of the death penalty and the manner in which contradictory information served to entrench them ever more deeply in their original position? If that were always to be the case, the situation would be a discouraging one.

Fortunately, there is good news. A variant of the death penalty experiment was carried out, but with one important difference. Before the research team let the test subjects read the reports about the effects of the death penalty on murder rates, they first gave them another task to complete. They provided each person with a list of possible personal values and asked them to select the three values that were most important to them. They were also asked to write something brief about each of the values they had chosen. What this effectively did was to mark out and strengthen the personal identity and value awareness – in other words, the personal territory – of the participants. The result: when they were now confronted with contradictory information, they were more inclined to nuance their opinions and take the new information seriously. Why? Because the value awareness exercise had made them more confident about who they were and therefore less fearful of the alternative values of others.

This is another theme that we will be looking at again later, when we explore how you can deal with opposition to your ideas and proposals. For now, suffice it to say that opposition is always a sign of uncertainty. And the more emotional the resistance, the greater the level of that uncertainty becomes, simply because the level of threat experienced towards the boundaries of your own territory is perceived to be greater. The best way to counter this in your stakeholders - as you will also read later - is to first build up their self-confidence, and only then present them with the 'threatening' contradictory information.

The emotional approach (feeling what the other feels) is indispensible in interpersonal relationships with family, friends and close colleagues, but involves a number of potential risks in a business environment. It often goes hand in hand with favouritism and with the tendency to go further than you normally would to maintain your existing good relations.[11] What you are, in fact, doing in these circumstances is strengthening your social territory (the people around you like you) at the expense of your personal territory. In the long run, this is seldom a good thing.

Perspective taking may seem self-evident, but it is not always as easy as it sounds. This is particularly true when the situation is heavily charged or when a great deal is at stake – as was the case in the following situation.

Robert McNamara was the longest serving minister of defence in American history. He was in office at the start of the Vietnam War and was also closely involved in the Cuban missile crisis that nearly led to a third (and potentially disastrous nuclear) world war in 1962. A few years ago, he recorded some of his memories for posterity.[12] Thanks to his testimony and other recordings of conversations in the White House that have now been made public, we can finally piece together with accuracy what happened during those momentous days that nearly brought catastrophe to us all.

In 1962, the Soviet Union intended to install a large number of nuclear missiles on Cuba. This was a direct threat to the 90 million Americans who lived within range of the rockets. According to the CIA, the missiles had not yet been installed but were still crossing the Atlantic Ocean in Russian ships. The US Navy blocked the approaches to Cuba and 180,000 American troops were mobilised. In addition, a massive airstrike was planned. Everyone was acutely aware of the danger and of the possible consequences of an attack of this kind: a nuclear war that would wipe Cuba off the map, but would also devastate a large part of the United States, which would no doubt retaliate against the Soviet Union in kind. Within the White House, opinions were strongly divided. Some leading figures, including President Kennedy, wanted to avoid war; others, including some of the military chiefs of staff, wanted to strike first and blow Cuba out of the water.

On 27 October, at the height of the crisis, two messages were received in Washington from the Soviet leader Nikita Khrushchev. The first said: 'If you guarantee not to attack Cuba, we will withdraw our missiles.' The second, received soon after, said: 'If you attack Cuba, you can be certain that we will respond with massive military action.' In other words, two contradictory messages in the space of a few minutes. The final solution to this potential devastating nuclear conflict was set to be the result of perspective taking!

One of the people in the White House crisis room was Tommy Thompson, a former US Ambassador to Moscow, who had met Khrushchev and his family on several occasions. He urged the president to respond to the first conciliatory message, even though this was against Kennedy's gut instincts. But Thompson persisted: 'Mr President, I still think we have a chance to preserve peace. The most important thing for Khrushchev is that he can say that to his people that he has saved Cuba and prevented an American invasion.' Thompson argued that Khrushchev had backed himself into a corner which left him with no room for manoeuvre without a loss of face that he could never accept. If they wanted to avoid a war, the Americans needed to help him find a way out. They had to allow Khrushchev to be a hero at home. He had to be able to say: 'Kennedy was on the point of destroying Castro and Cuba, and I stopped him.'

Kennedy was wise enough and confident enough to allow his initial opinion to be challenged by Thompson and eventually accepted his advice. He probably realised that he was too close and too personally involved in the crisis. He also understood that he lacked information that Thompson possessed by virtue of his prior personal contact with the Russian leader. Even so – as McNamara admitted – it still took a lot of courage from Thompson to go up against his commander-in-chief. We should all still be grateful to him that he did...

4   PARTNERSHIP: SHARING TERRITORY

In your acceptance matrix, you mapped out the position of all your different stakeholders in relation to your project. This allowed you to think about possible migration routes: who you could move from one sector to another, and when. The influence matrix is the big brother of the acceptance matrix. It makes it possible for you to map out how you can best position yourself in relation to the migrations you want from others. What must you do to make these migrations happen? It will not surprise you to learn that here again steering or impact is one of the most crucial dimensions.

You can mark all your influencing relationships on two dimensions. There is a proximity axis and a steering axis. Proximity says something about the closeness of your relationships with your stakeholders and is characterised by harmony or connectedness (or the lack thereof). Steering says something about the extent to which you are able to influence your stakeholders and give direction to what they think and/or do. If you combine these two dimensions, you get four prototype relationships.

Influence matrix

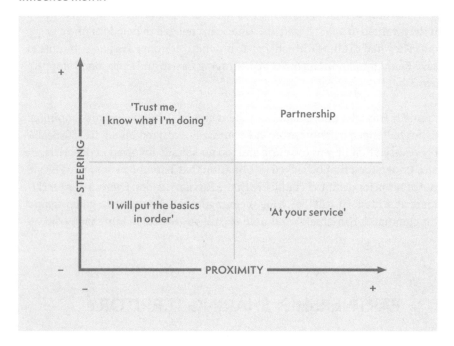

'I WILL PUT THE BASICS IN ORDER'

Departments like Maintenance, some sections of IT and General Service are often characterised by a combination of non-proximity and little steering. In other words, they are a long way off and only have little direct influence on others. In fact, in principle they should be invisible. They make sure that everything runs smoothly and they invest considerable know-how and experience to achieve this. Their positioning within the organisation is often a thankless one, because they only come into the picture when something goes wrong. And sometimes this means literally: no water coming out of the tap, no heat coming out of the radiator, no light coming out of the bulb, etc. It is very unfair, but people who carry out these functions seldom enjoy much prestige among their colleagues. Their contribution is as enablers. They create the conditions – put the basics in order – that make it possible for others to do things. They seldom make a contribution to the generation of profit. In fact, they are usually a cost. Hence their lack of influence. They are in the bottom left quadrant of the matrix.

'AT YOUR SERVICE'

Staff departments often find themselves in the bottom right quadrant. They see it as their task to support the business departments and take out of their hands all the work that is not essential for the direct creation of profit. They often gain their job satisfaction from their service orientation (their willingness and ability to help), their customer-friendliness and, if possible, customer delight (doing more than an internal or external customer expects). When talking of these matters they often use the word 'partners'. In many organisations, this involves functions like the HR business partner or finance partner. But this is not really a true partnership. There is little or no steering involved. De facto they are no more than the extra hands of the line organisation.

People who are positioned in the lower two quadrants know exactly how much effort and experience is necessary to do what they do and to do it well. On this basis, they often claim that they should be listened to more seriously than is generally the case. In other words, not only that their territory should be respected by their stakeholders, but also that these stakeholders should grant them access to parts of their own territories, thereby allowing them room to formulate a response that will be heeded and for which they will obtain the appreciation they feel they deserve. In practice, however, this doesn't happen very often, precisely because they define their own territory and professional identity as being at the service of others. But that is not enough to actively engage in steering. Steering continues to come from the upper two quadrants.

'TRUST ME, I KNOW WHAT I'M DOING'

It is in the top left quadrant where the real power is to be found. This can be either expertise or positional power. This means that the impact of people in this quadrant can be high, even if their proximity is low. What's more, this positioning assumes that there is primarily one-way traffic between those who possess expertise and power and those who don't. Before you get all indignant at this seemingly 'dictatorial' approach, first have a look at a few examples.

Imagine that you are working for a production company. You have ordered a new machine from an Italian supplier that will allow you to automatically extract minerals from sand. This is the most state-of-the-art technology and it costs a small fortune. In these circumstances, it is only normal to expect (and in no way dictatorial) that after the installation the supplier will detach some of his staff to show you how the wonder-machine works. This kind of one-way traffic is perfectly acceptable and even necessary, because the Italians have the knowledge and you do not. And that is how things work in every field of expertise.

Here is a different kind of example. Imagine now that you are the CEO of a logistical company. To keep your head above water, you are considering a huge investment in new technology. Its introduction will cost a lot of jobs, but if it fails it will probably mean the end of your financial independence as an organisation, since the scale of the investment will push you to the limit and many more jobs will also be on the line. All the calculations have been made, all the pros and cons have been weighed, all the consultancy reports have been read, the board of directors has been asked for its opinion. Yet even so, it still remains unclear whether the decision to invest will be the right one or not. In this situation, the ball is in your court as the CEO. And in no-one-else's. You are the only one who can take the decision. Alone and on your own responsibility. That is what you are paid for – and that is what your people expect you to do.

What both these examples show is that in certain circumstances stakeholders are prepared to voluntarily and/or out of necessity give up part of their territory. They are willing to do this because there is no other alternative. As a result, they have nothing to lose and all to gain. However, in order to use unilateral power of this kind efficiently and effectively, a number of conditions need to be met:

1   Your competence and your position must be beyond discussion.
2   It is possible to speak of unilateral dependence between the parties involved.
3   You have a clear mandate to make the final decision.
4   You can justify the decision in terms of the general good.

5   Your action is restricted to the initiation of a change, with the responsibility for implementing that change and for its proper functioning in the long run eventually being handed back to the other levels of the organisational hierarchy.
6   In the first instance, it is enough that people comply with your decision or that you are in a position to compel them. Whether or not they follow you willingly and will continue to do so is not (yet) relevant.

'PARTNERSHIP'

Partnership sits in the top right quadrant. It combines a high degree of proximity and connectedness with an equally high degree of steering ability. In these circumstances, you are a conversation partner who not only under-stands the wishes, needs and motives of others, but can also help them to take a positive step in the direction of all those things. This is what Tommy Thompson did during the Cuban crisis, when he dared to go against the opinion of President Kennedy. He respected the president, but was still able to successfully widen his perspective. He was not in agreement, made this clear in a reasoned manner, and was listened to as a result.

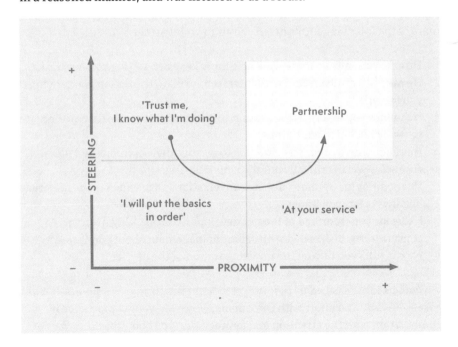

Gaining a position as a partner doesn't just happen. You can only acquire it if you can show that you are credible and trustworthy. To return to the matrix: you must first demonstrate that you can do a job in the lower two quadrants to a consistent and predictable standard of excellence and that you have relevant expertise (top left) that gives you the right to speak.

In other words, proximity, connectedness and knowledge are all prerequisites. People will only allow you into their territory and be prepared to surrender a piece of their autonomy if you can first prove that you are competent and are not working simply to serve your own ends.

Do you remember the acceptance matrix? First and foremost, you need the support of your Promoters to get things done and we looked at a number of behavioural indicators that allowed you to see whether their Promotership was genuine or just lip service.

Something similar applies for Partnership: there are also behavioural indicators you can use to check if a stakeholder really sees you and treats you as a Partner. This can help to protect you against too much wishful thinking. You can be confident that your Partnership is a real one if you can identify one or more of the following forms of behaviour in your Partner:

1. He asks your advice more than he simply keeps on setting you new tasks.
2. He asks you critically and with interest to explain the reasons underlying your advice.
3. He invites you as a sparring partner to also discuss themes that are only partially related to your project.
4. He sends you to other stakeholders to test out their opinions and ideas.
5. He allows you to critically question his own assumptions.
6. He modifies his opinions during conversations with you or does this later, but always lets you know.
7. He keeps you informed of further developments resulting from the conversations he has had with senior management about your project.
8. He consults you during the implementation of the project.

You will be most easily able to form Partnerships with your Promoters. It will cost more time and effort with Opponents. However, your competence in combination with the attention and appreciation you show for their ways of thinking and doing will gradually earn their respect, so that the possibility that they will at least give you the benefit of the doubt will grow.

You need Partnerships to ensure the viability of your project over time. It is the only solution when forcing your project through is not an option (or not desirable) or when a broad base of support is necessary for the project to be successful.

Let's return to the logistical organisation where a decision had to be made about crucial investments in new technology. In the real case on which this example is based the decision to invest was taken. It was a necessary decision, but in essence it was not much more than a way to create the conditions that would allow the organisation to be significantly more efficient and effective – if the project was properly implemented. This was by no means guaranteed, since this implementation was even more complex than the decision itself. The jobs of many hundreds of people were affected. The content and often the location of their work would change. Large scale re-training was needed. And all this was taking place under the eagle eye of pressure groups both inside and outside the company, each with their own different agendas. This is the kind of situation where you need Partnerships.

The building of Partnerships does not begin at the moment when you make a decision to implement a change or project. In this case, the company had been working for years to develop a good Partnership with the unions. It had consistently behaved with full transparency and had always first communicated any decisions affecting the workforce to the union council. All new and relevant information was shared; all changes were discussed in advance. Moreover, the company management was sensible enough to realise that union officials are elected and therefore need from time to time to show to their grassroots that they are properly defending their interests. In other words, the company understood that the unions would need to show 'resistance', even including short-term stoppages of work. Of course, this was not encouraged, but the union's right to do it was accepted. The goodwill that this created was later vital for the implementation of the massive change process that followed the life-saving investment.

In chapter 5 we will look in detail – right down to the micro level – at the best ways to form Partnerships. But first we need to do a little more exploring of the landscape in which stakeholders and stakeholder interests are found, a landscape through which you will need to navigate skilfully and successfully.

5 THE MOTOR OF PARTNERSHIP IS RECIPROCITY

Reciprocity is a mechanism and an automatism that is built into our genes. For many tens of thousands of years it was essential to our survival as a species. If the necessary means for survival are limited and if, at some point, you are fortunate enough to have a surplus of those means, it makes sense to share that surplus with those who have less, providing you can rely on them to do the same for your should the situation ever become reversed.

This is a lesson that even nowadays is still drummed into us as young children. Do you remember? If, as a toddler, a kind auntie gave you a sweet and you quickly turned away to shove it into your mouth, this attempt (in evolutionary terms) at 'flight' would soon be brought to a halt by the stern voice of one of your parents asking: 'What do you say?' This is formulated as a question, but is in fact a command. We all discovered quickly enough that a mumbled 'Thank you' would be enough to get us off the hook. At first, this was just learned behaviour, but after the process had been repeated hundreds of times the behaviour eventually became internalised. As a result, it is now second nature for all of us (well, nearly all of us) to say those two magic words as an expression of gratitude for the things we receive. And it is the same when we get older. We have all been there. You have been invited to a dinner party and are driving to your friends' house, when your partner says: 'I suppose you remembered to buy a bottle of wine for them?' Panic sets in for both of you when you reply: 'But I thought you said that you were going to do that!' This is the embarrassment we feel when we have broken the unwritten rule: if you get something (in this case, dinner), you need to give something back (in this case, a cheap bottle of plonk).

This is the rule of reciprocity. It says that giving is a social obligation, but that there is an equal obligation to receive what is given, as a result of which the receivers must then also give something in return. This rule is built into us. We do it almost without thinking and find it annoying if someone else breaks the rule. In the above example, you can almost hear your friends mutter 'ungrateful pigs' under their breath when you turn up at their front door without the obligatory bottle of wine (or box of chocolates, bunch of flowers, etc.). And it is the same on your way home, when you kindly give another car right of way, but the other driver races off without any form of acknowledgement, not even a raised hand. 'Arrogant swine!' you shout at his disappearing tail lights...

Whichever way you look at it, your success in whatever you do is dependent on the willingness of what is often a large number of stakeholders to cooperate. They will either demonstrate their goodwill towards you or they won't. And there is no way you can force this goodwill out of them. The most important thing you can do to get them on board is therefore to demonstrate your goodwill towards them. But you must mean it when you do it: if you try to trick them, they will soon see through you and pay you back in kind.

And quite right, too: because reciprocity always operates in both directions. If you help someone to be successful, it increases the likelihood that he will help you to be successful. But if you are only concerned with looking after your own interests, you can be certain that your stakeholders will only be concerned with looking after theirs. And where will that get you? This mechanism always works one-to-one – and not just with people. It also works with monkeys!

More specifically, capuchin monkeys. You let a group of capuchins look at two groups of two people playing out two different scenes (yes, for once the monkeys can study us, instead of the other way around!). One person wants to twist open the top of a glass jar containing sweets, but is unable to do so. With a look that is an obvious appeal for assistance, he passes the glass jar to the other person. In the first scenario, this second person opens the jar and takes out two sweets, one for each of them. In the second scenario, the second person just looks away when he is asked to help. Enter the monkeys. Having watched both scenarios, they are now put in the same room as the humans. Sweets are now offered to the monkeys: first by the person who they have just seen being helpful, and then by the person who looked away. The result? The monkeys were significantly more inclined to accept a sweet from the first person than from the second person. Why? Because they had been put off by the second person's egotistical behaviour.[13]

This has parallels with the real world. We are all constantly being watched when we interact with others: the way we do business, they way we play sport, even the way we talk about others. If you are cynical when discussing others or if you boast about how many times you have been able to fool them in the past, this will be mentally registered by everyone who hears you. And, as we all know, people love to talk. Before you know it, your 'bad' reputation as someone not to be trusted will have been spread far and wide, reducing the chance of your securing your stakeholders' goodwill.

In the reciprocity game, the more valuable the 'gift' you are able to give, the greater the likelihood that you will get something equally valuable in return. Within a project context, we are obviously not talking about financial rewards (at least, I hope not!), but about non-material benefits: time and attention, the swift communication of information, protecting a colleague's back, bringing them into contact with people in your network who may be useful to them. If you do this as a habit and not just when you need something, your efforts will be doubly rewarded, and perhaps even more. As we saw in chapter 2, goodwill is a currency – so use it wisely, and not as a counterproductive guerrilla tactic.

Additional comment

The giving and receiving of positive and negative gifts works asymmetrically. We remember much longer the 'good' things we have done for others, whilst tending to forget the 'bad' things. For the receivers, it is the other way around. You would be amazed how accurately people are able to keep a kind of emotional bank account in their head, with a detailed register of both debits and credits. This plays a crucial role in what is known as negativity bias: a negative experience weighs five to seven times more heavily than a positive experience. Of course, we all make mistakes in our relationships with others, but they require a disproportionally greater effort to make things right again.

TAKE AWAY

1 Always focus on the general good, and not simply on your own interests.

2 Ask your key stakeholders explicitly for their vision of your projects. Use a checklist as a guide.

3 Explain repeatedly and explicitly the connection between what you are planning and what your key stakeholders have told you is important for them.

4 Ask yourself with which themes your key stakeholders are emotionally connected. Do not overwhelm them with information on these matters that runs contrary to their own opinions. Give this information, if necessary, in smaller doses.

5 Listen carefully to what you hear in informal conversations when your key stakeholders are talking about others. Ask yourself what this says about the things that are important to them.

6 Check what your key stakeholders need to score with their own grassroots support and investigate how you can contribute towards this.

7 Position yourself as a sparring partner for your stakeholders, so that you become more than just another pairs of hands.

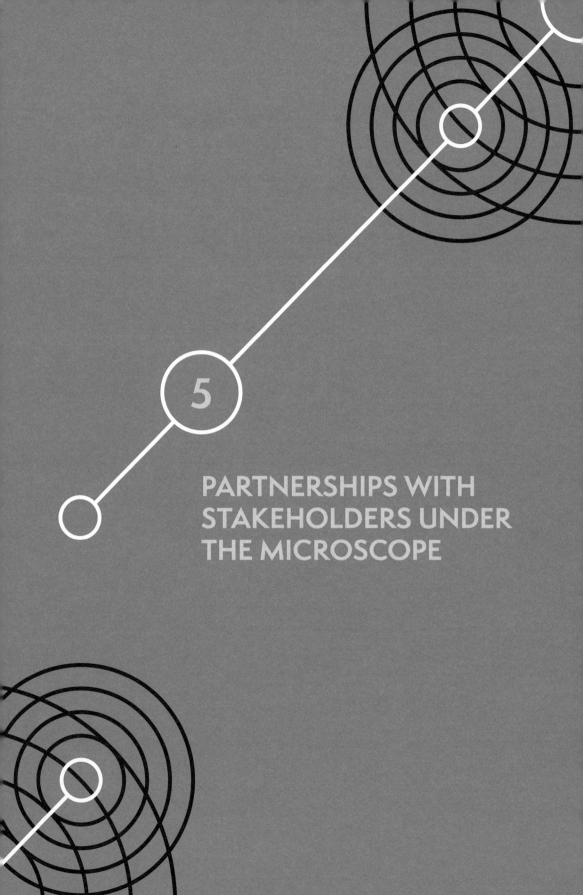

5

PARTNERSHIPS WITH STAKEHOLDERS UNDER THE MICROSCOPE

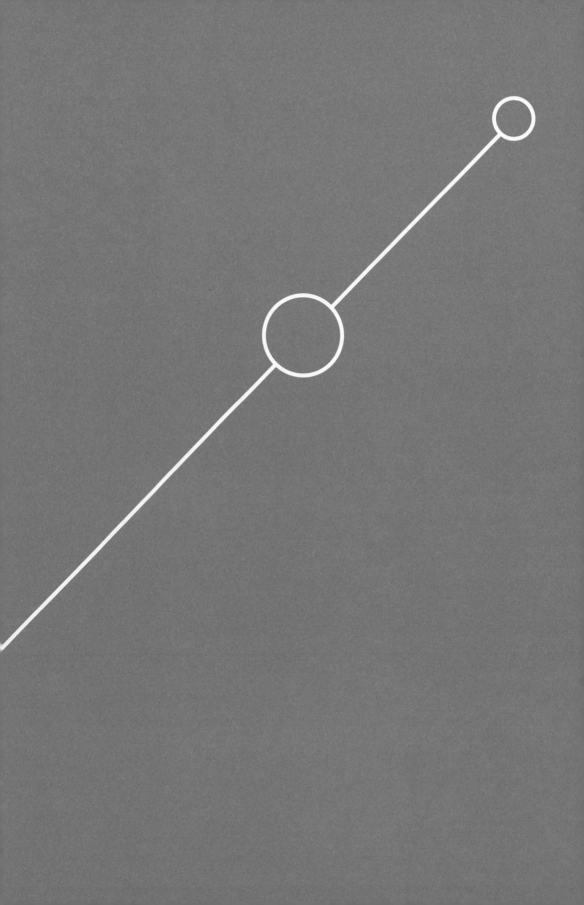

You cannot force your stakeholders to give their engagement. At best, you can ensure that they follow the normal rules and procedures in your organisation, since failure to do so may leave them open to sanction – although it is doubtful whether this possibility would worry them unduly. It certainly wouldn't get them on your side. No, if you want to get the wind in the sails of your project, there is only one way to do it: you need to persuade your stakeholders to follow you willingly. There are two possible reasons why they might be prepared to do this. The first reason is a business-minded reason: they understand that it is in their own best interests. In short, there is something in it for them. The second reason is more personal and emotional: they like you and are therefore prepared to do something a little extra for you. This is the foundation of the goodwill you so desperately need.

1   ## TRUST IS THE BASIS

'When I recruit people,' says investment guru Warren Buffet, 'I always look for three things. First and foremost, personal integrity. In second place comes intelligence. And in third place a high level of energy. For me, the relative importance of these things is clear: if you don't have the first, the other two will be your downfall.'

Thousands of years of evolution have equipped us with a highly sensitive radar for assessing other people. We attach most importance to two particular dimensions of their behaviour. The first dimension is our estimate of their intentions towards us. The second dimension relates to our valuation of their competencies.[1] Both of these dimensions are made up from a number of different characteristics (see table).

Intention	Competency
Fairness	Cleverness
Honesty	Efficiency
Tolerance	Intelligence
Mildness	Competence
Sense of justice	Foresight
Empathy	Expertise
Helpfullness	Creativity
Authenticity	Inventiveness
Trustworthiness	Skills

When we meet someone and form an idea about them, we are really not doing much more than viewing them through two different clusters or pairs of glasses. Together, these two clusters are responsible for 97 percent of the evaluations we make.[2] And you have probably already noticed just how closely they reflect the axes on the influence matrix: proximity (= intention) and steering (=competency).

Both these clusters are essential, but they are not of equal value. We always first assess a person's intentions before moving on to their competencies. The most crucial question is the most obvious one: are they a friend or an enemy? If the answer is 'enemy', the relationship goes no further. You immediately withdraw or pull up your defences.

If, however, you believe that their intentions are good, the next question is to assess whether or not the person is actually capable of doing what he says he wants to do on your behalf or for you. This is the competency question, but it only becomes relevant in the second instance.

There is also another important difference between the two dimensions. The assessments we make are asymmetric. When we assess someone as being trustworthy but it later transpires that this is not the case, our original assessment is overturned completely. We now regard this person as being 100 percent untrustworthy. It is a bit like the denouement in a dramatic film, when the hero says to the villain: 'Ha, your mask has fallen at last! Now we can see you as you really are!' We all know from our own experience just how damning and definitive this final judgement can be. The underlying reasoning is: 'If you are good actor, you can make me believe for a time that you are on my side. That is something you can fake. But you can't fake being untrustworthy. That is your true nature.' This harks back to some of the things we have already discussed previously: something negative weighs more heavily in our assessments than something positive and – think back to Kahneman and Tversky – the risk of losing something weighs more heavily than the desire to gain something.

Curiously enough, this phenomenon works in the opposite direction when it comes to the competency dimension. Once you have been labelled by someone as being 'competent', it is perfectly possible for you to make a mistake here or there without losing that label. You can see this, for example, in the stereotypical image of the 'absent-minded professor': the man is a genius, but sometimes he doesn't even know what day of the week it is. But once a professor, always a professor. In other words, this dimension is less vulnerable to change. Conclusion? You can occasionally risk playing fast and loose in matters relating to your competencies. But it is a bad idea to take risks in matters relating to your trustworthiness. No matter how many tricks you know and how persuasive you think you are, if you only use these competencies to serve your own interests and you get found out, your reputation will be shot to pieces overnight. What's more, it will never recover. People will no longer be willing to do anything to help you.

Because this dimension is so crucial, it is worth looking at some of the research results relating to trustworthiness.[3] For example, in one experiment a database was compiled with different images of the human face. The images were chosen because they are typically recognised – by white Westerners, at least – as being either trustworthy or untrustworthy. The test subjects were then shown the images in a random order, during which their brain activity was monitored by an MRI scan. The researchers were interested in answering three questions: how fast is the brain's reaction to the photos, how strong is this reaction and is there any measurable difference between reactions to trustworthy and untrustworthy facial expressions?

We all know the importance of 'first impressions' and how quickly they are made. Most of us assume that we are able to assess people in a matter of minutes. Some of us even think we can do it within the first 30 seconds. But what did the MRI show? Its measurements were at least objective – and that is what makes them so fascinating!

Believe it or not, the brain already reacts to both trustworthy and untrustworthy images in just 0.05 seconds! This is much too fast for us to be consciously aware of the process and it gives some idea of just how sensitive our 'intentions' radar has become in the course of our evolutionary development. The first assessment ('friend or enemy?') is made at lightning speed, because for many thousands of years that instant decision was crucial to our survival as a species. When our ancient ancestors bumped into something unexpected in the primeval forest, there was not much time for mature reflection or philosophical musings: 'Can I eat it or will it eat me? Hmm, let's just think about this for a moment or two...' No, that would not have been a particularly effective survival strategy. Instead, they needed to decide in a split second: fight or flight.

Yet while reaction speed is the same, there is however a difference in the intensity with which the brain reacts to trustworthy and untrustworthy images. This can be measured with the MRI scan, which monitors the extent to which the affected parts of the brain are activated. The reaction was significantly stronger for untrustworthy faces than for trustworthy ones. This provides yet further evidence that the negative nearly always weighs more heavily than the positive in human assessments. It seems that this is simply a built-in part of our evolutionary heritage.

2   FRIENDLINESS IS A BONUS

If you are interested in exploring the domain of interpersonal influence, sooner or later you will come up against the name of the American researcher Robert Cialdini. He has done much excellent work mapping out the (often unconscious) mechanisms by which influence and influencing operate. Importantly, his findings are always based on rigorous, empirical and scientifically sound investigative methods. If you are able to look beyond the strong marketing orientation of his conclusions, you can learn much of great value.[4]

It was Cialdini who devised the operational definition of the factors that determine whether or not we like someone and are therefore prepared to make a little extra effort on their behalf: 'We like those who like us and those who are like us.'

People who like each other often show this by smiling. It is a non-verbal code language that is instantly recognisable.

This was clearly demonstrated by a research study in the United States, where the service personnel in restaurants – the waiters and waitresses – are dependent for a substantial part of their income on the tips they receive from customers.[5]

There are informal rules about the size of these tips, but there is also a fair margin for individual interpretation. The study was set up in such a way that the same number of men and women were involved, so that gender would not make a difference. Two different scenarios were played out. In the first, the personnel carried out their duties with a big smile on their face. In the second, the smile was much less in evidence. The question was, of course, whether or not this would have an impact on the size of the tip the customers were willing to give. In this study, the impact was significant: a big smile yielded an average tip of 23.20 dollars; a minimal smile just 9.40 dollars. It is the kind of result that makes you think – especially if your income depends on it.

So what about this next example? 7-ELEVEN is a well-know convenience store chain in America and you can also find its stores in the larger European centres. Their concept is to provide the benefits of a local store at inner city locations. As a result, their shops are not too big, do not have a huge range of products and are typically located at the kinds of places you might pass on your way to and from your work. Ideal for buying your lunchtime coffee and a sandwich or a ready-made evening meal on your way home.

Some years ago, 7-ELEVEN launched a major coast-to-coast campaign in the US to improve their customer-friendliness. All their many stores and their tens of thousands of staff were involved. The idea was that everyone should follow a day of customer-friendliness training.

This is not necessarily as easy as it sounds, since customer-friendliness is a fairly abstract concept. If you want to train people in it, you have to find a way to make it tangible for them. 7-ELEVEN (being aware of the kind of research mentioned above) did this by focusing on two very specific acts of behaviour: engaging in brief conversation with customers and smiling at them.

Measuring is knowing. If you are investing on a huge scale in training, you want to know that it is having the desired effect. The use of mystery shoppers is an effective way to find out. They work for the research bureaus but visit shops and stores, pretending to be ordinary customers. This idea is that they visit their target locations a few days before and a few days after the training has taken place. In the case of 7-ELEVEN, their task was to count the extent to which the two key behaviours – chatting and smiling – were observable.

Imagine the pride of the project manager when half way through the project he was able to present a series of impressive intermediary results to the executive committee! The amount of chatting had increased from 33 percent to 58 percent and smiling from 32 percent to 49 percent. Applause all round.

Well, nearly all round. It was probably someone from IT who raised a hand to ask a question: 'Remind me. Why did we go to all the trouble of setting up this campaign?' Disbelieving looks from the other side of the table. 'Why? Why do you think? To improve our levels of customer-friendliness!' 'Yes, I know that,' continued the inquisitor, 'but why exactly do we want to improve our customer-friendliness?' Silence. Then, suddenly, the penny dropped. 'Ah, you mean the turnover...' 'Yes, I mean the store turnover. Just a minor thing, I know, but have you bothered to measure it?' More silence. Followed by panic. They had forgotten to measure the main reason for the whole campaign!

Fortunately, this was something that could easily be put right, because the cash registers identify each of the sales staff individually. And what transpired? The results showed that the sellers with the highest turnover were actually those who were least 'friendly', in terms of the two behavioural criteria for which everyone had been trained. They might not smile a lot or chat a lot, but they certainly sold a lot.

When you think about it, the explanation is easy, but that doesn't make it any the less important: you only have influence to the extent that the added value you give is relevant to the people to whom you give it. Customers clearly visit 7-ELEVEN with a different mindset from the one they use when visiting a restaurant. At a convenience store, they are not interested in chatting and smiling. They just want to get in and out of the place with their purchases as quickly as possible – and chatting and smiling slows this process down. It is different in a restaurant, where people have more time and are looking to relax and enjoy themselves. The moral of this story? Beware the perils of simplistic behavioural recipes and copy-paste tricks.

There are a couple of other reasons why artificial friendliness is not a good idea and can often have the opposite effect to what you intend. One of them is your own self-interest. Research has shown that people who work in service industries and who feel 'obliged' by the nature of their duties to be excessively friendly, like stewards and stewardesses on aircraft, can often find this very difficult after a time, particularly if authenticity is one of their most important values. This results in a higher incidence of burn-out and other physical and mental problems, simply because the people concerned feel increasingly alienated from their own personality and emotions.[6]

Another drawback to artificial friendliness is the fact that it is so obviously false. You cannot fake an authentic smile: the muscles around the eyes contract automatically as a consequence of the emotion you feel, in a manner that cannot be consciously controlled.[7] In contrast, the visible falsity of a bogus smile gives people the impression they are being deceived. But how does this work, exactly? We mentioned earlier how our inner radar is able to detect trustworthiness and untrustworthiness with great accuracy and speed. When someone fakes a smile, your radar will pick it up instantly. Inside our brain we have a group of cells known as mirror neurons. When we see an expression of emotion in someone else, these neurons – as their name implies – instantly copy it, so that we create that same emotion in our own selves. Once again, this is an automatic process over which we have no control. If someone feels obliged to pretend to be friendly towards us, this creates a certain internal tension in that person. This same tension is then automatically generated by our own mirror neurons, so that we immediately get the feeling that something is not right. We know that we are being conned – and which of us is happy with that?[8]

Additional remark

We know that there is a very specific area in the brain responsible for the recognition of faces. If you focus on this area during an MRI scan, it lights up on the scan screen when you show a test subject a photograph of someone. But it also does the same when you show them an emoticon. The reaction time for an emoticon is nearly as fast as for a human face, and much shorter than if you show the test subject abstract symbols that have nothing to do with faces (although, strangely enough, there is no recognition if the emoticon is inverted).[9] Even so, this is a remarkable performance. It took many millennia of evolution for our brains to react in the way it does to the faces of others. Emoticons have only been in existence for decades, yet the level of speed and recognition is already as strong. This opens the door to an obvious practical application: don't hesitate to use emoticons in your e-mails and text messages. The effect on readers will be the same as if they had seen you smile in person!

Keep your hands to yourself?

People who like each other not only smile at each other, but also touch each other. However, it goes without saying that you need to be very careful when it comes to matters of physical contact. Some people feel really uncomfortable if their personal space is infringed in this manner and in some cultures it is very definitely not done. Even so, there is no disputing that in the right circumstances it can have a powerful positive effect, as the following experiment in puritanical and politically correct America was able to show.

The study once again involved waiters and waitresses working in restaurants and was again set up in a way that ensured that the gender and number of both personnel and customers would play no role. This time the intention was to see what effect giving the customer a pat of the shoulder when bringing the bill would have on the level of the tip. Once again, there was a significant positive effect: a friendly pat on the shoulder was rewarded with a tip that on average was 3.5 percent higher.[10] Other research has demonstrated that this effect is even stronger in non-commercial contexts. Imagine, for example, that you want to persuade people to sign a petition or fill in a questionnaire. As with the restaurant experiment, you create two conditions: in the first, you briefly touch the upper arm of your conversation partner before making your request; in the second, there is no physical contact. The different scenarios are applied to equal numbers of people, with the necessary control measures to filter out the impact of gender. The results are now even more startling than in the restaurant study: with minimal physical contact, the number of people willing to sign the petition increased from 55 percent to 81 percent, while those willing to fill in the questionnaire rose from 40 percent to 70 percent.[11]

Hopefully, this will not lead you to the conclusion that you constantly need to be pawing your stakeholders. If you are daft enough to think that you can use touching as a persuasive 'technique', you are barking up the wrong tree and run the same risk as with a false smile: once people see that the contact is not spontaneous and genuine, it will actually increase the distance between you and the other person, rather than narrow it. That being said, if you are a natural 'toucher' – someone who does it easily and authentically – there is no reason why you should try to block out this impulse, unless there are cultural reasons for doing so. Of course, you always need to keep a close eye on how your 'touchee' reacts, because not everyone likes to be the subject of this kind of gesture, no matter how well intentioned. If you sense there is a problem, apologise immediately and don't do it again. But don't make the mistake of changing your behaviour in general: your habit of brief and appropriate physical contact will almost certainly bring you more benefits than difficulties. So don't suppress your natural impulse unnecessarily.

Be seen

In addition to smiling and touching, there is a third element that also contributes to liking and being liked. It is neatly summarised by a saying that everyone will know: 'Out of sight, out of mind.' In other words, you need to be seen. You need to remind people who you are, not just in mails and reports, but in person. It is this that can make the difference. You want proof? Consider the following experiment – which was carried out in an unusual setting.

In a university lecture hall, where students regularly attended courses, a life-size doll was always put on the same chair at the same desk. This doll was clearly intended to simulate a person, even though it had no facial features. The students were not told in advance why it was there; they simply had to accept its presence. And that is precisely what they did. What's more, after a time some of them even began to develop positive feelings towards their dummy colleague! This effect is known as 'mere exposure'.[12] The simple fact that you are more and more visible will result in people liking you more and more, as long as you give them no reason not to. This helps to explain, for example, why some politicians are prepared to sell their own grandmothers to get a few extra minutes of exposure on national television, certainly when elections are due!

The implications of this phenomenon for the successful completion of your project are obvious. That being said, this 'visibility' card is played much less frequently than you might expect, particularly in our Western culture. The basic rule is simple enough: make sure you are seen and seen often. This should be interpreted literally: you need to come into face-to-face contact with your stakeholders as frequently as you realistically can. This obviously happens in meetings, but you should make an effort to pop your head regularly around the doors of people's offices, even if only for a few seconds. If they are not in the same building, think about making use of Skype and video conferencing. Yet even though visibility can help you a lot, it is still not a popular option in the western business world. Consequently, people try to find all different kinds of rationalisation to avoid the need to do it, the most common being: 'I am more concerned with content than with my own PR!' Perhaps this makes a great sound-bite for outsiders, but it can really take the wind out of your sails if you are heavily dependent on the goodwill of your stakeholders.

3 'FLATTERY WILL GET YOU EVERYWHERE'

It is hardly a state secret to say that you will normally do a little bit extra for people who value you for who you are and what you do. Being valued is extremely important for us all, because it relates to the answers to two important questions that everyone should (hopefully) be able to answer positively. The first question is this: if I look at myself in the mirror and realise that I am never going to achieve divine (or even semi-divine) status, can I nevertheless live with myself? In other words, do I find myself okay? And the second question is this: if I think about the opinions that people I respect have of me, can I be reasonably confident that they will also find me okay? If you have doubts about one or both of these answers, you might be on the fast road to depression! Realising that you are valuable as a person is an essential component of our human well-being. It is vital to all of us that our personal territory (our identity) is appreciated and that we can share a common social territory with others. If these others can contribute to this process by expressing their admiration for us, this makes us feel so much better!

Laura is a fine colleague who told me that she had sent a price tender to a very good customer of ours, a prestigious IT company. Amongst the things mentioned in the company's reply, was a comment about her daily rate. She let me read the passage in question: '(…) I am certain that this tariff is a good reflection of your level of expertise, but may I nevertheless ask you as a gesture of goodwill to offer us a more favourable total price for your services.' Laura has been working with us for some time and knows all aspects of her job thoroughly, including the tricks that buyers use to lower the prices they have to pay. As a result, she recognised the IT company's tactic of first praising her skills to the heavens, before asking her to knock something off the bill. However, she was so proud to hear her professionalism so described that – against her better judgement – she did indeed agree to lower her hourly rate! Falling victim to the effect of compliments and appreciation is practically impossible to avoid.

William Lamb and Robert Peel were both British prime ministers during the reign of Queen Victoria. The two men were great political rivals. There is a story that a lady-in-waiting at the royal court dined with both men during the same month. Afterwards, she described both experiences to her friends. Of Peel she said: 'After dining with Peel, I was in seventh heaven. I was convinced that I had dined with the most intelligent man in the country.' Of Lamb she said: 'After dining with Lamb, I was in seventh heaven. I was convinced that he had dined with the most intelligent woman in the country.' Who would have had the biggest smile, do you think? And how would you have felt if you were Peel? Exactly.

When using compliments, the rule we have seen previously still applies: they are a very powerful tool, but only if they are authentic. If everything we do is applauded as being 'fantastic' or 'great', the effect soon wears off: none of us are always that good. In these circumstances, the 'praise' becomes little more than an exaggerated form of politeness, which actually creates more distance between the people involved and thereby weakens rather than strengthens their relationship. But it is important not to go to the opposite extreme: you can miss huge opportunities if you fail to tell your stakeholders when you genuinely appreciate something they have done. It only takes a small effort on your part, but it can be a massive goodwill lever.

If you want to maximise the effect of your compliments, you have to explain the reasoning behind them. An example. You send an e-mail and receive an answer back within an hour, to which you then respond with a further e-mail:

'Thank you for your quick reply!' Okay, there is nothing really wrong with this stereotypical phrase, but its use has become so commonplace that it has about as much meaning (in other words, very little) as your greeting and signature at the bottom of the mail. Look at the difference if you formulate your message in the following way: 'Thank you for your quick reply, which I much appreciate, because it made it possible for me to...' It is that 'because' clause that makes the real impact.

Of course, it is understandable that you sometimes hesitate to give compliments to people, because you anticipate their possible reaction ('What do you want from me?'). Naturally, the very last thing you want is to make them feel used. If you think that there is a real danger of this (but don't assume it too quickly), you might like to consider the following approach.

If you know that one of your stakeholders is a good friend of someone else you know, and you also know that the two of them see each other regularly, you can try to pass on your appreciation for your stakeholder through your common acquaintance. You can be fairly certain that this will happen: 'Hey, do you know what X said about you?' In this way, your stakeholder receives a compliment from an unsuspected source (and which of us can fail to be charmed when that happens!), while still allowing you to reap the rewards as the giver of that compliment, but without being suspected of ulterior motives. Once again, however, authenticity is the key. Do not regard this as simply another tactic you can use indiscriminately. If you do, it will come across as being too mechanistic, so that it risks losing its effect. This is not what you want.

It must appear – no, it must be – natural. How can you make sure this is the case? If you regularly reflect on the good things that you see happening in your environment, you will almost automatically find yourself saying positive things about others, so that you gradually build up a positive reputation of your own. In other words, you develop an attitude of mind that makes your complements seem credible when you give them, rather than being a strategic or tactical intervention from your management box of tricks.

If you can acquire this kind of mindset, the compliments will often come of their own accord. Imagine that you are in a team meeting where a number of different agenda points need to be discussed. The people present, including yourself, give their opinions on the various topics. When it is your turn, you might, for example, find yourself saying: 'There is another point I think we should consider, which builds on something that Rose just said, when she was talking about…' By mentioning Rose in this manner, you clearly imply that you attach value to her opinion. In other words, it is a compliment that you give her in public – and you can be certain that it will be appreciated by her as such. Once again, however, spontaneity is the key. You must not mention Rose (or other members of the team) in this same manner in every meeting!

The real power of a compliment is to be found in the recognition and attention it confers. It is almost as if you are saying: 'I see you and hear you as the person you are, and that is reason enough for me to value you.'

David's work takes him all over the world. A few months ago, he was at a conference in a hotel in the southern part of the United States. The hotel was huge, with several restaurants and a casino on the ground floor. The number of guests passing through the reception area each day was equally huge. During the first morning of his stay, David needed to have a document copied and asked the young woman behind the reception desk if she could help. 'Sorry, I'm afraid not, or at least not here,' came the reply. 'But if you are on your way to the business centre, there is a corridor on the right where you can find everything you will need.' Fine. Problem solved.

Two evenings later, David wanted to ask a question about one of the hotel's restaurants, so back he went to the reception desk. He failed to notice that it was the same young woman who had helped him two days before. She answered his question about the restaurant, but then added: 'And did you find everything you needed to make those copies?' David was amazed. How on earth could she still know that?

The effect of something like this is enormous. It gives you a feeling of: 'Gosh, I must be really important, if she can remember me out of all the many hundreds of customers she deals with!' In this case, David was so impressed that he went to see the hotel manager, not only to express his admiration, but also to ask how such a feat of memory was possible. The manager admitted that it didn't happen by magic. It was a question of training. When they come into contact with guests who are staying a number of days, the receptionists are trained to pinch themselves in the hand at the moment they give an answer to a question, whilst at the same time repeating to themselves the guest's name. In this way, they are able to anchor the contact in their mind. Impressive indeed!

This is comparable with a technique that sales staff often use. During every customer contact there is almost always a social preamble, when client and seller chat about this and that (the weather, the latest football results, etc.). This can often reveal lots of useful information for the seller. If you note down, for example, that your client is a big fan of Liverpool F.C. and is planning to spend his holiday this year in Parma, you can pleasantly surprise him when you mention these things again during a subsequent meeting: 'I see Liverpool won again… By the way, how was your vacation in Parma?' Just a trick? Yes and no. A trick certainly, but also something more than that. Do you remember our earlier discussion about the dynamics of reciprocity? What you demonstrate to the customer by using this technique is that you have made the effort: (1) to listen to what he said; (2) to note it down; (3) to consult your notes; (4) and to use the information again. You will be rewarded for this effort in the form of goodwill.

That the importance of giving attention and of valuing people for who they are is more than just a moral slogan has been convincingly illustrated by research carried out by Kaptchuk and his colleagues at Harvard. Their field of study is the placebo effect, an effect that is often grossly misunderstood.

One of the many experiments conducted by the group around Kaptchuk involved patients with a stomach complaint known as irritable bowel syndrome.[13] The patients were divided into three groups and were followed over a period of six weeks. One group received no treatment; they were simply put on a waiting list. The second group were given acupuncture. The third group were given acupuncture +. The difference between the second and third conditions was that the patients in the + group not only had needles administered to them, but were also talked to in a particular way (which will become clear later). Something else unusual was also going on. The 'acupuncture' was not really acupuncture at all. The needles were especially made so that they retracted automatically into a sheath when they came into contact with the skin. It was this sheath that stuck to the skin, giving the impression that a needle had been inserted, whereas in reality this was not the case.

First, the results. At the end of the six-week period, all the patients were asked whether or not their condition had improved. This was the case with 28 percent of the people on the waiting list, a figure that rose to 44 percent for the patients who had received 'normal' acupuncture, increasing yet again to an impressive 62 percent for the acupuncture + group. These are significant differences.

So what exactly did acupuncture + involve? The doctors had been specially trained to behave in the following manner with each of their patients:

- To ask them at length about their symptoms and about the impact of the condition on themselves and their families.
- To use a friendly tone of voice.
- To use the techniques of active listening (open questions, summarisation, etc.).
- To express empathy with and sympathy for the patient.
- To take time in the presence of the patient to read through in silence the extensive notes made by the doctor during the treatment session.
- To express positive expectations about the future progress of the treatment and the improvement of the condition.

The most important lesson of all this? Giving attention to people cements strong relationships.

Additional comment

The more you believe in your own expertise and the more you allow your identity to be dependent on your status as an expert, the more likely you are to undervalue and underappreciate the efforts and abilities of your stakeholders.

My colleague Lisa regularly tries to help project managers with their problem situations. Recently, she received the following request from one of them: 'How do you deal with idiots?' Of course, to most of us this sounds blunt to the point of rudeness, but unfortunately it is a question that often plays on the minds of specialists when their expert advice is not automatically and immediately followed by everyone else. If you are troubled by similar thoughts, consider the following comment by American humorist, journalist and Pulitzer Prize winner Dave Barry: 'I can win any argument on any topic against any opponent. People know this and steer clear of me at parties. Often, as a sign of their great respect, they don't even invite me.' This is frequently what happens when you try to be the smartest kid on the block.

Perhaps it is useful here to summarise what you have already read about compliments and flattery:

1. Smile and also answer the smiles of others with a smile.
2. Only do it if you mean it.
3. Make use of emoticons.
4. Maintain eye contact when you are listening to others.
5. Make the physical distance between you and the other as small as is comfortable for both of you.
6. Briefly touch the other person's arm when saying hello or goodbye.
7. Make sure you remain visible to others.
8. If you are able to show genuine appreciation for a stakeholder, don't hesitate: just do it!
9. Consider communicating compliments through a third person.
10. Make your compliments more meaningful, not only by expressing them but also by explaining your reason for expressing them.
11. Express your satisfaction and gratitude for any progress made in a project or collaboration in which you are involved.
12. Show that you understand and value the feelings and opinions of others, as well as understanding the things to which they relate.
13. During discussions in meetings, refer positively to comments that others have previously made in the same meeting.
14. Remember details about people. Write them down and use them again later.

4 WE LIKE PEOPLE LIKE US – BUT WE LIKE OURSELVES BEST OF ALL

In order to feel comfortable with yourself, there are two questions to which you need to be able to answer 'yes':

1. Taking all things into account, do I feel that I am generally okay?
2. Do people whose opinions I value also generally find me okay?

This might seem like two different questions and therefore a kind of 'double test', on the outcome of which a great deal depends. But if you are clever, you can find a way to roll both questions into one *and* more or less guarantee that you get a positive answer. The magic formula that makes this possible? Auto-poiesis. 'Auto what?' I can hear you asking.

The term comes from the world of biology and refers to the tendency of every cell to replicate itself. In other words, to make a copy of what it already was.[14] Biologically, this means that we are capable of reproducing ourselves at the cellular level. To make ourselves double what we currently are. Sociologists now make use of this same mechanism to explain the tendency of human beings not only to reproduce their cells but also their ideas.[15] And how exactly do you do this? By searching for people who think the same way you do. Certain parts of town attract the same kind of people. Certain groups of like-minded colleagues form cohorts within even the most coherent teams. As for friendship, it is almost exclusively based on autopoiesis.

We all try to find people who we can talk to, who immediately understand us, who we feel comfortable with. In fact, what we are doing is trying to find ourselves in others. This offers numerous advantages. It makes us feel safe, prevents us from being confronted with the unpredictability of divergent opinions and therefore avoids the need for us to constantly question and defend our own ideas and way of life. Most important of all, if we spend most of our time with people who are the same as us, we not only receive confirmation of our own identity but also acceptance of that identity by our immediate environment. Hey presto: both our important 'okay' questions answered in one fell swoop!

This is the way in which social territories are formed. It is the mechanism of the tribe and it provides us with something crucial: a social identity. It allows us to belong to a group that is close-knit, offers us protection, and is different from other groups. Of course, this means that we will have to adjust to the norms of the group, if we want to belong. But if others make things difficult for us, they had better look out – because the group will know and will soon be after them.

Additional comment

Social media and dating sites fully understand the power of this mechanism. They both make use of people's desire to search for matches: 'If a potential dating partner gives the same answers as me to the following three questions, then surely I can't go wrong!' This opens up the interesting (if somewhat lurid) possibility that dating sites are actually encouraging people to go on a date with themselves, or at least with their alter ego!

Here is a little experiment you might like to try. Ask a number of your acquaintances or business contacts from here or abroad (it doesn't matter which) to type the search term 'Zambia' (or something similar) into their search engine and then to mail you their first screen shot. If you compare these screenshots side by side, you will be amazed by the number of differences you see. So why is this? It is because each of these people has a different search history that has been memorised by the search engine, so that they are repeatedly fed 'more of the same'.

Long before the Cambridge Analytica affair hit the headlines, revealing the systematic online manipulation of the Brexit referendum and the American presidential elections in 2016, publicist Eli Pariser was already complaining about something similar.[16] Although he regards himself as a political progressive, he has always made attempts to keep abreast of what is happening in conservative America. If you like, he wants to hear the story from the other side, since he feels this helps him to better refine his own very different ideas. As a result, he regularly follows matters of 'conservative' interest online. Or at least he did. One day, however, he suddenly noticed that all the conservatives had disappeared from his Facebook feed. He soon discovered why. He had recently been clicking more frequently on the links sent to him by some of his more progressive friends than on links from conservative sources. As a result, the latter had now vanished from his screen, as if by magic. Abracadabra: gone! So much for his attempt to keep in touch with ideas from a different political camp.

There is something slightly sinister about this. An analysis of the sites clicked on by 376 million internet users over a period of six years has revealed just how few different news sites are consulted by most people. Even if they do consult more than a few sites, they are usually all of the same (political) persuasion. This leads to a situation where two people whose views initially might only have been slightly divergent gradually become ever more divergent, because they are being selectively and systematically exposed to news that only confirms 'their' view of the world and deliberately ignores other opinions.[17] Welcome to the wonderful world of polarisation! Selective exposure of this kind is relatively easy to organise and direct. Research has shown that a medium like Facebook can predict with 88 percent certainty whether or not you are homosexual or heterosexual, simply on the basis of your 'likes'. The success rate for political preference is 85 percent.[18] This is then followed up by the application of the 'people like us' principle, so that you are only fed online information that conforms with your profile, thereby effectively cutting you off – at least without a serious effort on your part – from all other shades of opinion. This is what happened to Eli Pariser. It is also what happened to voters in Great Britain and the United States.[19]

But most of all, we like ourselves

In addition to our search for a social identity (we want to belong to a tribe of like-minded people), we are also continually striving to develop, establish and maintain a personal identity. We want to be unique and we want to be valued because of that uniqueness. We have already referred to this earlier in the book as your 'personal territory'. As a source of motivation, this desire to be 'you' is perhaps even greater and more fundamental than the desire to be 'one of us'. What's more, it can also manifest itself in some curious ways.

Jozef Nuttin was a Belgian professor of social psychology. One day, as he was driving along in his car, he noticed that his attention was particular drawn to the number plates of other cars that contained the letters of his name. Curious as he was (and as all scientists are), he wondered whether or not this phenomenon was subject to any laws. He decided to set up an experiment to find out – and so the name letter effect was born.[20]

If people are given a choice between a letter that appears in their name and a letter that does not, they will systematically choose the former, especially if that letter happens to be one of their initials. This means, for example, that if someone had ever asked Nuttin before he stumbled across this idea whether he preferred the letter 'J' to the letter 'M', he would have opted for the 'J' from Jozef. The same would have applied, of course, for the 'Z' and the 'F'. What's more, subsequent experiments have shown that this is not only true for the Dutch language, but also for eleven other European languages that use the Roman alphabet, as well as for Greek and Japanese.

Oddly enough, there is a comparable effect for numbers. You will have a pref-erence for numbers that appear in your date of birth, as opposed to random numbers that hold no meaning for you. This mechanism is completely uncon-scious and is found in all different kinds of people (young children, students, expert professionals, etc.) and in all different cultures.

It is taking things a step too far to label this phenomenon as narcissism, which has a negative connotation, although research has shown that there is nevertheless a clear correlation between the strength of the name letter effect and a high sense of self-esteem. This is interesting, but more important still is the fact that this effect seems to be strongest of all in people who come from a warm and positive family background rather than from a background where the parents were controlling and over-protective.[21] In other words, it is a healthy mechanism.

The same is true of people's desire to be unique and to be valued for who they are. This is not only a strong source of motivation, but also has power-ful positive effects. That people wish to protect their identity is self-evident. Even within your tribe of like-minded kindred spirits, you still want to be a special individual and to be recognised as such. But when you want to form an alliance with someone else to create a common territory, this will only be possible when you show that you understand what is important for the other and demonstrate your respect for it. This applies both to the group to which he belongs and to his values and identity as an individual. You do not nec-essarily have to agree with these things, but you do have to make clear that you are aware of them and that you recognise their right to exist. This will be sufficient to generate the goodwill you need.

If you want to connect with someone else's identity, there are many different ways you can do this, since there are many different facets to each individual person. Sometimes it can be useful to have a few handles on which to rely. What kind of person is he? What kind of person are you? On which aspect(s) of your respective personalities might you be able to find a connection? On the following three pages you will find three questionnaires. On each line there are two alternatives from which you can choose. The idea is that should put a cross by the one that best describes you in your work situation. Bear in mind that these pairs of options are seldom likely to be 100 percent 'either... or', as though you always do one of the options and never do the other one. Even so, you will generally find that your preference leans more in favour of one of the two directions.

But before we start, let's be clear. This test is not a matter of life and death. Your future success and the well-being of your family does not depend on it. It is simply a list of questions that will clarify a number of your preferences in your working environment and perhaps show you how they relate to each other. The purpose is to give you pause for thought and to encourage reflection. No more than that. With this in mind, it is a good idea to count up the number of crosses you set in each column and note down the total at the bottom. Leave out the questions where you feel there is no clear answer that applies to you.

Another equally effective way to approach the test is to first read through all the options in both columns and then decided which column as a whole you think best describes you. It is perhaps also a good idea to give a copy of the questionnaire to a trusted colleague and ask him to fill it in as he sees you. This often provides interesting results, because it is sometimes easier for someone else to be more objective about the way you think and behave. After completing the third list, you will find instructions about how the questionnaire can be scored and what these scores mean.

Dimension 1	
I ...	
☐ am good at implementing projects	☐ am good at designing projects
☐ can deal well with procedures	☐ see the need for procedures, but find them limiting
☐ like detail and precision	☐ lose my interest if there is too much detail and often don't take the time to be precise
☐ like solving problems that are simple and clear	☐ like solving complex problems
☐ am good at developing here-and-now solutions	☐ am good at developing long-term solutions
☐ usually reach conclusions step by step	☐ usually reach quick conclusions in leaps and bounds
☐ usually work at an even pace	☐ work in fits and starts, with periods of energy alternating with periods of more limited activity
☐ like a well-defined way of doing things and like to stick to what we have done before	☐ don't like always doing the same things
☐ like to optimise what already exists and works well	☐ like to innovate
☐ like to fully enjoy the success we have achieved	☐ soon become restless after a success and quickly need a new challenge
I recognise myself above all in ...	
☐ 1a	☐ 1b

I ...

☐ am strongly focused by nature on the content quality of measures

☐ am strongly focused by nature on the acceptance of measures by all concerned

☐ have a tendency to follow principles consistently

☐ have a tendency to adjust principles to the situation of those involved

☐ have a strong eye for the effect that people and human factors can have on a task

☐ have a strong eye for the effect that a task can have on people

☐ am strongly task-oriented by nature

☐ am strongly process and person-oriented by nature

☐ take decisions with a certain detachment, based purely on business logic and deductive reasoning

☐ take decisions based on my experience of the situation for those involved and my own subjective values

☐ sometimes hurt the feelings of others without knowing it

☐ attach great importance to the building and maintaining of harmonious human relationships

☐ easily give corrective feedback

☐ easily give positive feedback

☐ attach more importance to respect between people than to warmth

☐ attach great importance to interpersonal warmth

☐ react to criticism in a business-like manner

☐ take criticism personally and react emotionally

☐ am good at putting forward facts and opinions

☐ am good at listening and empathising

☐ am not too worried by conflicts, as long as they don't affect the implementation of the task

☐ find conflicts in a work setting highly stressful

I recognise myself above all in ...

☐ 2a

☐ 2b

Dimension 3

I ...

☐ like streamlining, predictability and control	☐ like flexibility
☐ attach great importance to honouring agreements	☐ attach great importance to completing the task as successfully as possible, even if this means using an approach different to what was originally agreed
☐ find it difficult to revise a decision that has been agreed	☐ find it difficult to follow a rigid course
☐ like to commit myself to a clear direction	☐ like to keep open as many options as possible
☐ deal with what needs to be dealt with	☐ have a tendency to postpone unpleasant tasks
☐ attach great importance to setting fixed priorities in advance and then sticking to them	☐ can easily deviate from my plans or priorities, if this gives me the possibility to exploit opportunities
☐ do not go in search of new information once I have formed an opinion	☐ remain curious and am constantly in search of new information
☐ feel at home in a structured environment	☐ feel that my desire to explore is often frustrated in a structured environment
☐ primarily focus on the end result	☐ primarily focus on the journey to the end result
☐ find it annoying to have to delay a project I have started, in order to do other more urgent tasks	☐ am sometimes busy with more than one project at the same time, but have no problem to complete them all

I recognise myself above all in ...

☐ 3a   ☐ 3b

The lists that you have filled in relate to different typologies, a typology being the division of people into groups.[22] You always need to be careful with typologies. In fact, you have already read some critical comments on them in chapters 1 and 2. They are extremely useful – as long as you don't always believe what they tell you! Extremely useful, because they offer you a differentiated way to look at people. This is not always as easy as it sounds, because to do this we are often inclined to use an unwritten rule, which more or less goes like this:

1   What are people like?
2   They are the way I am.
3   Or that, at least, is the way they should be.
4   If they are not the way they should be, I will do my best to set them back on the right path; in other words, my path.

Okay, it's not very scientific, but you get the idea. And it is not so surprising that we use this 'methodology', if you think back to a number of things already mentioned earlier in this chapter, such as the way it gives people certainty if other people are like they are, because this strengthens their own sense of identity.

The disadvantage of typologies is that they have a tendency to work as definitions. Someone is either this type or that type. This tends to blind us rather than make us aware of the rich diversity of human behaviour and the ways in which people can develop and grow, not only in the course of their life, but also in the course of their career, as they receive different responsibilities in different functions.

It would be a great shame if you assumed that what a typology says about you carries the same crushing weight as a biblical commandment. If you think this way, there are two things that might happen that you really need to avoid: (1) the typology gives you a perfect excuse to carry on doing what you are currently doing, including the non-productive elements of your behaviour; (2) the typology gives you no reason to develop the other aspects of your personality, because 'that's the way I am.' Make sure you don't make either of these mistakes.

That being said, typologies also have clear advantages as well. They invite us to look at people in a differentiated manner and encourage us to explore the logic and identity of others, rather than simply seeking for confirmation of our own logic and identity. This is a good idea, if we realise that to achieve our objectives we need the goodwill and support of others for our project. In these circumstances, it makes no sense to condemn the logic and identity of others, simply to confirm our own.

It is against this background that you can now give a score to the questionnaires you have just filled in. These score will focus the spotlight on four different kinds of typology: Diamond Cutters, Emergency Doctors, Teachers and Scientists. If you put a tick in box 1a and 3a, you are a Diamond Cutter. The combination 1a and 3b means you are an Emergency Doctor. For Teachers the combination is 1b and 2b, and for Scientists 1b and 2a.

You can regard each of these types as a kind of family. There are a number of members who have certain characteristics in common, but there are also numerous cousins, nieces and nephews who can be very different from each other. If you read the descriptions given below of each of the families, you will always find a reference back to our central formula for the exercising of influence: $I = Q \times A$. The Impact you can exert is equal to the Quality of what you say multiplied by the level of Acceptance for your message. As you read, you will notice that the nature of the different families means that they sometimes have a preference for a certain element in the formula and also for other aspects on which they will focus their special attention. So here are the families and how you can interpret the 'language' they speak.

Characteristics	Speaking their language	Examples
In the formula I = Q x A, they focus first and foremost on the Q. Their basic question is: HOW (precisely?). They are serious, realistic and task-oriented. They like structure, hierarchy, schedules and procedures. They are extremely accurate and reliable. They are loyal to the organisation. They are concerned for continuity and, as a result, recognise the importance of procedures. They believe more in step-by-step change than in leaps and bounds. They are almost automatically focused on avoiding things that can potentially go wrong with any innovation, and they avoid risks wherever possible.	Be precise and detailed. Start with the known facts and use them in your reasoning to reach your conclusion step by step. Point out potential risks and indicate in detail how they can be anticipated or avoided. If you put forward a new idea, make clear how this idea builds on what already exists and works well. Indicate how the organisation as a whole will benefit from the idea you are proposing. Always respect deadlines and agreements. When you propose an innovation to them, show how it has already proven its worth in a comparable environment.	Avoid surprises: send information in advance and offer to go deeper into this information before it is formally placed on the table. Always indicate clearly in advance which points and in which order you wish to deal with things, and abide by this. If you put forward a plan, always propose a detailed Plan B as well, in the event that your first plan, for whatever reason, should fail to work. Name and value their attitude of 'due diligence', praising their unwillingness to take unnecessary risks. Show that information has been double checked or give them the chance to do this themselves, before going public.

STAKEHOLDERING

Emergency doctors

Characteristics	Speaking their language	Examples
In the formula I = Q x A, they quickly focus on the I. Their basic question is: why NOW? They usually make excellent and action-oriented crisis managers. They are capable of being flexible and pragmatic in negotiation and can quickly achieve results. They are impatient with routines and procedures. They have no problem to amend agreements that have been made, providing it leads to a better result. They want to be challenged to achieve concrete results quickly. They are not always cautious in their approach.	Point out the urgent nature of what you are proposing to them and the necessity of achieving tangible results in the short term. Emphasise the level of freedom they have to take initiatives and find solutions. Provide support in the form of colleagues who can accurately record and document what they have elaborated. Make clear they have discretion to adopt a hands-on approach to problems. Indicate the opportunities that may result from finding a good solution to a difficult situation.	Conceal from them your concern about their ability to honour deadlines and trust that these deadlines will be met, even if often only at the last moment. Give them the freedom in the short term to deal creatively with non-essential rules and procedures. Ask them explicitly to let relevant parties know whenever they do something to solve a problem that is different from what had originally been agreed. Value their talent for improvisation and the originality of the solutions they find.

They focus primarily on the short term and are confident they can overcome difficulties, when confronted by them.		

Teachers

Characteristics	Speaking their language	Examples
In the formula $I = Q \times A$, they focus first and foremost on the A. Their basic question is: (for) WHO? They take first and foremost account of people: their well-being and development. They focus on harmony between people, which they can achieve by virtue of their capacity for empathy. They are strongly value-driven, with authenticity, integrity and autonomy as major priorities.	If you propose a project or initiative, emphasise the likely positive consequences for people and for mutual collaboration, especially in the long term. Show how your proposal not only reflects the company's value, but also their personal values. Show that you are aware of, understand and value not only their motives, but also those of their stakeholders.	Storytelling is a very useful way for communicating messages to them; personal anecdotes and examples involving family or friends work particularly well. If they are a member of your team, you can send them to put your proposal and gauge the opinions of stakeholders with whom you do not get on well. They are ideal as conversation partners for the target groups of your project who are by nature easily intimidated and/or find it difficult to make their voice heard.

They easily develop a feeling of sympathy for the underdog and feel personally responsible for his/her well-being. They find it difficult both to give and receive critical feedback. They can easily create consensus by organising participation.	Show your appreciation for their personal effort. Allow them to set their own boundaries and respect these boundaries, once set. Appeal to their abilities as mediators in cases where there is friction between stakeholders. Make clear your appreciation for their service-mindedness.	Ask them first for their gut feeling about a particular problem, before you ask them for specific suggestions about possible solutions.

Scientists

Characteristics	Speaking their language	Examples
In the formula $I = Q \times A$, they focus first and foremost on the Q. Their basic question is: WHY? They are focused on the long term-future.	Appeal to their capacity for 'out of the box' thinking. Accentuate the complexity of the problems you present to them.	Begin your communication with them by summarising the main lines of your proposal, which you should only later support with more detailed explanation.

Their powers of conceptual thinking make it possible for them to deal easily with complex issues and to separate the essential from the less relevant.

They are capable of initiating change that results in a break with the past.

They are often highly critical of others, but are even more critical for themselves, setting their personal bar very high.

They first need to understand the why of a measure or project, before moving on to look at the how.

They are ready and willing to challenge others, including authority figures.

Set the general framework within which solutions need to be found, but leave them with plenty of room to use their creativity.

Ensure that the logic of your reasoning is coherent.

Always state your starting point and working hypotheses when putting forward your proposals, as well as the other principles you have considered but rejected, and why.

Ask them explicitly to provide long-term solutions.

Point out that their impact will be greater if they can be patient enough to explain their reasoning step by step, with illustrative examples.

Ask them to signal and analyse trends that are potentially usable for the organisation.

Invite them to make critical analyses of the methods and ways of thinking that have become embedded in the organisation.

Regularly ask for their ideas about initiatives that might increase their own competence.

If you work your way through these four families, you will probably find something in each of them that reminds you of yourself. This is one of the good things about working in organisations: you are almost obliged to make use of every tool in your intellectual toolbox, if you wish to develop and make progress. In practice, one-dimensionality will get you nowhere. And it is the same with your stakeholders. At times, they will show you the full range of what they have to offer.

Something else that you will probably have noticed is that some families appeal more to you than others. You often value in others the things you find important in yourself. And, knowing as you do that it is always more pleasant to be in the company of kindred spirits, it will not surprise you to learn that you will find it easier to work with members of your own family than with others. Of course (and as we have seen), there is nothing wrong with this, apart from the fact that the amount of time and energy available to you is limited, which means that you will necessarily be driven to make choices about how and in whom you will invest more or less of that time and energy. As long as you can keep personal preference and functional necessity separate in your own mind, this should not be a problem.

If you want to have an idea accepted by someone else, you will have a good reason for doing so. Implicitly or explicitly, you have played around with various ideas, developed and refined them further, added helpful new elements and discarded unnecessary ones, until you are now satisfied with the end result. While you are working your way through this process, you have held your ideas up to the light on numerous occasions. You re-evaluate them constantly, checking if your reasoning and the decisions you have made are still valid enough and relevant enough to justify the effort of pursuing them further. To do this, you will use some form of measure. In part, this measure will be an objective one, but only in part. It is impossible to avoid also making subjective judgements based on the things that are important for you.

If you know that other people measure these things in a different way, because, for example, they belong to a different family, you can predict that not everyone will find your ideas as meaningful as you do. Not necessarily because they are not meaningful in absolute terms, but because your argumentation in their favour reflects your own logic, which will almost certainly not carry the same weight with these other families. This is where having a summary of the characteristics of the other families can be useful. Not to change your line of reasoning, but to focus the spotlight on those aspects of your ideas that do have meaning in the logic of the family concerned. And who in particular in that family? Your stakeholders, of course.

How can you find out to which family (logic) your stakeholders belong?

Observation is the most reliable source of information. What you can actually see your stakeholders do is more valuable than what they say about what is important to them, because the latter might be influenced by the need to give socially responsible answers to your questions. The underlying thought is that people – all people – behave in accordance with patterns or automatisms. There is a very good reason for this: pattern-based behaviour is economical. If you are able to do a large number of things on automatic pilot, as it were, this frees up extra capacity in your brain that allows you to stop and reflect on more important matters, before taking well-grounded decisions. Just imagine if you would need to make a conscious and justified decision about everything you do, starting with which eye to open first when you wake up in the morning. This would make life almost impossible. Patterns of behaviour are therefore a necessity. They are also the basis for each of our typologies. The good thing about this is that it means that most people's behaviour is predictable, up to a point. This, in turn, opens up some interesting avenues for forming partnerships.

Imagine that you regularly have discussions with the same group of people; for example, a steering group. Make it a habit after each meeting to write down who asked what questions and made what comments. Don't wait until a few days have gone by; do it immediately. Do the same for the next meeting and then compare what you have written down for both meetings for all the people present. After just two meetings you will be able to see for each person a certain overlap between their questions and reactions. This is a pattern that will make their questions and reactions in the next meeting to some extent predictable. Once you have mapped this out, you can make your own prepa-rations for the meeting in a much more targeted manner, which will relieve you of a good deal of stress. The more predictable a situation is, the safer it becomes. Do this analysis for all your stakeholders, so that you can marshal your resources for use where you most need them. Remember what we said earlier: 'choose your battles wisely'.

Additional comment 1

The true nature of individuals and therefore also of families comes most sharply into focus when they are under pressure.

This mechanism works as follows. Pressure increases uncertainty. When we feel uncertain, we reach for the security of the things with which we are most familiar: 'our' way of doing things, our automatisms. At the same time, our tolerance decreases for those who do not work in accordance with our methods and logic.

In these circumstances, there is a possibility that unnecessary friction will occur. This is hardly surprising, since even in normal situations a field of tension exists between the different families. Diamond Cutters believe in continuity. Scientists favour innovation. Emergency Doctors focus on short term improvisation, which is not really compatible with either continuity or innovation. Similarly, Diamond Cutters expect procedures to be respected, whereas Teachers will gladly make an exception to procedures if they think this can benefit someone. These same Teachers will seek to promote harmony and mutual support, while the Scientists see value in challenge and, where necessary, confrontation. As you can see, there is plenty of diversity and plenty of potential fields of tension. And once these fields of tension are put under pressure, the differences become even more pronounced – and visible. Map them out and use them to steer your way successfully through your dealings with your various stakeholders.

Additional comment 2

Speaking someone's language increases the likelihood that they will accept your idea. The more important your idea, the greater this need for linguistic affinity becomes. There is, however, a snake in the grass: the more you believe in an idea and the more passionate you are about it, the greater the chance that your capacity for self-criticism will diminish.

One of the consequences of enthusiasm is that we often fail to have our ideas critically checked by others before we launch them, or else we only have them checked by kindred spirits; in other words, by members of our own family. In this latter instance, we are not really looking for critique; we are looking for confirmation. Although this is understandable, it is not usually a good idea, especially when a lot is at stake. Hopefully, there will be someone in your vicinity who values you sufficiently to look at your idea objectively and also has the courage to tell you if something is not right. The implicit message communicated in these circumstances is a significant one, because it effectively says: 'I know that you have the ability to accept and deal with criticism, because you are someone who wants to produce an idea of the best possible quality.' You are fortunate if you have someone around you to do this. Make them your friend and do everything to keep it that way.

Additional comment 3

The typologies sketched above are intended to broaden and diversify your knowledge, so that you can better position the behaviour of others. At the same time, they are also an important tool that will allow you to better prepare yourself to deal with their reactions towards you and your project, in the hope that you will see these reactions for what they are and will not take them personally.

TAKE AWAY

1   If you genuinely appreciate something a stakeholder has done, tell him and explain in what way his contribution has made a difference.

2   Ask yourself to which psychological family does each of your stakeholders belong. Use checklists to help you reach your conclusions.

3   Unless they belong to the same family as you do, approach your key stakeholders in a manner that accords with their logic and sensitivities rather than your own.

4   Note down the comments and questions of your key stakeholders and see which issues recur regularly, as indications of the things that are important to them. Be prepared for them to ask similar questions and make similar comments in subsequent meetings.

5   Find someone you can trust to help you prepare for crucial meetings with key stakeholders. Choose someone who thinks in a different way from you, so that he can point out your blind spots. Do this especially when you are under pressure.

6

POWER: A COMPLEX
TERRITORY TO NAVIGATE

If you want to know everything about people and their motives, all you need to do is look at Greek mythology. It's all there. Each figure in this marvellous pageant of legends and tales personalises an aspect of human nature, reveals to us what really makes us tick. What's more, by concentrating each aspect in just a single figure, the message is amplified and becomes crystal clear. Myths expose the workings of the human spirit, just as the great anatomist Vesalius exposed the workings of the human body. He was the first to reveal our intricate structure of muscles and nerves by opening up their outer 'packaging', our skin. Greek mythology opens up the packaging of our mind.

You want an example? Try this one. On Crete, there were two brothers who were always arguing with each other. Amongst other things, they argued about who should be the rightful king. In stories of this kind, there is always someone who is a little bit smarter than the rest or has better connections in his places – which in Greek mythology means the gods. In this case, the smart one was the brother named Minos. He asked Poseidon, the god of the sea, to send a sign that would make clear that he, Minos, was the rightful heir to the throne, and no-one else. Poseidon agreed to his request and sent him a large and beautiful white bull as the requested sign. There was just one condition: the bull had to be sacrificed immediately.

This is where the problems started. Minos thought that the bull was so magnificent that he couldn't bring himself to kill it. He preferred to keep it for himself, and so he hid it in secret. However, Poseidon soon got wind of what Minos was doing and, as you might expect, was not amused. Humans are not supposed to disobey the gods! With typical Olympian fury, he devised a typically Olympian punishment to teach Minos a lesson. He made Pasiphaë, the wife of Minos, fall in love with the bull and nine months she later bore its child. (We will leave the details to your imagination! Suffice it to say that the ancient Greeks were not famed for either their morals or their political correctness!). It was now Minos's turn to be singularly unimpressed. Poseidon had saddled him with a 'son' who was half man and half bull. This creature was named Minotaurus, but he was not the kind of creature you would like to cuddle. On the contrary, he was a nasty piece of work. He terrorised the countryside and was only satisfied if he was fed on human flesh.

As one of his twelve works, Hercules was given the task of capturing this beast and delivering it to Eurystheus, the king of Mycene, who made the capital mistake of letting the Minotaur free again – for which the Minotaur thanked him by promptly resuming its reign of terror.

The end of the story? The Minotaur was captured again and returned to Minos, who locked his son away in a specially constructed labyrinth. As a gesture of paternal affection, Minos arranged for seven young men and seven virgins to be fed to his troublesome offspring each year, until one of the intended victims, Theseus, killed the Minotaur and escaped from the maze.

What you have read in this book so far has been more or less straightforward: what territories are, how powerful territorial behaviour can be, and how you can convert it into partnerships from which everyone can benefit. But now things are going to get a bit more complex – because now we need to discuss the nature of power.

Power is a fourth dimension that is always present in the above mentioned processes, a compound which binds itself to each of the elements as in a chemical reaction. Depending on how you use power, the results of these chemical reactions will be different. Power is a box, containing a huge amount of energy: a large and beautiful white bull. You have power when you are in a position to influence the fate of others at your own discretion. Or if you can enter their territory at will. In other words, power is a social phenomenon: it takes place between people.

Whether or not you have power is something you cannot decide for yourself. Power is something you are given by others, just as it was given to Minos by Poseidon. You can be given power out of goodwill and sympathy, or because people believe that you can do something useful with it that will also benefit them. You are given promotion, for example, because your bosses think that in your new position you will be able to contribute even more to the organisation. You are elected president because a large group of people hope that you will listen to their concerns and improve their lot. When you are given power, it is expected that you will use it to the benefit of others. In short, that you will sacrifice the white bull.

This, as Minos discovered, is the decisive moment. Do you do what is expected of you or have you become so fascinated by what you have been given that you decide to keep it for yourself? If you take the second option, this is when the trouble begins. From the beautiful white bull is born a flesh-eating monster that can no longer be controlled: the Minotaur. Even in captivity, you still need to keep it fed with human sacrifices. It takes heroic courage (from your internal Hercules) to cage this monster, but as soon as your relax your grip, as the king of Mycene did, the misery starts all over again. As terrifying and destructive as ever before. And even if you can eventually kill the beast, it still lives on. Thousands of years later the Minotaur is still a recurring theme in the work of artists, like Pablo Picasso.

This illustrates that dealing with power is a constant struggle, a struggle that is an essential part of who we are as human beings. The choices that we make about power will determine whether or not we can build successful common territories with others. It is never simple, but it is always important. In the following pages, we will explore the dynamic that confronts you when the white bull enters your life, both from the perspective of those who have power and those who are subject to it.

Because you are a social creature, you will always have to deal with both aspects. At the same time.

Because power is so all-defining, we learn how to deal with it very quickly. The 'no!' phase begins in children from the tender age of just two years. What a wonderful way to experience the awakenings of your own strength and explore its boundaries! Yet even before things get this far, we have already built up a whole repertoire of tricks to steer our parents in the direction we want. We know that if we tilt our head at exactly the right angle and look at them with our puppy dog eyes, they will do almost anything for us. And when, later on, we can add an imploring 'pleeeeease!', it seems as though there are almost no limits to our power!

Even so, right from the very beginning we also learn that power is as much a curse as a blessing. We want the power to be our autonomous self, yet on the other hand we remain dependent on the goodwill of others to give us the things we need and cannot provide for ourselves. This, again, is something that starts very early. You can get your parents and your siblings to do all kinds of things for you, almost with your eyes closed, but you can't do without their care, their cuddles and their smiles.

Power is an endless dance of giving and receiving. It is a tightrope that you must walk your whole life long. The challenge, of course, is to keep your balance: learning to deal with the white bull, whilst at the same time giving the reality of your own vulnerability the right to exist. This is no easy task, but how we confront that task makes us what we are. As Abraham Lincoln put it: 'Nearly all men can stand adversity, but if you want to test a man's character, give him power.'

2   POWER BRINGS OUT THE WORST IN PEOPLE

A word in advance

If you want to understand what power and powerlessness can do to people, there is plenty of scientific research that can help you. This is particularly the case for the field of social psychology, where numerous experiments to explore this theme have been conducted. These experiments usually consist of two groups of test subjects, with one group being given power and the other denied it. The researchers then see how this distribution affects both groups' behaviour.

Different methods are used to achieve these conditions. Sometimes the test subjects are put in game situations, where they can reward or punish others for their actions and behaviour. Sometimes they are asked to remember very detailed situations in which they had power. Sometimes they are simply asked to read words that are associated with power. Each of these methods has been proven to be an effective way of engendering the feeling of power.

The advantage of experiments is that the situation can be kept under tight control, so that you can clearly see the effect of changing just a single element. The disadvantage is that this all takes place in laboratory conditions. In other words, the situations are artificial. For this reason, the social psychologists also conduct a considerable amount of supplementary field research. They first accurately observe people's behaviour in the 'lab', make predictions about their behaviour and what it means, and then seek to verify these predictions in real-life situations.

If you read through the results of this social psychological research, you will note, however, that the conclusions always relate to groups of people as a whole, and never to individuals. If a study reveals that power has this or that effect, it will never say that this will always be the case and that it will always apply for everyone. This means that all you can be certain of is that the effect is a substantive one (it is not just a matter of chance) and will usually be valid for most people.

This 'general' nature of the conclusions relates to the fact that human behaviour is the result of many different factors that are all capable of influencing each other. This means that the behaviour of a single person cannot be predicted with precision. In this way, the human sciences are no different from, say, medicine. If you have a medical complaint, you will be treated on the basis of a trajectory that on average offers the best prospects for a cure. Even so, your doctor will continue to monitor you closely, since each patient reacts in a different way to the 'standard' trajectory. As a model, this is very different from what usually happens in professional domains, where individual situations can be predicted. If, as an engineer, you tell people that you are confident that on average the bridge you are building won't collapse, you are unlikely to persuade many people to travel across it!

Power and empathy do not make good bedfellows

Paul Piff and his colleagues conducted revealing research into the effect of wealth on the behaviour of people who have money.[1] The relationship with power is not difficult to see: especially in countries with a capitalist economy, power often leads to the possession of money, while, conversely, the possession of money is also often the basis for the exercising of power. The results of Piff's studies corresponded closely with the results of power experiments carried out in laboratory conditions (more about that later), although his findings were perhaps a little more telling, since they were not based on a group of test subjects, but on the behaviour of many thousands of ordinary American citizens from all walks of life. Here is one of his experiments.

Imagine a crossroads. Each of the four roads leading into it has a 'Stop' sign and there is a separate lane for cars turning right. What the researchers wanted to know was how many of the drivers in the 'turn right' lane would give priority to crossing traffic, as specified in the California highway code.

In total, 274 cars were observed. What made this different from an ordinary traffic study was that the cars were divided into five classes, on the basis of their perceived prestige, taking account of make, model, year of construction and general appearance. Additional control measures were also put in place to ensure that traffic density and the age and gender of the driver would not affect the results.

And these results revealed some very interesting correlations. For example, there was a clear connection between the number of traffic violations and the prestige of the car. The higher the status of the car, the greater the number of infringements, with the highest category of car some distance ahead of the rest. The drivers in the top-class models were three times more likely to cut in where they shouldn't than the drivers of more everyday vehicles.

Piff then organised a follow-up experiment (with the same car categories and control measures), this time for the purpose of answering a subsidiary question: how many drivers would be prepared to stop for pedestrians waiting to cross at a zebra crossing? 152 cars were observed in the early afternoon over a three-day period and a similar tendency was again noted, although this time with a wider spreading. In total, some 35 percent of the cars were prepared to stop. Cars with the lowest status nearly always stopped, with the percentage of non-stoppers gradually increasing through the categories, with only one in two of the drivers in the top category willing to pull up for the pedestrians.

Let's be clear on this: not every driver of a Mercedes, BMW, etc. is a road hog who carves up his fellow car-users and mows down unsuspecting wayfarers as they attempt to cross the road. Even so, the correlation is clear: the more prestigious the car, the more likely it is to happen. Does this mean that if you have more power (or money) you are less concerned about others? That certainly seems to be the implication. Not convinced? Consider the following situation.[2]

Take a number of test subjects, divide them into two groups and create a single difference between them. The difference? In one group you try to give its members a feeling of power; in the second group you do nothing. Next, you show both groups a series of photographs, telling them in advance that each one will display a different human emotion, such as happiness, fear, anger, sadness, etc. Ask them to write down which emotions they see with each photograph. The aim this time is to see whether a feeling of power affects people's ability to accurately assess the way other people are feeling. The answer is: it does. Significantly. Because power has a tendency to make people emotionally blind.

But there is more, much more. The following experiment brings things closer to home, since it moves beyond trying to create an artificial feeling of power in a laboratory.[3] This time a group of test subjects were asked to reflect on their lives in general and on their relationships, both at work and elsewhere. Based on these initial assessments, the test population was then divided into two cohorts: one consisting of people who generally felt powerful and one containing people who generally felt powerless.

Both groups were asked to write down a particularly sad or painful experience that had happened to them during the past five years. Once this had been done, the groups where split up into duos, one to do the telling and the other to do the listening. The task of the teller was to try and explain what he had felt during the painful experience. The task of the listener was to try and understand what the teller was saying while he was saying it.

The focus in this research was more on the listener than on the teller. In particular, it was hoped to find the answer to two questions: how much understanding or empathy was the listener able to show and was the level of this empathy affected by whether the listener generally felt powerful or powerless in his own life? Once again, the results were crystal clear.

The sadness of the teller was often strongly felt by listeners who felt powerless in their personal context. This level of fellow feeling fell for listeners who scored high on the power scale. The same trend was also evident when it came to empathy: the more power a listener had, the less sympathy and understanding he showed for his teller. Further analysis revealed that the underlying reason for both trends was the limited desire of powerful people to enter into an emotional relationship with the teller. Other research in situations that are more similar to those found in the professional world has since confirmed this.[4]

One of these experiments worked as follows. The researchers divided up the test population into small groups, with one person in charge of each group. These leaders were also divided into categories: some leaders were instructed to lead through punishment and rewards (this is the power category); others were told to lead through their ability to persuade and to form collaborative relationships. All the groups were then asked to carry out a similar task. Each group was allowed to do this in its own way, following which everyone was given the opportunity to have a drink together and discuss what had happened – all, of course, under the watchful eyes of the researchers. What they observed was interesting: during the drink, the 'power' leaders seemed much less interested in social contact with their team members that the 'persuasive' leaders.

The fact that power seems to go hand in hand with less empathy and less interest in others leads to a fascinating paradox, which we will examine in a moment.[5]

But first, let's return to a number of the central concepts in this book. The fate of people with little or no power is decided by the people above them who have a lot of power. In other words, there is a relationship of dependence. This means that the people with less power develop skills that allow them to 'read' the power holder. By predicting the power holder's behaviour in this way, the 'subordinates' know how to avoid getting on the wrong side of their 'superiors'.

We also know that if you want to get the support of others for your project, you can best do this by building a common territory with them. This is possible by framing your project as a contribution to the things that really matter for them. Your first task is therefore to identify what those things are. The only way to this is by trying to understand 'their' world, the environment in which they live and work. And this, in turn, is only possible if you can again learn how to 'read' them. Or to put it in slightly different terms: you get more influence with others by giving them more attention and showing them more empathy. And this is where we are confronted by the paradox: if you have the power and influence you need to lead, this goes hand in hand with a loss of empathy and interest in others. In these circumstances, it almost seems as if other people are simply a means to achieve your ends and that, as soon as you have reached those ends, those who helped you to get there are no longer important enough to warrant your concern. They are just a tool you have used for as long as was necessary.

This might sound hard, even confrontational, but, as we have read above, there is plenty of research to support this conclusion.[6] Time after time, researchers have consistently produced the same findings: the more power you have, the greater the tendency for you to regard others as jigsaw pieces that need to fit into your personal puzzle.

This power paradox seems to be more typical for the human animal than for other types of mammals. Frans de Waal, who coined the term 'alpha male', has spent thousands of hours observing chimpanzees. He has described what happens when a chimp is on its way to acquiring alpha status. It does exactly what a human would do: it gives plenty of extra attention to its fellow-male chimps, charms the chimp mothers by fondly cuddling their babies, and attempts to form coalitions. In short, it does its best to make itself popular in the group. It almost sounds like a politician at election time!

But then comes the big difference with humans: once the chimpanzee has become an alpha, it continues to show its concern and care for the rest of the group. What's more, it does so six times more than apes who are lower down in the pecking order.[7] Is there something we can learn from this, do you think?

Additional comment 1

Before we get bogged down in gender stereotypes, it may be useful at this juncture to point out that research has also confirmed that the correlation between more power and less empathy is not an exclusively male preserve. Power does something to us all, irrespective of gender.

Additional comment 2

When you read about the less endearing aspects of power, remember that power is nearly always situational. All phenomena take place in contexts in which people either have power or feel powerful. This does not necessarily say something about who these people are as persons in their own right. It simply says something about how they behave when they are in a position to exercise influence over others.

For example, you have probably come across leaders who are authoritarian and compelling when dealing with their own team, but who meekly follow like a lamb as soon as they come into contact with senior management. And this doesn't just apply to work situations. Bob has a leadership function in a multinational. He is tough on the people who work for him, but he often needs to be, because his regional office was in a mess when he took over. But as soon as he tries the same tactic at home, he gets a flea in his ear from his wife: 'Don't you try that here, mister. You're not at work now!' This imme-diately makes clear who the boss is in the home territory – and it isn't Bob. Sometimes even leaders have to follow!

Power and social and ethical norms also do not make good bedfellows

If you have power, you pay less attention to others. As a result, it is hardly surprising that your behaviour becomes increasingly asocial. The traffic situations we described earlier are a good example. At the same time, your standards of decency also begin to slip.

Let's go back to Paul Piff and his research team at the University of Califor-nia in Berkeley.[8] This time their experiment involved a game of Monopoly, but a game of Monopoly with a twist. In total, more than two hundred pairs of students took part, all of whom were unknown to each other. They were asked to play the game against each other, but with a number of special rules. Before the game started, one player was deliberately made rich and the other was made poor. This was decided by the toss of a coin. The basics of the game were the same as always, but the rich player received double the start money, double the money when he passed 'Go' and was allowed to throw two dice for each turn against his opponent's one. Piff let them play for an hour and, nat-urally, the rich player always won. We will look a little later at what happened next, but first a few brief comments on social decency.

While they were playing, there was a bowel of pretzels on the table. Not only did the rich players eat more of the pretzels, but more of them spoke to their opponents with their mouths full, which is not really good manners, not even in America. They were also significantly brusquer in their interactions with the poor players. When they moved their piece around the board from square to square, they did so with aggressive thumps and frequently made reference to their wealth and their opponent's poverty: 'I've got more than enough money to buy that'; 'Your soon going to lose everything'; 'I'm going to buy up the whole board'; ' You haven't got enough money to pay for that'; etc. In fact, their behaviour was embarrassing and asocial, so much so that the players – at least the poor ones – often had no desire to see their playing partner again.

So power certainly seems to have a negative effect on standards of decency. Okay, that is not pleasant for those on the receiving end, but it is not exactly the end of the world, is it? But what if power also has a corrupting effect on standards of morality? That would, indeed, be much more serious – and the idea is not as far-fetched as it might seem. A Dutch-American research study has revealed that people who feel they are in a position of power find offensive jokes about handicap, race and gender less inappropriate, less insulting and more amusing.[9] This suggests that the step from leadership to improper behaviour is a potentially small one. This seems to confirm a famous quote with which you will probably be familiar: 'Power tends to corrupt, and absolute power corrupts absolutely.' But is that really so? If you look at the available research, you could again be forgiven for thinking it is. Here are some examples.

You bring together a group of people whose social origins are known to you. You describe to them a list of situations and ask them if they would have behaved in the same way as the persons in those situations. Here are just a few of them:

- 'You work in a fast-food restaurant in the centre of town. It is against the rules to eat food here unless you pay for it. You have just arrived from a meeting with someone and haven't had time to eat, so that you are very hungry. Your supervisor in not around and so you quickly make yourself a hamburger and eat it without paying.'
- 'You do administrative work in an office. You are alone and are making some photocopies. You suddenly remember that your supply of paper at home has run out and so you slip a pack of the firm's paper into your rucksack.'
- 'You have been standing in a queue for 10 minutes to get a coffee and a muffin. When you are a few streets away, you realise that the girl behind the till has given you change for 20 dollars instead of the 10 dollars you gave her. Instead of going back, you enjoy your coffee, muffin and the free 10 dollars.'

If you filter out the effects of ethnicity, gender and age, the results show that there is a strong correlation between rising social class and an increased willingness to make unethical choices.

This last piece of research was about estimating behaviour (What would you do?). The following experiment dealt with real behaviour. Innocent behaviour, but with an interesting story to tell. This time the test subjects were put in a room and asked to complete a task. On the table there was a dish of sweets. The participants were told that the sweets were intended for a group of children who would be taking part in a different experiment a little later on, but that they were free to decide whether or not to eat some of them. The outcome? Yes, you've guessed it: the higher the participant's social class, the more of the children's sweets they 'stole'. It seems that people who have a lot still want more, even at the expense of others.

And it is exactly the same with helpful behaviour. Another group of unsuspecting test subject were brought one by one to a laboratory. Some of them were rich; some were poor. They were each given 10 dollars and were told that they could either keep it for themselves or share it with someone who they did not know and would never meet. The poor cohort, who earned less than 25,000 dollars a year, gave 44 percent more money to others than the rich cohort, who earned between 150,000 and 200,000 dollars a year, and for whom 10 dollars means very little.[10]

This previous test was a matter of choice. It involved no dishonesty. But the next one did. A group of test subjects were sat in front of a computer screen. With the press of a button, they could roll five dice on the screen. They were told that the higher their total score, the more credits they would receive and the greater the chance that they would win a 50 dollar prize. What they were not told is that the game had been rigged so that the maximum score for the five dice could never be more than twelve, which is a pretty lousy score. They were asked to count up their score and tell it to one of the researchers. This was a reliably objective way to discover how many cheats were among the test population. And by now it will probably not surprise you to learn that the richer the candidates, the greater the likelihood that they would lie.

You think it can't get any worse? Well, you would be wrong. An experiment by researchers at the University of Tilburg added a moral dimension to the equation.[11] But the general conclusion remained equally unfavourable for those from the higher social classes: the more money and power people have, not only are they more likely to lie and cheat, but are also more likely to develop a double moral standard. They can easily overlook their own lying and cheating, but are furious when they discover others doing exactly the same thing.

This battery of test results would seem to underline the wisdom and importance of President Lincoln's words. If you want to find out what someone is really like, if you want to test them to the utmost, just give them some power.

As we have seen, dealing with your own power is difficult. It is extremely tempting to do things that are not okay and to then justify your actions afterwards with spurious reasoning. This is made even more complex (and delicate) by the fact that people with power can have such a strong impact on others, either directly or by virtue of the decisions they make. All of which makes your task as a project leader no easier, because you will always be involved with people who have power. But at least you now know the kind of factors you will have to contend with.

Additional comment

Baboons look every 20 to 30 seconds at their alpha mail to see what he is doing[12] (and with people it won't be much different). This is hardly surprising, if you remember our definition of power: the position that makes it possible to influence the fate of others.

If you are dependent on someone in this way, it makes sense to keep an eye on him. What does he think is important? If you know this, you can adjust your behaviour to reflect it. And how can you know it? By observing him closely. The things that people with power do are always magnified and exaggerated. If you are in a position of power, you will always (whether you want to or not) 'lead by example'. It makes no difference whether you are a parent, a teacher or a project manager. You will constantly need to come to terms with the Minotaur in you and the people over whom you have power will need to adjust to your way of doing things, to your way of exercising your power. For ill, but fortunately also – as we shall soon see – for good.

3   POWER ALSO BRINGS OUT THE BEST IN PEOPLE

We have seen that concern for others does not seem to be the main considera-tion of people with power. So what is? The short answer is: effectiveness. One of the models that helps to explain a lot about what people do is the model which posits that every act of behaviour is the result of two opposing forces. Psychologists refer to the first of these forces as the approach force. This is the force that prompts us into action to achieve what we want. It is directed by our desire for satisfaction and reward. On the other side of the spectrum is the avoidance force. This ensures that nothing unpleasant happens to us.

Both these forces are always present. If we were always directed exclusive-ly by the approach force, we would follow our every impulse. I want to eat now, so I go to the kitchen now or find a restaurant now and eat what I want now. Perhaps not the best idea. But then neither is the opposite. If you are so worried about what can always go wrong that you are almost afraid to get out of bed, never mind actually do anything, you will never get anywhere. And it wouldn't be a lot of fun either.

No, a kind of balance needs to be achieved. In this balance, the approach force – thanks to its associated effectiveness – is usually stronger than the avoidance force. The approach force is also more visible, which is again due to its action-oriented nature.[13] Or to express it in territorial terms: more power leads to a greater desire to explore and conquer new territories. We have al-ready mentioned the great importance of this desire: it is the source of all en-trepreneurship, growth, progress and innovation. It is absolutely essential if you wish to ensure that groups of people can book results and move forward.

Power gives direction, it brings order to interaction and focuses attention and deeds on what is most important. Power makes behaviour predictable. It gives people something to hold on to and prevents too much energy from being wasted on things that don't really matter. This is not only true in the professional world, but also in families, sports clubs, groups of friends, etc.

'There can be no collaboration without hierarchy,' says behavioural biolo-gist Mark Nelissen:[14] 'In a research project, people were allocated a random dominance status. They were given a lot of power, no power or something in between. After that, they were divided up into groups of three, who either all had the same power status – low, medium or high – or else all had a different power status; in other words, a hierarchy.

All the groups were given the same task. To begin with, each individual had to write down as many sixteen-letter words as possible, following which the group had to make as many sentences with those words as it could. This was an elegant experiment, in the sense that the task was clearly defined, individuals needed to perform both in isolation and in a group, and the results of all the groups were easy to compare. What transpired? The groups with a clear hierarchy, where one member had more power than another, performed better: they made more sentences than the groups where everyone was equal in terms of power. When a different task was set, one which required no collaboration, there was no measurable difference between the performance of the different types of groups.'

In a professional environment collaboration is always a crucial element, as are (or so one hopes) power and hierarchy. People with power develop qualities and characteristics that serve them well in terms of their ability to achieve their objectives. In short, it helps them to get things done.

Power and the feeling of 'being in control' go hand in hand

Psychologists are familiar with the notion of the 'locus of control', which refers to a conviction (often more implicit than explicit) that people have about why things turn out good or bad. People with an external locus of control assume that their lot is determined by factors outside of themselves, making them effectively the playthings of chance. If the stars are favourable, they will have luck and succeed. But if the stars are not favourable... Fatalism and a certain degree of passivity are then the predictable results.

Consider, for example, the story of Frank. He has just been taken into hospital following his second heart attack. Of course, the doctors are concerned about his condition and have discussed with him at length the need to change his way of life: better food, more exercise, less booze and no cigarettes. Otherwise, a third attack is inevitable – and this time it could be fatal. Frank listened politely, nodded in all the right places and took home all the folders he was given. As soon as he got there, he threw them all in the bin. Why? Because Frank knew better. There was a history of heart disease in his family and he had seen others live to a ripe old age without all this 'improve your life' nonsense. With a bit of luck, this most recent incident would be his last. And if not, *que sera sera*.

Against the background of this conviction, there is little likelihood that Frank will make the necessary effort to change his habits. There is a much greater likelihood that he will contribute, unintentionally but nonetheless actively, to his own death. This is an attitude – although with a potentially less dramatic outcome – that you are probably familiar with from both your home and work situations. When things go wrong, the first thing that people with a strong external locus of control do is to complain about how everything and every-one was against them. And indeed, it can sometimes happen that circum-stances do conspire against you. But if you focus exclusively on this, you not only increase your feeling of powerlessness, but also fail to learn from the situation, so that the chance that you will repeat the same mistakes becomes ever greater. What's more, it creates a general atmosphere of gloom and doom around the 'victim', which makes nobody any better or happier.

In contrast, people with an internal locus of control implicitly assume that they are the most important element in deciding what happens to them. Like their less self-assured counterparts, they too will sometimes experience fail-ures that are the result of various factors. Some of these factors they will be able to influence; others they cannot. No matter how small this first group of factors is, these are the only ones that truly interest them – because these are the only ones they can do something about.

So which is better? An internal or an external locus of control? The results of research are very clear. In many areas, you are much better off with an internal locus than an external one: you will achieve more, be less troubled by depression and will bounce back quickly after setbacks.[15] If people with power have one thing in common, it is their strong conviction that they have the ability to shape circumstances, rather than being shaped by them. In other words, they have a strong internal locus of control. This explains why they are often capable of doing things that we never imagined were possible.

Sometimes, however, this desire to be in control can take extreme and illog-ical forms – as this following experiment illustrated. A group of people were asked to predict which number would be face up on the top of a dice once it had been rolled. They were then asked to say whether they would prefer to roll the dice themselves or let someone else do it. In reality, of course, this makes no difference. The outcome will be purely a matter of chance, irrespective of who does the rolling. In other words, it is beyond human influence.

Before the rolling began, the larger group was split up into three smaller groups: one group in which a feeling of power was stimulated, one group in which a feeling of powerlessness was stimulated and a third group in which nothing special was done. You can probably guess what happened. In the third group (the control group), 69 percent chose to roll the dice themselves. In the 'powerless' group, this figure fell to 58 percent. And in the power group? 100 percent. Every single one of them.[16]

Does this mean that they are all control freaks? No, not necessarily. But is does demonstrate a high degree of confidence in their own ability to affect things.

This is where you need to be careful. Sometimes your belief in your own ability can carry you away, so that you push things too far or lose a proper sense of perspective. Do you remember the monopoly game, where the rules were changed so that one of the two players was always certain to win, no matter what he did? When these winners were asked afterwards to explain the reason for their success, the most common answers were all egocentric: their own skill, insight, boldness, etc. The fact that the game was fixed, so that they couldn't lose, was never mentioned! This was curious, to say the least: success was explained exclusively in terms of factors that the player had under his control, whereas in reality this was not the case. In the laboratory conditions of the experiment, this was almost amusing. But in real life it can be less so. Has it ever happened in your company that someone high up in the organisation takes all the credit for the latest glittering success, even though he was hardly involved? It is precisely the same phenomenon. Only this time, it isn't funny.

Power and action-mindedness: a potent mix

It is perhaps only logical that someone who has belief in his own abilities to affect things should also be action-minded. You can see this in lots of different places: the laboratory, the negotiating table and in crisis situations, to name but three.

Let's begin with the lab. You select a group of people and give half of them a feeling of superiority by telling them that they will have power over someone else. With the other half you do the opposite, informing them that at some point in the test they will be subject to someone's control. You then take them one by one to a work room, where they are asked to carry out a number of tasks. There is a fan on the table, which blows cold air directly into their face, in such a way that the effect is unpleasant. So what would you do? More than two-thirds of the 'power' group either turned it away or turned it off. In the 'powerless' group, significantly fewer than half had the confidence to do this.[17]

This confirms what we have already seen: people who feel powerful will act quicker to improve their own lot. Nothing wrong with that. More worrying is the fact that people who feel powerless actually increase their feeling of powerlessness by failing to take action and simply suffering in silence instead. Later in the chapter you can read what you can do to avoid this, should you ever find yourself in this position at work, where you may sometimes be faced with situations that you cannot control or in which you are heavily dependent on people with more power than you.

From the laboratory to the negotiating table. Here it often happens that a feeling of power leads to an action that significantly increases the chances of the negotiator to achieve what he wants: opening the negotiations with a quick and aggressive opening bid.

If you are familiar with negotiation (and you should be – we all do it our whole life long), you will know that striking the first blow is half the battle. Whoever makes the first offer or is first to take up an initial position immediately takes the initiative. This pushes the other party onto the defensive and also allows you to profit from the anchoring effect.

Earlier in the book we referred to this as the 'blitzkrieg', a tactic that is often used by people with power, as has been repeatedly demonstrated in recent years by President Trump. It is doubtful if the president does this for didactic reasons; it is more likely that he just wants to show who is top dog. But whatever his reasons, he has certainly made this much used power tactic far more visible than ever before.

No matter what the subject, he takes up an initial position that is so far from what any reasonable person might expect that at first it is hard to believe it is anything more than a publicity stunt designed to appeal to his die-hard sup-porters. Is he really serious? You bet! And to prove it, he repeats his position is his loudest voice several times over, in even more ominous tones. By now, the other parties are starting to realise that the playing field on which they are negotiating has been dramatically expanded. What's more, the president has moved the goal posts! It seems as though the territory of the United States has suddenly got bigger, while everyone else's territory has got smaller. This im-mediately put the others on the back foot, which, of course, is precisely where Trump wants them. After that he can moderate his position slightly (although it is still extreme in comparison with the original pre-negotiation situation), in the expectation that his negotiating partners will be glad to secure any con-cessions, however small. But when this happens, he immediately demands a new favour in return: you scratch my back...

Reading all the above, you might be forgiven for thinking that people with power are only concerned with and actively pursue their own best interests. Fortunately, that is not the case – not by a long chalk. Imagine the following situation. A car is driven by accident into a river. In no time at all, there are 20 to 30 spectators, but nobody dares to dive into the water to try and help the occupants. Everyone wrings their hands and says how terrible it is, but nobody does anything. Psychologists (as well as the fire and police services) know this phenomenon very well and refer to it as 'spectator apathy'. The cause of this 'inefficient' behaviour is a feeling of uncertainty that quickly spreads from one spectator to another. Everyone is waiting for someone else to take the initiative. As a result, their attention is focused on each other, rather than being focused on the crisis situation.

You see this form of apathy much more frequently in people with a low level of power. But you seldom see it in people of real authority. In fact, this is the advantage of what we condemned at the beginning of this chapter as a lack of empathy in power holders. Here you can see the beneficial side of the phenomenon: people with power do not allow themselves to be influenced as much by the opinions and behaviour of others. They decide for themselves what to do. If they feel there is a need for action in a crisis, they will act – no matter what anyone else thinks, says or does. And so they dive into the river...

Additional comment 1

It was the legendary Dutch footballer Johan Cruijff who made famous the phrase 'every disadvantage has its advantages'. We know that a feeling of power often goes with only limited interest in the feelings of other people. However, this can be a huge plus point at the negotiating table, since it makes a negotiator much more immune against the commercial pressure of other parties,[18] against group pressure from within his own ranks,[19] and against the emotional tantrums (outbursts of anger, tears, etc.) of his negotiating partners.[20]

Additional comment 2

Building on the previous comment, we can also say that in people with power effectiveness is a far more decisive factor than empathy.

Imagine that you have a group of supervisors who need to complete a difficult task with their team. To one half of the group you give a primarily production-oriented task. Your instructions to them are twofold: 'Your first responsibility is to ensure that your staff work as productively and as efficiently as possible, so that they can achieve their objective. Secondly, however, it would be no bad thing if your staff also feel involved in what they are doing and its organisation.'

You also give the other half of the group a double instruction, but this time with the emphasis reversed: they must first ensure there is a good working atmosphere and only in the second instance keep an eye on productivity. Their primary objective is therefore people-oriented.

What do you find by the end of the first day? The supervisors with a production objective can remember very little about the individual characteristics of their team members and sometimes even get them confused with each other. That was not the case with their colleagues with the people-oriented objective. They knew all about the qualities of their different team members and had no problem in telling them apart. Conclusion: power does not lead automatically to less attention for people; it all depends on the nature of the situation. If an objective is task-oriented, individuals are relatively unimportant; if the objective is people-oriented, attention for the people involved is a means to attain that objective, so that more attention will be given by leaders to individuals.[21]

If you ask managers what is the most important aspect of their policy imple-mentation, it is nowadays the done thing to answer that 'people' are the most important. To deny this would not be politically correct. But often this claim is nothing more than fine words. To really know what their most important focus is, you should examine instead the nature of the subjects that they dis-cuss most frequently at their weekly and monthly meetings with their bosses, so that you can see in what proportion task-oriented and people-oriented themes appear. These proportions will usually tell you more about the true focus of their attention than anything they say. It often happens that 'soft' subjects only find a place on the agenda when the realisation of task-related objectives is in danger.

The reverse is also often true: if a manager obtains his satisfaction from a good working atmosphere, staff engagement and regular consultation, and if he is not challenged in this order of priorities by his superiors, it might be hard for you as one of his team members to persuade him to devote much agenda time to topics that contribute to greater efficiency and return.

The feeling of being in control and action-mindedness increase the willingness to take risks

Imagine that you are playing a game of blackjack. We all know the rules: you are dealt two cards and can then ask for new ones, with the aim of getting as close as possible to a total of 21. If your score exceeds 21, you are 'bust' and lose everything. In a research study, the cards were rigged so that after the in-itial deal the test subjects had a total score of 16. The question was, of course, whether they would now ask for an extra card or not? It was also arranged that the next card would be a ten, but that was not really relevant. It was all about the extra card and who would take the risk of asking for it.

Once again, the results leave no room for doubt. 92 percent of the players in whom a feeling of power had first been generated asked for the extra card. For the players who had not been encouraged to feel powerful, the figure was only 58 percent.[22] This suggests that if you feel powerful you are more likely to take risks, not only because you are inclined to assume that things will turn out well for you, but also because you are less concerned about the possibility of failure.

To gain deeper insight into these matters, we need to return to the power model that we discussed at the beginning of this chapter. People who feel powerful are more driven by approach forces. These forces are focused on the obtaining of rewards rather than the avoidance of punishments. What's more, it is hardly a surprise that people who have power are more optimistic and therefore more willing to take risks. This willingness is all the greater because they have greater confidence in their ability to bounce back, should things unexpectedly go wrong.

This effectively becomes a self-reinforcing mechanism: greater belief in your own ability to influence outcomes leads to greater confidence in ultimate success, which leads to a greater willingness to take action, which leads to the increased exploration and acquisition of new territories. You do not begin the exploration of a new territory unless you are convinced that there is some-thing worthwhile to find there. It is hard to imagine that new worlds were discovered by people who set off across uncharted oceans with only thoughts of possible failure in their heads. Just as today it is hard to imagine that new technologies are invented by people who doubt whether it is possible to im-prove on what already exists. When innovations make a break with the past, rather than simply building on the present, this is always based on a strong belief in a better future. People with power are better able to think in this positive way than others who do not have the same confidence in their ability to change things.

Last but not least, it is also to be expected that people with power find it easier to think in abstract and conceptual terms, are more inclined to focus first and foremost on the final objective, and are less easily distracted by practical details and operational difficulties.[23] This way of thinking offers huge possi-bilities for the development of visions and the inspiration and mobilisation of people to create a better future. The slogan 'Yes, we can!' has given many people the necessary energy to overcome all the many difficulties on the road to that better future one by one.

You probably know the story about the man who went to a medieval construc-tion site, where he saw two labourers hard at work. He asked them what they were doing. The first said: 'I am cutting stone.' The second, whose task was exactly the same, answered: 'I am building a cathedral.' If you can let your project be carried forward by the élan of this kind of leader, it will open up new horizons that you might never have explored without them.

It is time now to return to King Minos and the choice with which he was faced: would he use his white bull (his power) as a sacrifice to serve others or would he keep it for himself? Actions are often a mix of both these motives, but one or the other will inevitably gain the upper hand.

If the needs of your own ego (prestige, status, narcissism, personal satisfaction, etc.) are your most important motive, your power makes you highly vulnerable. If you are forced to surrender part of your power, you are also forced to surrender part of your self-esteem. A desire to continually increase your power is like trying to fill a bottomless pit. Your power serves only to exhaust you and to increase the defensiveness of everyone around you. In these circumstances, power quickly becomes a prison, both for the person who possesses it and for those who are subject to it.

When the needs of ego are the motive, the desire for power is often born out of a fundamental uncertainty. It is this uncertainty that makes the pit bottomless and explains why the urge to cling on to power is so rigid, bringing with it fear and suspicion of everyone and everything that might undermine that power. However, this fear works both ways: it is the only reason for people to continue following you. Power of this kind seldom lasts for long; only for as long as the power holder is able to maintain his position on his shaky pedestal.

On the other side of the spectrum stands power that is based on motives that go beyond individual interests. And these motives do not necessarily need to be found in the social sphere. Consider, for example, the story of Catherine Verfaillie. She is a doctor, a professor and a world authority on stem cell research. To give you some idea of the level of her ability, a Japanese colleague of hers was awarded the Nobel Prize for Medicine on the basis of research in which Verfaillie was the pioneer. Even so, she generously admits that the method developed in Japan was much more efficient than hers.

She leads a group of researchers who have the greatest admiration and respect for her. What drives her forward has nothing to do with personal success or even with a desire to make a contribution to medicine (although she clearly does: her work has led to improved treatment for many thousands of cancer patients).

No, what motivates her is her need to know. Science as knowledge. Is she pleased that her work has had positive consequences for many people? Of course she is – but that is not her main driver. Does she have power? Yes, plenty of it, but that is not what interests her either. Does she use this power to secure funding to expand her research facilities and increase her number of staff? Absolutely! Does she influence the thinking and the lives of the people who work with her? To a significant degree. In fact, all the positive power characteristics that we have read about in this chapter can be found somewhere in her career. And the negative aspects we have also discussed? No, very few. And why it this? It is because she mobilises all her power to serve a higher purpose. Many people in many different fields who have achieved something important, not just once but their whole life long, share this same passion. The content of what they do may be different, but it always goes much further than their own person. And they do it with all their might.[24]

If your projects are situated in an environment that is coloured by the Catherine Verfaillie's of the world, you should think yourself very lucky. Often, however, you will need to operate in much less favourable circumstances. You will frequently bump into power in one of its less attractive forms, which will slow down rather than speed up what you are trying to achieve. To deal with this, you will need to develop two new skills: you must find ways to mobilise your own power, while combining this with strategies that will allow you to turn power figures into allies.

How you use power also depends on your nature

What are the things that are important to you? This has a lot to do with the strength of your D-factor.

German and Danish researchers have discovered that a number of the less pleasing aspects of human nature are interconnected.[25] These aspects include egotism, Machiavellianism, narcissism, the feeling that the world revolves around you (or at least should do), psychopathy and several other 'qualities' of a similar kind.

Their interconnectedness means that when you possess one of these characteristics to a significant degree, you are likely to have a high score for some of the others. In other words, there is an underlying or connective factor. This is what the researchers call the Dark or D-factor (perhaps they were also fans of Star Wars!).

The effect of the D-factor can be summarised by saying that those who possess it behave in accordance with the following principles:

1   I do what is good for me and gives me satisfaction. This might be power, money, status or pleasure. It doesn't matter, as long as it meets my personal needs.
2   If I wound or disadvantage someone as a result, that is their bad luck. It was probably their own fault, anyway.
3   I have developed in my head a perfectly cogent reasoning to justify the previous two points.

This research has helped us to understand the actions of power holders in a more nuanced way. This involves an interaction of not one but two different factors. The first of these factors is situational: having power in a particular context. The other is person-related: the strength of the D-factor.

It should be obvious that the combination of a strong D-factor with strong situational power is a potentially explosive cocktail that does not bode well for the outcome. To make matters worse, it is also a situation that is very difficult to correct, both for the person concerned and for his environment. The D-factor is a disposition that is firmly anchored in the personality of the power holder, which therefore needs to be protected and maintained by a self-confirmatory mindset that justifies the power holder's own actions. We have already seen earlier in the book just how much resistance to change this can generate.

POWERLESSNESS PARALYSES

22 December 1999. Shortly after take-off, a Korean plane crashes in a field near London. A nightmare scene. The destruction is total and all the crew are killed. The commission of experts investigating the crash eventually comes to the conclusion that it was caused by a combination of factors. One of these factors was worthy of particular note: the relationship between the pilot and the co-pilot.

The captain was a former air force colonel who had many hours of experience flying the Boeing 747 that crashed. The first officer was much younger and only had 200 hours of experience in this type of plane. One of the things that most puzzled the experts when they listened to the cockpit conversations on the black box flight recorder was why on earth no-one had reacted when a number of alarms began to sound. Both pilots must have known that they would be killed unless someone did something, but instead they just sat there as the plane plummeted to earth.

The mystery became even greater when the technical analysis revealed that a crucial piece of the equipment in the captain's console had not been working, but that the same piece of equipment in the first officer's console had been functioning perfectly. This is a scenario that occasionally happens, but every pilot has been trained and retrained to deal with this situation.

The standard procedure says that the co-pilot must inform the pilot that his (the pilot's) equipment is malfunctioning and that he (the co-pilot) is taking over control of the aircraft, so that it can land safely. But that is not what hap-pened in this case. The reason? Power relationships.

In Korea, if a pilot transfers from the air force to the civil aviation company, he retains his military rank. Pilot Park was a colonel, which meant that he was immediately made a leading pilot, without the need to first acquire experi-ence of civil aircraft as a co-pilot. A few months prior to the accident he had already been given a warning for failing to follow the correct procedures. This had wounded his honour, something that he could not allow to be repeated. As a result, on that fateful day he blindly trusted what his instruments were telling him, even though he must have known they were faulty. The in-flight engineer had told him as much and the alarms flashed out the same disquieting message. Park was under additional stress because the take-off of his flight had been delayed and so he was in no mood for discussion once the crisis broke. Justifying yourself to others who are lower in rank is simply not done, at least not in Korean culture.

Sadly, the younger co-pilot was also imbued with the same philosophy. Lower in rank, he remained faithful to the code of discipline. He preferred to die, rather than to confront his superior officer and challenge his authority, with all that this would imply. In much the same way, the captain preferred to die rather than risk a further reprimand from his own superiors or – heaven forbid – suffer the indignity of being corrected by a subordinate. Power relationships can have serious and even fatal consequences – and this was not the first time for Korean Airlines. A few years earlier, another of their planes had crashed in Guam for much the same reasons, this time killing over 200 people.

The accident in London was the last straw for the company's senior management. They had learnt their lesson and now made huge efforts to change the commercial culture within their organisation and on board their aircraft, with an emphasis on more open and equal communication. And, thankfully, it worked: since then, the company has experienced no further tragedies of this kind.

Power gets under your skin and it consumes you completely when you are confronted by figures who have even more power than you do. If you are not careful, your attitude and your behaviour become complementary: the greater the power of the other person, the more subservient you make yourself, because you do not wish to incur the wrath of this powerful other.

However, the price you pay is a high one. By making yourself 'invisible' in this manner, you not only reduce the likelihood that you will be valued by others, but you also risk harming your intellectual capabilities. This is not a pleasing prospect, but is nevertheless one that has been confirmed many times by research studies.

We have already seen the basic set-up previously: you divide your test subjects into two groups, giving one group a feeling of power and the other group a feeling of inferiority. Everyone is then given the same task. This time, the task is far from easy. Various options are possible. For example, the subjects might be seated in front of a computer screen, on which different series of random letters briefly appear. They are given the following instruction: 'As soon as you see a letter that appeared in the last set of letters but one, press the button as quickly as you can.' This means that you need to sort out very quickly which new information is relevant for your objective and which is not. Psychologists refer to this as updating the working memory.

A similar test – again on a computer – involves the display of the names of colours. Sometimes the name appears in letters with the same colour as the name – for example, the name 'blue' in blue-coloured letters. Sometimes the name and the colour are different. The task is to indicate as quickly as you can whether the colour and the name are the same or not.[26]

There are several other tests of this kind, but it doesn't really make a difference which one you use: the results are nearly always the same, and they are not very encouraging. People with less power are systematically less able to update their working memory; less able to distinguish between what is relevant and irrelevant; less able to assess new information critically; and, as a result, less able to plan well. In other words, such people often find themselves in positions in which they have little or no influence. If this has a further debilitating effect on your intellectual capacities, it eventually results in a self-fulfilling prophecy: you end up proving that you are indeed capable of less.

If you are a position of utter powerlessness, you risk falling prey to a condition referred to by the psychologists as stereotype threat.[27] This mechanism is wholly unconscious but can have a serious limiting effect on its victims. It works like this.

Imagine that you are talking a mathematics test. You are sitting in a large auditorium with many other men and women. In your culture, there is a perception (rightly or wrongly) that women are less good at mathematics. Before the test starts, the examiner gives an informal introduction, as part of which he mentions two things: firstly, that the test will be a difficult one; and, secondly, that in his opinion that standard view about women not being as good at maths as men has never been satisfactorily proven. As a result, the women in the auditorium will now start to worry, because the idea that women and maths is not a marriage made in heaven has been activated in their minds. This is bad enough, but the next step is even worse. Because they have activated this stereotype, they unconsciously begin to conform to it, so that they do actually perform worse than their male colleagues in the test, even though there is no objective reason why this should be the case.

From the laboratory to the workplace

Luke was the director-general of a government service. He was a brilliant engineer but not a very nice person. He used to criticise his departmental managers mercilessly in public, branding them without exception as being 'incompetent'.

It goes without saying that you don't get to become a departmental manager if you are incompetent. At an intellectual level, his managers were all excellent. However, if you are constantly being told that you are useless, this so increases your fear of failure that the chances of you making a mistake also increase, giving your boss new ammunition for his accusation of incompetence. In this particular case, no-one had the courage to speak out against the DG. This was strange, because on the face of it they had no objective reason to be afraid. In this government department, you almost need to shoot someone before you might be considered for downgrading, let alone dismissal. This instinct to crawl into their shell was not the result of a balanced assessment of the risks involved, but was an instinctive emotional reaction that led to an ever greater degree of helplessness.

Additional comment 1

If you are in a position of power, you are faced with a double dilemma when it comes to information: you are temperamentally less well suited to gathering information from your environment and your environment will have a tendency to edit the information it passes on to you, so that you only hear the things people think you want to hear.

Nathalie was the CEO of a telecommunications company. She was an outstanding business woman, but also had great personal charm and charisma. You could often find her at the company coffee bar, having a friendly chat with some of her people. A large part of the company's business involved dealing with private customers and she knew that customer contacts of this kind work better if the staff involved feel comfortable with what they do and with their surroundings. This meant that ensuring a good working atmosphere was always one of her key priorities.

To make sure that she continued to keep her finger on the pulse of internal opinion, she decided to have informal conversations with at least one member of each team each year. Since there were a lot of teams, this meant making a heavy commitment in terms of her available time, but she thought that it was warranted. This was an exceptional step for someone at her organisational level to take, but that was part of her charisma. There was, however, one thing that she failed to take into account. Each year the teams had to decide who to send to see her: not an easy choice. 'Natalie is so unbelievably positive that we've got to send her someone who is positive as well!' As a result, and notwithstanding her good intentions and her investment of time, Nathalie only got to hear a fraction of what was really being said inside the company.

Additional comment 2

If you are dealing with staff from a position of power, there is almost no room for relational error. Rebecca can tell you all about it. She is an engineer in the sales department of a large logistics company. She is by no means a shrinking violet, but even so she once found herself in the following situation.

'I was at a meeting of the company's middle and senior managers. Someone from the senior management committee gave us the opportunity to ask questions. One of my colleagues asked a fairly straightforward question, a question of the kind one of our customers might ask, but the big boss didn't know how to answer it. He hummed and hawed for a few minutes, before quickly moving on to the next question. At the drinks reception after the meeting, the woman who asked the question was standing with a group of us when the senior manager came up to her and asked point-blank what she thought she was playing at, trying to embarrass him like that with her smart-ass questions.'

Of course, an incident of this kind spreads around an organisation like wildfire. In no time at all, people had reached the collective conclusion that from now on it was smarter to sit tight and say nothing during future question-and-answer sessions with the top brass.

If a power figure makes this kind of mistake, it is almost impossible to correct – on both sides. In these circumstances, not even an apology works. If it can happen once, it can happen again. And once bitten, twice shy! 'I'm certainly not going to take the risk,' said Rebecca. 'After all, that man has the power to decide whether or not I will be able to afford to pay for my kids to go to university!' Viewed objectively, that is a massive over-exaggeration, certainly for a highly competent engineer like Rebecca, but that is exactly how people in her situation experience these things.

5 YOU CAN ALWAYS STRENGTHEN YOUR OWN POWER

Simon has just become a father for the first time. When he and his wife took their baby home from hospital after the birth, they left with a huge amount of information and advice. The first day had not yet passed before Simon started to worry about the child's eating habits. Both he and his wife had noticed that the baby was not drinking as much as they had thought it should. And that was when the doubts begin. Is this normal? Should we be worried? Should we phone the hospital? No, perhaps not yet. Simon and his wife were both well educated and they didn't want to appear as panic-stricken idiots. Besides, the people at the hospital have more important things to do than deal with over-anxious parents. If drinking a bit less than normal was likely to be a problem, surely someone would have told them, wouldn't they? Two days later, their baby was admitted to A&E with serious dehydration…

At the opposite side of the spectrum, we have Helen. Helen is a young and promising project developer, who works on a self-employed basis. She was recently offered the chance of a lifetime: a long-term contract with a major furniture manufacturer. The contract that she was asked to sign looked fine to her, but she thought she would let her accountant have a look at it, anyway. After all, he was experienced and was known to be a skillful negotiator. In particular, he knew how big companies deal with young professionals, making use of their youthful ambition and enthusiasm to serve their own interests.

He told her that the contract was full of restrictive conditions and demands. He suggested that she tell the company this was not acceptable. After that, she could make a few small concessions and would eventually end up with a much better deal. Helen didn't really understand what all the fuss was about, but if a man with his experience told her that this was the best thing to do, who was she to doubt him? She therefore decided to make an appointment with the company for later the same week. The meeting was short but not very sweet. Ten minutes later, Helen was back on the street, with her dream of a contract in ruins. She had overplayed her hand by being too demanding and was immediately shown the door.

In situations of this kind, it is difficult to find the right balance. On the one hand, how do you avoid, like Simon, paying a high price because you allow yourself to be intimidated by people who you regard as authorities? And on the other hand, how do you avoid, like Helen, challenging authority in a manner that ultimately does you more harm than good?

How to avoid playing the power game

If you are confronted by power, it is not really a good idea to try and make yourself as small and inconspicuous as possible. But it is an even worse idea if you try to take on the power holder at his own game. Fortunately, this latter option doesn't happen very often; most of us know instinctively that this can only lead to disaster. You don't challenge an alpha wolf and get away with it unpunished. Even so, our desire to rebel is never far away: it is hidden rather than suppressed.

Do you remember what we said earlier about territories? People with power can enter your territory and diminish your autonomy. Your initial emotional reaction is a desire to resist. Your survival instinct will tell you to what extent this is a good idea. Fighting to preserve a territory can be worthwhile, but only as long as this does not expose you to reprisals that can cause you serious pain and harm you in other territories that mean even more to you than the one you are defending. For this reason, it is generally more promising to try and make allies of power figures. We will look a little later at some of the strategies to achieve this. However, they will only work if, at the same time, you can find ways to strengthen your awareness of your own power and value. That is the key to success. No matter how useful it is to learn how to deal with power, by making yourself neither too subservient (small) nor too threatening (big), this does nothing to change the power dynamic in which you are trapped. You remain locked within a framework in which someone has power over you and dictates your behaviour. Whichever way you look at it, in these circumstances you remain power dependent. The only way you can break out of this dynamic is by greater self-awareness. And there are a number of practical ways in which you can do this.

Amy Cuddy is a professor at the Harvard Business School. She has made a remarkable contribution to research into the somewhat abstract notion of 'presence'. By training, she is a psychologist, but much of her methodology is based on concepts from biology. Here is a brief summary:[28]

1   Animals and humans all make use of the same body language when they wish to impose themselves: they make themselves bigger.

2   Adopting this expansive body language is instinctive, also in humans. When we win in a race, we raise our hands in the air and stick out our chin. This is a posture we all adopt, even people who have been born blind and have never seen anyone else do it.

3   If you feel powerless, you do the opposite: you make yourself physically smaller, by hunching your shoulders and pulling your head down.[29]

4   When you assume an expansive posture, two hormonal changes take place in the body: your level of testosterone increases and the level of cortisol falls. In everyday language, you become simultaneously more dominant and more relaxed.

5   This combination of high testosterone and low cortisol is a distinguishing characteristic of effective leaders.

6   By adopting an expansive posture deliberately for no longer than two minutes, it is possible to replicate this hormonal effect. These are the postures that you can see illustrated on the following page.

7   You want to do an experiment to confirm all this? Ask half of your test subjects to adopt the expansive position for two minutes. Ask the other half to do the same with the defensive position. Next, submit everyone to a rigorous job interview. Record the conversations and show them to a panel of assessors who are not aware of your test conditions and

the theories on which they are based. Ask the panel to say who they assess positively and who they assess negatively. In other words, which candidates would get the job? You don't need to be a genius to guess the answer: the people who adopted the power position before the interview are systematically chosen in preference to the others.

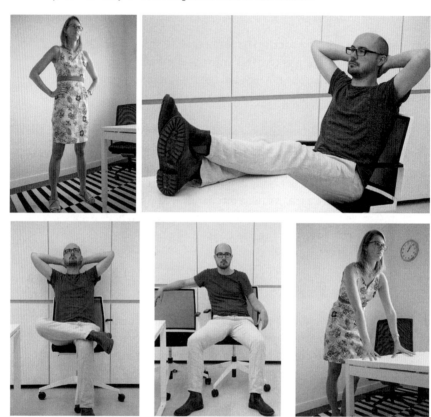

Using this two-minute technique is an excellent way to prepare yourself mentally for dealing with people with power. It puts you in the same frame of mind as them, and therefore prevents you from selling yourself short.

If you want to take things a stage further, you can combine this technique with what we now know as mindfulness. This is a methodology that has its roots in Buddhism and has measurable positive results in terms of reducing stress.[30] Mindfulness teaches you how to remain fully in the moment, in the here and now, rather than clinging on to or being carried away by the thoughts and emotions that are raging inside you. You can achieve this by paying careful attention to your body, your posture and your breathing. The more you train yourself in this method, the more it will become a habit and a way of moving through life, with clearly documented benefits both for you and your environment.

If meditation is taking things just a little too far for you, but you nonetheless wish to prepare for important meetings, you can use a short version in combination with Amy Cuddy's two-minute technique.

1   Go to a place where no-one can see you, so that you can prepare without the need to take account of cynical looks and raised eyebrows. A toilet can often be the perfect location.
2   Assume one of the positions in the photographs. Choose the one that suits you best.
3   Feel yourself sitting or standing: you must quite literally sense and experience your body. Do this as consciously and as accurately as possible for two minutes.
4   If you note that your attention is wandering, that is okay. Just bring your thoughts back to the sensing of your body. Do this again and again.
5   As you approach the end of the two minutes, try to imagine exactly what contribution you can make for the person or group that you will shortly be meeting.
6   Go to the place of the meeting and do what you must do.

There is nothing remarkable or exotic about this technique, but it does have a number of beneficial effects:

1   By influencing your hormonal activity, you increase your presence.
2   By sensing your body in this way, you give yourself a message: 'I am who I am. Not bigger or stronger than I am, not weaker or smaller. I am me.' In this way, you establish your own right to exist and escape from the power dynamic of others. Power games always take place between people. You can break through this by concentrating intensely on yourself.
3   By focusing on your possible contribution, you adopt a positive mindset towards the other(s), so that the chance of building a constructive partnership increases.

You will soon know if this technique can work for you or not. The worst that can happen is that you will waste two minutes of your time. On the other hand, it might be the best two minutes you ever spend. The potential gains are clear and once you have mastered the technique its use will become almost automatic. Because that is how our brain works: we repeat the things that bring us benefit. Effortlessly.

6 STREET SMARTS: HOW SHOULD YOU DEAL WITH STAKEHOLDERS WHO HAVE POWER?

For the success of your projects, you will inevitably need the support of key stakeholders in powerful positions. As an absolute minimum, you must give them the space that they need to do whatever is necessary. In the best case scenario, they will become your allies. In this case, you will build a common territory with them.

In this chapter, you have been given insights into the psychology of power. These will now be translated in the following paragraphs into a number of practical suggestions. You can regard these as pointers for your diplomatic offensive. Read them and pick out the ones that best suit your preferred way of doing things. These will give you the best chance of success. Good luck!

1 Be prepared to act like a 'mama bear'

You will be less easily steamrolled by power figures if you have a clear idea of what is important for you. If your goal goes beyond the protection of your own self interests, this will give you extra strength, precisely because you will then be defending the interests of a wider community. Just like 'mama bear' protects her young.

2   Frame what you can do as a direct contribution to the objectives of
    the other

You can only do this once you know the answers to the questions in
point 1. You can then approach this in two ways: you can either explain what he can gain by your contribution or else what loss he can
avoid. The more strongly you are able to quantify this, the greater
will be his willingness to listen and the more powerful the impact of
your message.

3   Be prepared to act like a 'mama bear'

You will be less easily steamrollered by power figures if you have
a clear idea of what is important for you. If your goal goes beyond
the protection of your own self interests, this will give you extra
strength, precisely because you will then be defending the interests
of a wider community. Just like 'mama bear' protects her young.

4   Ask power figures for advice

By asking advice, you achieve two things: you demonstrate your willingness to behave in a humble and respectful way, whilst at the same
time winning an important ally. Giving advice increases a person's
status. What's more, it is very difficult for someone to refuse to give
advice, when they are asked. And once the advice is given, it makes
him a co-owner of your project. In other words, he now shares in
your territory and will take the necessary steps to defend it.

5   Be visible

If you want to gain in influence, simply doing a good job is not
enough. If people do not know what you have done, your impact
will remain minimal. So keep putting forward new ideas and make
sure people with power see the contribution you are making to the
organisation's objectives.

6 Build up your credibility

Someone with power will only listen to you if you are credible. He will measure this credibility against your reputation and your proven past performance. Be certain to approach him in the right manner: first explain how you can contribute towards the things that are important to him and only then explain why what you say is credible. In an environment where it is 'not done' to talk about your own successes, try to get the same messages across via a third party, preferably before your first meeting with your key stakeholder. In this way, your reputation will precede you, creating a positive mindset in your conversation partner before you even arrive.

7 Be modest when you are praised

Thank the person explicitly for their expression of appreciation, but seek to play down your own merits. Like John did, for example: 'Thank you for your kind words. If my father had heard them, he would have been proud. If my mother had heard them, she might even have believed it, too.' Modesty after a success increases your status.

8 Never apologise

Sometimes you will make mistakes and these will be pointed out to you by figures in authority. Thank them for their comments and tell them what you have learned from them. Apologising only makes you smaller than you need to be. So don't do it. Saying sorry is only useful if you have made a moral error.

9 Use your passion as an explanation for infringing on someone else's territory

If you have perhaps pushed things a little too far when dealing with power figures, immediately take a step back and explain your over-enthusiastic behaviour as an expression of the passion you feel for your project. Say that you will try to control this enthusiasm better in future. It is difficult for others, even authority figures, to criticise someone for having too much passion.

10 Give power figures alternatives

Telling people in authority what they 'must' do or giving them no alternative seldom works. Power figures think that decision-making is part of their territory. So offer them a number of options, but give a clear recommendation for your favoured option, providing reasons for your choice but stating explicitly that the final decision is down to them. In this way, you increase the likelihood that they will go with your recommendation.

11 Never directly praise the performance of people with power

Assessing performance is only done by people with a higher position in the hierarchy. Giving praise is a form of assessment, so don't do it. If you want to show your appreciation for someone in authority, ask, for example, how he has managed to achieve so much in his career so far. This gives him the opportunity to assess his own performance, stressing the parts that are most important to him. Expressing your praise for him to others in his network is a good idea, because there is a good chance that they will pass the message on. In this way, your praise reaches him indirectly and from an unsuspected source, which suggests that you are not expecting anything in return. As a result, your appreciation will only have positive effects.

12 Talk with power figures about objectives rather than expressing feelings

Power makes people very goal-oriented. This means that they often regard things that do not contribute towards their objectives as being irrelevant. Unless the objective is person-oriented, the discussion of feelings is at best a distraction and at worst an irritation (if the feelings are negative). It is appropriate, however, to express your pride at what the organisation or part of it has achieved.

13 Never overshadow a power figure

Never embarrass power figures, and certainly never in a public setting, where a loss of face may potentially be involved (to his colleagues, superiors, staff, etc.). Even though your arguments might be strong, never try to prove your bosses wrong. Instead, offer them a convenient escape route and time to use it; for example, by telling them that you have found new information you would like to bring to their attention, which will allow them (as always!) to take the right decision. Never enter into discussion with them in public. Instead, try and talk to them before meetings, saying that you will get all the necessary extra information to them in advance.

14 Never brag about your successes

If you succeed in persuading a power figure to change their mind, make sure that you always depict this in a light that is favourable to him and not to you. At best, you should only say that you may have provide some of the elements that led him to take this wise decision. Bragging always boomerangs on the bragger and is never appreciated, especially by potential colleagues, since they will now be convinced that you are only out for personal power and glory, so that they will be less inclined to trust and work with you.

15 Express your self-esteem in your non-verbal behaviour

Never bow or scrape when you meet someone or shake their hand, unless they are royalty or a power figure from an Asian culture. Instead, make eye contact and smile. Give them the opportunity to speak the first words of greeting. Leaving this initiative to them confirms and strengthens their status.

7

WHEN THE GOING GETS TOUGH: A TOOLKIT TO CREATE OR REPAIR SHARED TERRITORIES

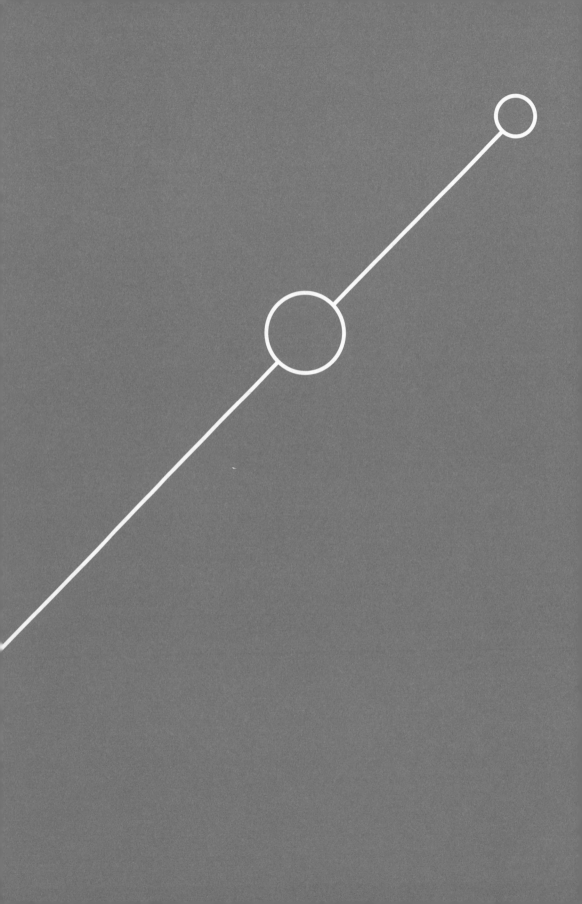

This book has a single central theme: the acquisition and protection of terri-tories as a basic need of all people, either as individuals or in groups. Because none of us works in a vacuum and we are all dependent on others to get things done, it is necessary to get the territories of different people moving in the same direction. This is always difficult, since a territory by definition implies separation. If you want to achieve collaboration, it is essential to understand the processes that can make this possible. And that is what this book has been about.

Yet while it is essential to understand these underlying processes, it is just as important to understand your stakeholders. This is also something that has been covered in all its many different nuances in the previous pages. The problem is that the more the situation becomes pressurised and the more this pressure is felt by the different actors, the greater the tendency becomes to retreat into yourself, so that you do not explore how the world looks from the perspective of others.

1 AN ORIENTATION

William Ury, together with his colleagues Fisher and Patton, has developed the Harvard Negotiation Model.[1] Their work has left a lasting impression on the way people and organisations negotiate with each other. The most impor-tant field of application for their ideas is diplomacy. In particular, the model has often been applied by American negotiators in international conflict situations. The following extracts from the TED talk by William Ury will give you some notion of how their system works.[2] One of the first things you will notice is this: there is always a way out. There is always a different approach that will solve a seemingly unsolvable problem.

'Well, the subject of difficult negotiation reminds me of one of my favourite stories from the Middle East, of a man who left to his three sons seventeen camels. To the first son, he left half the camels; to the second son, he left a third of the camels; and to the youngest son, he left a ninth of the camels. The three sons got into a negotiation: seventeen doesn't divide by two. It doesn't divide by three. It doesn't divide by nine. Brotherly tempers started to get strained. Finally, in desperation, they went and consulted a wise old woman. The wise old woman thought about their problem for a long time, and finally she came back and said, "Well, I don't know if I can help you, but at least, if you want, you can have my camel." So then they had eighteen camels. The first son took his half: half of eighteen is nine. The second son took his third: a third of eighteen is six. The youngest son took his ninth: a ninth of eighteen is two. Nine plus six plus two makes seventeen. They had one camel left over. They gave it back to the wise old woman.'

Ury continued:

'Let me tell you a little story from my own negotiating experience. Some years ago, I was involved as a facilitator in some very tough talks between the leaders of Russia and the leaders of Chechnya. There was a war going on, as you know. We met in The Hague, in the Peace Palace, in the same room where the Yugoslav war-crimes tribunal was taking place.

The talks got off to a rather rocky start, when the vice president of Chechnya began by pointing at the Russians and said: "You should stay right here in your seats, because you're going to be on trial for war crimes." And then he turned to me and said: "You're an American. Look at what you Americans are doing in Puerto Rico." And my mind started racing: "Puerto Rico? What do I know about Puerto Rico?" I started to react. But then, I tried to remember to go to the balcony. And then when he paused and everyone looked at me for a response, from a balcony perspective, I was able to thank him for his remarks and say: "I appreciate your criticism of my country and I take it as a sign that we're among friends and can speak candidly to one another. But what we are not here to do is to talk about Puerto Rico or the past. We're here to see if we can figure out a way to stop the suffering and the bloodshed in Chechnya." The conversation got back on track. That is the role of the third side, to help the parties go to the balcony.'

Masterly and respectful.

2 PREVENTATIVE MAINTENANCE FOR COLLABORATIVE RELATIONSHIPS

The framework

Ury's comments relate to extremely difficult situations in which the parties are dug into deeply entrenched positions that are highly politically charged. Fortunately, these kinds of situations are few and far between. But even in your environment you will come across relationships that are blocked. Later in this chapter, you will find a number of tips to unblock them. Suffice it here to say that your first concern is to ensure that the collaboration is not derailed. But how? The great psychologist Kurt Lewin once said: 'Nothing is as practical as a good theory.' If you want to make your interventions efficient and effective, it is useful to start with a theoretical framework. In the case of the following example it is the concept of 'social dilemmas'.

We all know how fishing quotas are supposed to work: fishermen agree to limit the amount of fish they catch – in other words, to limit their income – so that there will still be enough fish over for their children and grandchildren to earn a decent living from the sea. Social dilemmas deal with the following question: how can you ensure that people find a balance between concern for their private interests and concern for the general good? Or to put it another way: between their own territory and society's common territory.

We can speak of a social dilemma when the following conditions apply:

1   Individuals or groups are dependent on each other; what you do has consequences for me and vice versa.
2   There is a built-in field of tension between private interests and the collective interest.
3   Individuals and groups are ultimately able to decide independently for themselves what they will and will not do.

We are talking here of a dilemma in the most literal sense of the word: if you choose to favour your own interests, the community will suffer and vice versa. Fields of tension of this kind are always and continuously present, not only on a large scale (think, for example, of the situation in the EU relating to the migration crisis and the position of the different member states), but also in every workplace and family. These fields are incapable of definitive solution. There is a constant need to seek for a new dynamic balance that will allow you to move forward, a balance that needs to go further than meaningless promises and slogans.

You could, of course, say that only the collective interest should matter, but then you would be doing an injustice to the need of the individual to be 'special' within his group and also to the need of each group to have its own identity within the wider community. On the other hand, if you just let events take their course, there is a real danger that private interests and 'might is right' will predominate. In these latter circumstances, living together as a society or working together as a team would become very difficult.

Whether people opt for communal interest or their own profit depends to some extent on their nature as a person. Research suggests that in the first instance more than half are motivated by communal interest. Slightly more than a third put their own interests first, while a third group of roughly 10 percent have a slightly different driving force: they either want to have more than others or lose less than them. These are the competitive spirits.

After reading chapter 6, it will probably not surprise you to learn that power also plays a role in all this. Generally, you can expect that power is more closely associated with self-interest or competition.

Because social dilemmas are so difficult to solve in practice and because it is often not possible or acceptable to leave the settlement of important issues to individual preferences, a great deal of research has been carried out to assess the factors which can ensure that the collective interest will always remain part of the equation. Private interest needs no such help: it will always find its place on any agenda. The elements that can work to the benefit of collectivism include the following:[3]

1   Discuss in advance what you will do if there is a social dilemma.

The social dilemma field of tension is nearly always inherent in teamwork. There is the interest of the project team as a whole, while at the same time there are also the interests of the functional teams from which the project members are drawn. For example, when these project members are only involved in the project for part of their working time, sooner or later there will inevitably be problems relating to their availability. The project leader needs them for something crucial on Monday, but so does the manager of their functional department. If you wait until this kind of conflict flares up, they are much more difficult to solve, since the situation very quickly becomes emotionally charged. For this reason, it is better to sit down and discuss possible flash points before the project starts and agree what you will do to defuse these potential explosive incidents. This makes it possible to give mutually acceptable undertakings without being under the pressure of the moment.

2   Make explicit promises

Once you have agreed the undertakings referred to in this first point, it is useful to include these in a project charter, which should be explicitly and personally endorsed by everyone involved. If you can get everyone to confirm the undertakings they have given at a moment when there is relatively little social pressure, there is more chance that they will honour these undertakings if or when difficult situations arise. In this way, you make use of the internal consistency mechanism we discussed earlier in the book.

3   Make the group as small as possible

If you have a fishing fleet of two hundred boats at sea, there is a greater likelihood that an individual fisherman will feel less of an obligation to abide by the quota restrictions than if there were only twenty boats. 'What difference can it make if I catch just a little bit more? In such a big group nobody will notice.'

The larger the group, the likelier it is that this kind of reasoning will come to the fore. And if a significant number of fishermen all think the same thing, the quota will never be met. But if there are only a few of trawlers, each individual case of overfishing will be much more easily identified, so that the pressure to stick to the quota is much greater.

The smaller the group, the greater the feeling of solidarity within that group. In this way, the group feels more like your close family than your extended family; more like your own team as opposed to the company as a whole. You can increase identification with the larger group by making the results of the next highest group level as visible as possible.

4   Make individual behaviour visible

A prototypical situation might be that of a football team. Of course, the collective result – the score – is easily known. So too are a number of the key parameters (amount of possession, shots on goal, etc.). When you want to improve the team's performance, there is a further parameter that coaches need to consider: the contribution of each individual player. Each player is monitored individually and the results are analysed and discussed. This makes it harder for 'lazy' players to hide behind the collective effort of the team.

You should think about introducing a similar practice in your project or work group. Of course, this means that you have to accept internal competition between individuals as a consequence. Whether this is possible in your case will depend in the first instance on the culture of your organisation.

5   Guarantee that collaboration will have no negative effects

When emotions are involved, people learn fast and often what they learn they don't forget. Fiona has her objectives within the project; so does Eric. Two of the members of Fiona's team fall sick and will not be back at work for weeks. As a result, her deadlines are in danger. She asks Eric if she can temporarily borrow one of his team. Eric is a good colleague: 'Of course!' he replies. But as a result of this collegiality Eric fails to meet his own deadlines, which gets him a rocket from his manager. This means that next time anyone asks him for help, he is more likely to refuse.

Don't make the same mistake as Eric's manager. You cannot seek to encourage collaboration and then punish someone for showing their goodwill. If you do, news of the incident will soon spread throughout your organisation and will remain fixed in people's memories. And not without good reason: there is nothing people hate more than making themselves vulnerable by showing their goodwill, only to be 'rewarded' for their generosity by being penalised.

6   Keep everyone informed of the results of good collaboration

If you are dependent on each other, this means that what one person does or does not do makes a difference for all the others involved. We often assume that everyone in the team knows this and will bear it in mind, but this is frequently not the case. The reason for this is more a matter of poor communication than an unwillingness to collaborate.

Because situations can change quickly, it is a good idea to periodically take the time to discuss in a structured manner the practical arrangements for your collaboration. You might consider the following process, which should help you to deal with problems before they arise.

The process

1   Hold a meeting (generally one and a half to two hours long) in a separate room with all the people who need to collaborate with each other. Face-to-face contact is essential.

2   Explain to them the conceptual framework of social dilemmas and point out how difficult it is in practice to manage these dilemmas. Underline the continuing importance of keeping each other informed of the practical consequences of good and poor collaboration for all concerned.

3   Ask them to note down in key words (not pages) the following matters for anyone present in the room with whom they have a functional interface:

    • 'You could help me or make my task easier by...'
    • 'This is important for me because it would make it possible to...'
    • 'One practical way that you could do this is...'
    • 'A possible system to follow this up is...'

4   Wait until everyone has finished writing and then ask them to exchange what they have written.

5   Ask them to start a series of one-to-one conversations with all the people for whom they have made notes. This will usually take about an hour.

6 During these conversations, ask them to stick to the following rules:

- Do not react to what the other person has written, but ask for its clarification first. Do this above all for the things that are at stake for the other person: the 'why' of his requests.
- Be realistic: avoid later disappointment by not making promises you cannot keep; sometimes your answer will have to be 'no'.
- When you have to turn down a request, explain why this is the case and, if possible, suggest an alternative that is more feasible and can perhaps still help your colleague to make progress.
- Only move on from one conversation to another when you have made concrete arrangements about the what, how and when of the first step.

By allowing the conversations to take place on a one-to-one basis, you avoid creating group pressure and increase the likelihood of voluntary and long-lasting engagement. However, at the end of the session you can always ask the meeting as a whole what kind of arrangements have been made and in what way they are useful. A few examples will suffice.

Plan this type of dialogue in advance, roughly once every six months. It is an excellent investment of your time, since it results in greater understanding, cohesion and belief in the group's self-regulating abilities. Above all, it helps to create and strengthen collective territories.

3 MEDIATING IN TERRITORIAL CONFLICTS

The process described above serves a preventative purpose. Sometimes, however, territorial disputes will already have broken out – as was the case with two quality control departments in a pharmaceutical company. One department had been given a wider competence than the other by senior management, because they were at the critical phase in the testing of a new product. As a result, the other department felt limited in its autonomy and invested a huge amount of energy in its attempts to defend the boundaries of its territory against the 'invader'. At first, they did this in a passive manner, by saying that they would help, but then hiding behind a barrage of procedural 'difficulties', which effectively meant that they did very little or nothing. Later, the conflict became more open, including regular shouting matches at co-ordination meetings. Something clearly needed to be done. But what?

What does not work

In conflicts of this kind, management sometimes decides to transfer a few members of staff from one department to another. The underlying idea is that in this way it is possible to introduce the thinking of one group into the other group, and vice versa. It is hoped that, as a result, mutual understanding will be increased. Unfortunately, it is not that simple. The newcomers need to be accepted by their new group. They need to become 'one of us' as opposed to 'one of them', and this can only be achieved by acceptance of the group's existing informal norms. One of these norms will inevitably be that the newcomers' former department is 'no good'. The outcome is predictable: they will have no option but to accept this new norm, so that in a few days time the situation is back to the way it was.

When groups are competing or are in conflict with each other, there are one or two things that always happen. To begin with, their image forming changes in a predictable manner, in both directions. You are probably familiar with the mindset mechanism or the 'mental glasses' that you wear to look at things. If you are pregnant, you suddenly start noticing how many other pregnant women there are in your neighbourhood. If you have just bought a new car, you suddenly start seeing the same model everywhere in traffic. This is the first law of mental imaging: whatever matches the mental glasses you are wearing will encroach on your vision. It has always been there, but suddenly you see it, because you are now more directly concerned with it.

If your group regards another team as its enemy, two things will happen to your mental glasses: of all the different things you are able to observe – both in your team and in the other team – certain things are selectively exaggerated; namely, the negative aspects of the other group and the positive aspects of your own group. The fascinating thing about this process is that it is entirely unconscious. You think you are basing your view on objective facts. And, indeed, sometimes you are, but you remain unaware that you are collecting these facts on the basis of selective observation. There are many other facts that you are no longer seeing. Result? Your opinion of your own group becomes increasingly more positive and of the other group increasingly more negative. This simply gives you more reason to turn against the other group, so that the distance between you and them becomes ever wider. This gulf is further widened by the fact that you seek support for your own opinion within your own group, which confirms the 'correctness' of the image you have formed. Of course, exactly the same thing is happening in the other group.

During the next step in the process, the boundaries of both territories are defined with increasing sharpness. The division between 'us' and 'them' becomes more pronounced. The net result is that contact between the groups is reduced still further, so that the image forming becomes even more exaggerated in the absence of any reality check.

A huge contribution to the social psychology that sheds light on the dynamics of this phenomenon has been made by the research of Muzafer Sherif and his colleagues.[4] Their team brought together two groups of young boys at a summer camp. Both groups were comparable in terms of age, talents and physical abilities.

In phase 1, both groups were kept apart and the group identity was strengthened by allowing them to play games and carry out tasks together. As is often the case with young boys, a team spirit developed quickly. In no time at all, they had even thought up names for their respective groups: one was the Rattlesnakes and the other was the Eagles. Because both groups had their camp in the same vicinity, they gradually began to become aware of each other's presence, so that a first early form of mistrust began to raise its head ('Do they respect the infrastructure of the camp that we also need?'). At the same time, the camp leaders were increasingly asked to try and arrange competitive activities against the other team.

In phase 2, this latter wish was granted. Each group was given the same task, and at the end a winner was announced, with a trophy and prizes being awarded to the best team. What's more, the prizes were not just medals, but included lots of fun things that boys love, such as penknives and model cars. To make matters worse, the award ceremony was very public and explicit, as was the fact that the losing team got nothing. The injustice of it all! From this point onwards, things began to move rapidly. Each group made its own flag and planted it on its own territory. Each group made signs proclaiming 'No entry here!' Threats were made about what might happen if flags were stolen or boundaries crossed. In short, territorial behaviour *pur sang*.

In phase 3, the two groups were brought together in the same hall. The result was not difficult to predict. Insults and recriminations flew back and forth on a daily basis. Both groups even made up scurrilous songs or slogans to torment their opponents: 'We'd rather starve than eat in the same room as that lot!' Things quickly went from bad to worse: flags were effectively stolen and burnt; dormitories were raided and prizes stolen. A full scale fight between the groups was becoming ever more likely. It was time to intervene – but initially this intervention had little success.

In phase 4, the two groups were brought together in situations that would allow them to get to know each other better: watching a film, setting off fireworks on the national holiday, playing board games, etc. The researchers' working hypothesis was that if they could learn more about each other, there would be more mutual understanding, so that the problems between them would eventually solve themselves. But that is not the way things happened. Most of these reconciliatory activities ended in shouting matches and food fights.

This is a second kind of intervention that never works. When a territorial conflict between groups has escalated, it does not help to 'force' them into each other's company. The image-forming mechanisms are still working at full tilt. Arranging meetings simply gives both sides further ammunition to demonise the other group.

What does work

Fortunately, in the above experiment a way was eventually found to make a breakthrough. The camp leaders arranged for the water supply to be regularly cut off, although the official version was that vandals were responsible. It was soon clear that this could lead to serious problems for everyone, in both camps. They were therefore given the task of working out together how sufficient water could be found to keep the camp supplied.

As a first step, everyone set out to explore the surroundings. Initially, the groups operated separately, but in each other's general vicinity. After some time, one of them found a large water tank, which seemed to be full but had a defective tap that was difficult to repair. Both groups then put their heads together to see how this problem could be overcome. A smaller group of 'experts' was created with members from both teams to focus specifically on the tap issue, while all the others kept a watching brief (as a single group), until a solution was eventually found. Everyone now had water again, thanks to a collective effort.

From this moment onwards, the group dynamic changed completely. Henceforth, goodwill was displayed on both sides. Joint activities became fun instead of a battle. The key to this transformation was the solution of a common problem that had concerned everyone in both teams, which they had only been able to solve by using their combined talents. In other words, a common territory had been created and this led to a shared success.

It was much the same story with Fred and Willy. Although they were neighbours, they hardly ever spoke to each other, except to complain when one of them had put out his dustbin just over the boundary line between their two houses or if their shared hedge had not been properly trimmed. It had been going on like this for years: at best, an armed truce; at worst, open warfare. Until the roadworks started. At last, something was going to be done about the through traffic that made life in their neighbourhood hell!

Unfortunately, it soon became clear that the local council's plans would actually make the problem worse rather than better. The neighbourhood committee were determined not to let this happen and who were the first two volunteers to man the barricades? Fred and Willy! Suddenly, they had a common purpose and, just as importantly, a common enemy. Each day, they talked to each other over the now perfectly cut hedge ('Nice job, Willy.'), exchanging observations and making plans. In fact, they talked more to each other in the first week than in the previous ten years!

Once you understand this dynamic, you can probably guess the kind of thing the pharmaceutical company did with their two competing departments. The management gave them a common task that was crucial for the next step in the development of another new product. Everybody knew that the results of their collaboration would be judged by the company's executive committee, so that failure was not an option. This managed to concentrate their minds wonderfully!

Finding an overarching task is a powerful strategy to bridge the gulf between territories. But if the situation precludes use of this method, your only option is to try and mediate between the rival groups. You can do this as follows:

1   Make sure that the initiative is taken by a neutral third party and that both the conflicting groups or individuals are willing to take part in an exploratory conversation with someone who will attempt to mediate between them. This mediator can never be from one of the two rival parties.

2   First listen to each party separately. What you will hear is two versions of the same events that are perfectly coherent and explain in detail why they are right and the others are wrong. As mediator, it is crucial not to pass any kind of judgement at this stage.

3   Invite both parties for a joint conversation on neutral ground, with a number of clear rules to which both parties must feel able to agree in advance:

   •   The purpose of the conversation is to exchange information and better understand each other.
   •   Both sides agree not to immediately put the blame for the situation on their rival. If everyone is only concerned with trying to prove their own point, a solution will never be found. Worse still, their respective positions will become even more deeply entrenched.
   •   The outcome of the conversation will be a number of small-scale and short-term agreements that serve as a first step, with a follow-up meeting planned for an agreed date.

4   Circulate these rules to both parties in advance and emphasise the fact that everyone is free to decide whether or not to take part in the conversation under these conditions.

5   During the conversation, make use of the following scenario:

   •   Underline that the presence of both parties is an expression of their positive intentions.
   •   Specify the common interest they share.
   •   Recognise the complexity of the situation.
   •   Remind them of the agreed rules and the reasons behind them.

- Give them time to prepare in writing answers to the following questions, which they should then exchange:
  - *'I sometimes have difficulty with the fact that you...'*
  - *'It is difficult when you do this, because the consequence for me is....'*
  - *'What would make things easier for in this situation, is if you could..., because...'*
- Allow the parties to ask each other in turn for further clarification of these written comments, explaining the reasons for their respective behaviour and assumptions.
- As mediator, ensure that the agreed rules are respected; in other words, that the parties listen to each other in the hope of learning more, without critical or contradictory reactions.
- After this exchange of information, ask the parties to suggest a number of very small, feasible and visible measures that may be a first move in the right direction. Again, let both sides have their say.
- Fix a date for a follow-up meeting within a maximum period of three months.

Some crucial points for the attention of mediators

The first point is respect. You can show this by explicitly referring to the complexity of the situation. 'If it was all so easy, we wouldn't be sitting here trying to sort it out.'

The second point is that the perceived intentions of both parties must be exchanged. Often, the things we find most irritating are not what people do, but the reasons we have in our head for why they do these things. In other words, their underlying motives. These assumptions are seldom checked to see if they are right, as a result of which they soon start leading lives of their own, making them the perfect excuse for behaving even less co-operatively with the other party. Naming these assumptions and verifying them is the most important key to unlocking a territorial conflict.

The last and most important point that you need to remember as a mediator is that at the start of your intervention there will be little confidence in the solvability of the problem, simply because the wounds are deep and long-standing. This makes it vital in the early stages to only aim for the smallest possible improvements. Because they are so small, these improvements should be achievable. In this way, you can prove to the parties that they do have it within their power to change things, so that confidence in further and more complex changes can grow. Having broken through the negative spiral, it gradually becomes possible to build up a more positive one. What's more, these early successes activate the dynamic of internal consistency: solving small and relatively easy problems is a good basis for later solving larger and more difficult ones. And the further you follow this path, the less willing you are to risk the gains already made by breaking off the dialogue with the other partner, even if the matters under discussion become increasingly delicate.

Also bear in mind that sometimes the relations between two parties have become so soured that face-to-face mediation is not possible. When this happens, you need to engage in a little 'shuttle diplomacy'.

Two heads of department. One was responsible for all digital projects; the other for budgeting. The project man was brilliant technically, but found it difficult to plan effectively. New priorities kept coming to the fore, as a result of which he had to keep going back to the budget man for more money. This meant scrounging around in other departments, to see where a bit of extra cash might be found. After a time, the budget man was sick of this. The next time the project man came knocking at his door, he refused to co-operate. And he wouldn't budge.

Irene was asked to mediate. She worked in another department and was one step lower on the hierarchical ladder than the departmental heads. However, in terms of prestige within the organisation, she was on the same level.

It was immediately clear to her that it would be impossible to get the antagonists to sit around the same table in the same room. Her only option was to go back and forth between the two of them. Suggesting ideas, checking what was possible, making clear whether a suggestion was hers or came from the other side, testing the water for possible solutions, watching for signs of a positive reaction. She did this first in one office and then in the other, time after time, until it finally became clear that a minimum form of modus vivendi was possible. But no more than that. The image forming of these two stubborn men had become too rigid for any further progress to be made. The only thing that would help the situation was if one of them changed jobs. Which is what eventually happened.

4   BRIDGING THE VALUE GAP

This is perhaps the most difficult task of all: doing business with someone whose values are diametrically opposed to your own. Sometimes you might feel like saying: 'I don't even want to talk to that man' and sometimes this might be perfectly understandable. But on other occasions you may have no choice. Whether you like it or not, to achieve your objective you will have to jump this awkward hurdle.

For example, you probably know that opinions about abortion in America are highly polarised. There are fervent opponents (the pro-life movement) and equally fervent supporters (the pro-choice group).

Imagine the following scenario.[5] You have identified in advance which of your test subjects are pro-life and pro-choice. You then tell them that they will soon engage in a conversation with someone about a subject that has been chosen at random and, in itself, has no further significance for the experiment. You then ask them to follow you to the conversation room, where their conversation partner is waiting. Of course, the test subject does not know that the whole scene has been deliberately staged (psychology researchers can be quite sneaky – but you have probably realised that by now).

When the test subject enters the room, the first thing he sees is a jacket hanging on the back of a chair with a badge on it, which can be either a pro-life or a pro-choice badge. Sometimes this badge will agree with the test subject's own convictions; sometimes it will not. The jacket is unisex, so that the gender factor does not have an impact. The second chair is placed against the wall. The test subject is told: 'Your conversation partner must have popped out to toilet for a few moments. Just take a chair. I am sure we will be able to start in a couple of minutes.'

The researchers were interested in the answer to two questions. First, if the test subject agrees to take a chair, how close to the chair of his unknown conversation partner will he put it? Second, to what extent is the resulting distance a reflection of a difference or a similarity in terms of their values? Of course, the answer to this second question was fairly obvious in advance: if the value orientation of the conversation partner was the same as the test subject's own, the chair was set on average 50 percent closer. In other words, a difference in values was indeed translated into physical distance, which in turn reflects a willingness to be influenced by the other person or not.

Values are probably our most intimate and personal territory. It is a territory whose boundaries no-one may touch. The reluctance to speak with someone who holds radically different values is therefore understandable. But what do you do if your success in something important depends on this person's co-operation?

To find the answer to this, we need to return briefly to chapter 6. This was where you learnt that you sometimes need to adopt a 'mama bear' attitude when you are confronted by people with power. Being a 'mama bear' means that you are highly motivated, not by your own interests but by something bigger and more meaningful. This is what you should also do when confronted with distasteful values: focus on the final objective and don't let yourself be distracted by personal preferences, no matter how passionately they are felt.

Many of you will have seen Steven Spielberg's much praised film *Schindler's List*. It is the story of Oskar Schindler, a German businessman whose ventures have often failed in the past. The Second World War offers him an unexpected opportunity for success, providing he is able to work for the German Army. Using a combination of bribery and flattery, he finally succeeds in winning an army contract to run a factory in Poland making pots and pans for German soldiers. He has but one aim: to make as much money as possible.

If costs are low, profits are higher. One way to cut costs is to employ Jewish labour. Jews are cheaper than Polish workers and there is an almost endless supply of them. Schindler needs no second thoughts. But gradually he begins to change his ideas. His witnessing of the atrocities in the Jewish ghetto in Krakow and the influence of his Jewish bookkeeper open his eyes to the true nature of the Nazi regime, so that from now on his desire to save Jews is greater than his desire to make money. How can he do this? By employing more and more Jews in his factory.

But this will only be possible if he continues to work with the Nazi officials he now despises. The most important of these is the local camp commander, part of whose daily routine is to randomly shoot a few of his prisoners before breakfast. Schindler want to stop this senseless waste of human lives.

When he decides to broach the subject with the commandant, he knows that there is no point in making moral arguments that will fall on deaf ears. This would change nothing and might cost Schindler his credibility in the commandant's eyes, so that he would no longer be able to save Jews from the concentration camps by employing them in his factory.

For this reason, Schindler adopts a different strategy. His conversation with the commandant is about power. Schindler knows that this is the commandant's most important motivation. Trying to talk him out of this power is pointless. So instead he tries to show understanding. 'Of course, power feels good. That's only natural. It feels good to have so much power that we can shoot people. But that is not real power. At best, it is justice, because they get no more than they deserve. But real power is different. Real power is what a Roman emperor had. A worthless criminal is thrown down at his feet and the emperor can have him killed just like that. But if he wants to, he can also pardon this man for his crimes with just a click of his fingers. He lets him go, even though he is both guilty and worthless. That is the real power: having the power to kill but not killing...'

Schindler did not set out to try and show that his morals were better than the commandant's. This might have massaged his own ego, but would otherwise have got him nowhere. To save the lives he wanted to save, he had to give a different twist to the commandant's own values. But he first needed to make himself credible, so that the commandant would be willing to listen. Of course, he abhorred the commandant's values, but he succeeded in finding a way to use them to serve a higher purpose. By recognising that the commandant's obsession with power had a right to exist and by offering an alternative way to satisfy that obsession, by shifting the focus from ordinary power to absolute power, as the emperors had, he was able to change the mind of a wholly irrational man.

Accepting the existence of other values, but trying to give them a different context and content, while always remaining focused on the final objective: these are the keys to success. What Schindler gave in this scene was a master-class in analysis and self-management.

'If all you have is a hammer, everything looks like a nail.' Having a broad repertoire of different behaviours and being able to use them differently depending on the position and priorities of your stakeholders: this is the secret of diplomatic skill. So how can you make sure it is a skill that you possess?

Let's return briefly to chapter 3 and the necessary ingredients for successful change that we discussed there: an experienced need, a clear vision of where you want to go, the capacity to change and the ability to make it happen. Applying the lessons in this book will also mean a change in the way you usually approach matters. Carrying through this behavioural change requires lots of extra energy. It would be folly to make this investment if you have no clear idea of the added value this will bring you in both the short-term and the long-term. If you only wish to apply a few of my tips 'for fun' (as it were), just to see what happens, your experiment will not last for very long. Existing habits are much stronger than vague intentions, certainly when you are under pressure – which in a working environment is nearly always the case.

I have no doubt that you will have the capacity to change. The insights found in this book will help you and the behavioural skills you need to apply them are not overly difficult. Many of them you already have and use, although perhaps in other contexts than projects. Empathy, for example, is an important ingredient in your dealings with family, friends, neighbours, acquaintances, etc. The same is true of your efforts to try and find out more about their way of looking at things and your willingness to deal tactfully with the issues that are important to them. If you do not possess these basic skills, then you will indeed find some parts of this book difficult to implement. Fortunately, that likelihood is relatively small. The real trick is to know how to transfer the skills you already possess from their current personal contexts into a work context.

But if you really wish to make the contents of this book useful for yourself, your biggest challenge will be to close the gap between knowing and doing. This is dependent on two factors.

You have probably heard of Carnegie Hall in New York. It is the Valhalla of the American music scene. Every orchestra, pop star or jazz musician of standing wants to play there and perhaps have their performance recorded live. Legendary places also have their legends. One of them says that one evening a young man was trying to find his way to the famous concert hall. He stopped to ask a passer-by: 'How do I get to Carnegie Hall?' To which came the reply: 'Practice, practice, practice.'

We all know that it supposedly takes ten thousand repetitions before we finally master something. But which of us has time for that? No-one, unless you become truly fascinated by something, unless understanding the diplomacy game becomes a real passion (like trying to unravel a complex game of bridge or chess), unless you notice that by expanding your behavioural repertoire you can also let your knowledge, your expertise and your experience come to their full and proper fruition. When this happens, you will also notice that stakeholdering increasingly becomes a reflex; an automatism that appears with increasing frequency on your radar.

The second crucial factor is less tangible. Diplomatic skills are more than just a collection of tips and tricks to get others to do things that work to your benefit. No, using these skills is a respectful and attentive search for ways to bridge differences and find solutions that do justice to the things that are important for everyone. This means that all those involved, including you, must be willing to allow themselves to be influenced by others, so that a meaningful exchange of ideas and opinions can lead to new and better perspectives.

I have mentioned on several occasions that this is not easy, because we all have the tendency to seek confirmation for our own ideas, especially when these ideas differ from those of others. But it is at precisely that moment that diplomatic skills are relevant. If you were always to agree with everyone, you wouldn't need them!

Growing into these skills is more a question of maturity than the use of techniques and devices. Being aware of your own motives and emotions, and being able to give them direction: these are the keys. Is it easy? No. But practice and persistence will pay off in the end. As a friend of mine once said: 'It's not so simple during the first hundred years, but after that it gets better!'

If you want to give yourself an extra push in the right direction, allow yourself the time to actively explore the material in this book. Apply its ideas in

your projects that are still on the drawing board and do it for preference with
a group of like-minded colleagues. They will be able to show you what you
fail to see for yourself, so that your learning process – and theirs – can move
forward as quickly and easily as possible.

And if you wish to do this 'with a little help from your friends', it will be our
privilege to assist you. You can find us at stakeholderingacademy.com.

STAKEHOLDERING

WORD OF THANKS

Writing a book is a curious process. It is a mix of rational and non-rational elements, as well as being a path towards a particular destination that the author never walks alone. There are always others involved; sometimes with physical help, sometimes as a source of inspiration.

The basic inspiration for Stakeholdering has been a never-ending search to find and understand the motives of human behaviour; in this case, specifically within organisations. Curiosity is the motor from which it has been possible to distill a particular angle of approach: the dynamics of collaboration.

As soon as this focus is chosen, a wonderful process is set in motion: you see things that you never saw before; you remember conversations that were long forgotten and are suddenly given a new meaning; you read what you never had the time to read. Somewhere along the way, pieces of the puzzle start falling into place and a kind of order begins to emerge, almost as if by magic. New insights are born, new avenues of thought are opened up, new ideas are revealed. Yet even though this process is quasi-autonomous, it is always fed by people. In my case, lots of them.

When you are writing a book about people, no-one in the author's vicinity is safe. What neighbours say in good faith can be cited as examples, and the same applies to family, colleagues and customers: all are used shamelessly, sometimes even to the smallest of anecdotes. I apologise to everyone who I have 'misused' in this way.

In addition to the professional and scientific literature, the organisations with which my colleagues and I have had the privilege to collaborate are the most important sources of information. I cannot thank them enough for their many years of trust.

A special word of thanks must go to Alexander Italianer for his contribution to the content and for his longstanding friendship, to Adri Van der Vurst for his critical assessment of the manuscript, and to Patricia Degeest for her dedication and accuracy in preparing the book for printing.

Thanks also to Pieter Vandendriessche for taking over my work while I was writing, and to Koenraad Coel for his patience with the many amendments and corrections.

There can be no book without a publisher who believes in it and is prepared with his team to give it every chance of success. My gratitude goes to Lannoo-Campus and in particular to Niels Janssens, Lotte Demeyer, Lisette Aerts and Tim Moriën for their unstinting hard work and professionalism.

Jan Van der Vurst

ENDNOTES

Chapter 1

1 Pfeffer, J. (1992). *Managing with power: Politics and influence in organizations*. Harvard Business Press.

2 Lombardo, M.M. & Eichinger, R.W. (2004). *FYI: For your improvement*. Center for Creative Leadership. One Leadership Place, PO Box 26300, Greensboro, NC 27438.

3 Pollard, R. (2008). Home Advantage in Football: A Current Review of an Unsolved Puzzle. *The Open Sports Sciences Journal, 1*, 12–14. See also: Pollard, R. & Pollard, G. (2005). Home Advantage in Soccer: A review of it's Existence and Causes. *International Journal of Soccer and Science, 3*, 28–38.

4 See, for example: Boyko, R.H., Boyko, A.R. & Boyko, M.G. (2007). Referee bias contributes to home advantage in English Premiership football. *Journal of Sport Sciences, 25(11)*, 1–28. For further information, see (2002). *Opta Football Yearbook 2001–2002* Carlton Books.

5 Nevill, A.M., Balmer, N.J. & Williams, A.M. (2002). The influence of crowd noise and experience upon refereeing decisions in football. *Psychology of Sport and Exercise, 3*, 261–271.

6 Neave, N. & Wolfson, S. (2003). Testosterone, territoriality, and the 'home advantage'. *Psychology & Behavior, 78*, 269–275.

7 Territorial behaviour amongst animals has often been described, for many species. Wolves are an excellent example. If you would like to know more, please see: Mech, L.D. & Boitani, L. (Eds.) (2003). *Wolves. Behavior, Ecology and Conservation*. The University of Chicago Press.

8 http://homepage.smc.edu/zehr_david/desmond_morris

9 For thinking about territories, I owe much to: Bakker, C.B. & Bakker-Rabdau, M.K.(1973). *No Trespassing! Explorations in human territoriality*. Chandler & Sharp Publishers.

10 Stajkovic, A.D. & Luthans F. (1998). Self-efficacy and Work-Related Performance: A Meta-Analysis. *Psychological Bulletin, 124*, 240–261.

11 For a summary and an analysis, see, for example: Harry Harlow (2013). A Science Odyssey. PBS. Web. 11 (https://www.pbs.org/wgbh/aso/databank/entries/bhharl.html).

12 Ryan, R.M. & Deci, E.L. (2000). Self-Determination Theory and the Facilitation of Intrinsic Motivation, Social Development, and Well-Being. *American Psychologist, 55*, 68–78.

13 Seligman, M.E. (1972). Learned helplessness. *Annual Review of Medicine, 23(1)*, 407–412.

14 See, for example: Seligman, M.E. & Csikszentmihalyi, M. Positive psychology: An introduction. In: Csikszentmihalyi, M., & Larson, R. (2014). *Flow and the foundations of positive psychology* (pp. 279–298). Springer Netherlands.

15 Rodin, J. & Langer, E.J. (1977). Long-term effects of a control-relevant intervention with the institutionalised aged. *Journal of Personality and Social Psychology, 35(12)*, 897.

16 See, for example: Whitney, D., Cherney, J., Trosten-Bloom, A. & Fry, R. (2004). *Appreciative team building: Positive questions to bring out the best of your team*. iUniverse.

17 Van Dyne, L. & Pierce, J.L. (2004). Psychological ownership and feelings of possession: Three field studies predicting employee attitudes and organizational citizenship behavior. *Journal of Organizational Behavior: The International Journal of Industrial, Occupational and Organizational Psychology and Behavior, 25(4)*, 439–459.

18 Renes, R.J., Van den Putte, B., Van Breukelen, R., Loef, J., Otte, M. & Wennekers, C. (2011). *Gedragsverandering via campagnes.* Literature study commissioned by Public Information and Communications Service, Ministry of General Affairs. The Hague.

19 Kahneman, D. (2012). *Thinking, fast and slow.* Business Contact.

20 Cioffi, D. & Garner, R. (1996). On doing the decision: Effects of active versus passive choice on commitment and self-perception. *Personality and Social Psychology Bulletin, 22(2)*, 133–147.

Chapter 2

1 Bolkan, S. & Andersen, P.A. (2009). Image induction and social influence: Explication and initial tests. *Basic and Applied Social Psychology, 31(4)*, 317–324.

2 Katie, B. & Mitchell, S. (2017). *Vier vragen die je leven veranderen.* Boekerij.

3 A good summary can be found in: Furnham, A. & Boo, H.C. (2011). A literature review of the anchoring effect. *The Journal of Socio-Economics, 40(1)*, 35–42.

4 Tversky, A. & Kahneman, D. (1974). Judgment under uncertainty: Heuristics and biases. *Science, 185(4157)*, 1124–1131.

5 Burnham, G., Lafta, R., Doocy, S. & Roberts, L. (2006). Mortality after the 2003 invasion of Iraq: a cross-sectional cluster sample survey. *The Lancet, 368(9545)*, 1421–1428.

6 Englich, B., Mussweiler, T. & Strack, F. (2006). Playing dice with criminal sentences: The influence of irrelevant anchors on experts' judicial decision making. *Personality and Social Psychology Bulletin, 32(2)*, 188–200.

7 Galinsky, A.D. & Mussweiler, T. (2001). First offers as anchors: the role of perspective-taking and negotiator focus. *Journal of Personality and Social Psychology, 81(4)*, 657.

Chapter 3

1 Block, P. (2012). *Flawless Consulting, Enhanced Edition: A Guide to Getting Your Expertise Used.* John Wiley & Sons. Olander, S. (2006). *External Stakeholder Analysis in Construction Project Management.* Lund University.

2 Knoster, T., Villa, R. & Thousand, J. (2000). A framework for thinking about systems change. In: R. Villa & J. Thousand, *Restructuring for caring and effective education: Piecing the Puzzle Together* (pp. 93–128). Paul H. Brookes Publishing.

3 There are different methods for identifying opinion leaders. A description and comparison of these methods can be found in: Valente, T.W. & Pumpuang, P. (2007). Identifying opinion leaders to promote behavior change. *Health Education & Behavior, 34(6)*, 881–896.

4 For a detailed description of the working of focus groups, see: Berkowitz, B. (2018). *Community Tool Box.* Center for Community Health and Development at the University of Kansas.

Chapter 4

1 Lord, C., Ross, L. & Lepper, M. (1979). Biased Assimilation and Attitude Polarization: The effects of Prior Theories on Subsequently Considered Evidence. *JPSP*, 37, 2098–2109.

2 Campanario, J.M. (2009). Rejecting and resisting Nobel class discoveries: accounts by Nobel Laureates. *Scientometrics*, 81, 549–565.

3 See, for example: Nicholson, N. (1998). How hardwired is human behavior? *Harvard Business Review*, 76, 134–147.

4 After: Davis, M.H. (1980). A multidimensional approach to individual differences in empathy. *JSAS Catalog of Selected Documents in Psychology*, 10, 85.

5 Galinsky, A.D., Maddux, W.W., Gilin, D. & White, J.B. (2008). Why it pays to get inside the head of your opponent: The differential effects of perspective taking and empathy in negotiations. *Psychological Science*, 19(4), 378–384.

6 Epley, N., Keysar, B., Van Boven, L. & Gilovich, T. (2004). Perspective taking as egocentric anchoring and adjustment. *Journal of Personality and Social Psychology*, 87(3), 327.

7 Pruitt, D.G. & Rubin, J.Z. (1986). *Social conflict: Escalation, impasse, and resolution*. Reading (MA): Addison-Wesley.

8 Neale, M.A. & Bazerman, M.H. (1983). The role of perspective-taking ability in negotiating under different forms of arbitration. *ILR Review*, 36(3), 378–388.

9 Galinsky, A.D. & Mussweiler, T. (2001). First offers as anchors: the role of perspective-taking and negotiator focus. *Journal of Personality and Social Psychology*, 81(4), 657.

10 Davis, M.H. (1983). Measuring individual differences in empathy: Evidence for a multidimensional approach. *Journal of Personality and Social Psychology*, 44(1), 113–126.

11 Batson, C.D. & Ahmad, N. (2001). Empathy-induced altruism in a prisoner's dilemma II: What if the target of empathy has defected? *European Journal of Social Psychology*, 31, 25–36.

12 Morris, E., Robert, C., Donahue, P. & McNamara, R.S. (2004). *The Fog of War (2003): Eleven Lessons from the Life of Robert S. McNamara*. Sony Pictures Classics.

13 Anderson, J.R., Kuroshima, H., Takimoto, A. & Fujita, K. (2013). Third-party social evaluation of humans by monkeys. *Nature Communications*, 4, 1561.

Chapter 5

1 Cuddy, A.J., Fiske, S.T. & Glick, P. (2008). Warmth and competence as universal dimensions of social perception: The stereotype content model and the BIAS map. *Advances in Experimental Social Psychology*, 40, 61–149.

2 Wojciszke, B., Abele, A.E. & Baryla, W. (2009). Two dimensions of interpersonal attitudes: Liking depends on communion, respect depends on agency. *European Journal of Social Psychology*, 39(6), 973–990.

3 Freeman, J.B., Stolier, R.M., Ingbretsen, Z.A. & Hehman, E.A. (2014). Amygdala responsivity to high-level social information from unseen faces. *Journal of Neuroscience*, 34(32), 10573–10581.

4 Cialdini, R.B. (2017). *Pre-Suasion. A Revolutionary Way to Influence and Persuade*. Random House Business.

5 Tidd, K.L. & Lockard, J.S. (1978). Monetary significance of the affiliative smile: A case for reciprocal altruism. *Bulletin of the Psychonomic Society*, 11(6), 344–346.

6   Pugh, S.D., Groth, M. & Hennig-Thurau, T. (2011). Willing and able to fake emotions: a closer examination of the link between emotional dissonance and employee well-being. *Journal of Applied Psychology*, 96(2), 377.

7   See, for example: Meyer, P. (2010). *Liespotting. Proven techniques to detect deception*. St. Martin's Press.

8   See, for example: Gallese, V. & Goldman, A. (1998). Mirror neurons and the simulation theory of mind-reading. *Trends in Cognitive Sciences*, 2(12), 493–501.

9   Churches, O., Nicholls, M., Thiessen, M., Kohler, M. & Keage, H. (2014). Emoticons in mind: An event-related potential study. *Social Neuroscience*, 9(2), 196–202.

10 Crusco, A.H. & Wetzel, C.G. (1984). The Midas touch: The effects of interpersonal touch on restaurant tipping. *Personality and Social Psychology Bulletin*, 10(4), 512–517.

11 Willis, F.N. & Hamm, H.K. (1980). The use of interpersonal touch in securing compliance. *Journal of Nonverbal Behavior*, 5(1), 49–55.

12 Zajonc, R.B. (2001). Mere exposure: A gateway to the subliminal. *Current Directions in Psychological Science*, 10(6), 224–228.

13 Kelley, J.M., Lembo, A.J., Ablon, J.S., Villanueva, J.J., Conboy, L.A., Levy, R., & Riess, H. (2009). Patient and practitioner influences on the placebo effect in irritable bowel syndrome. *Psychosomatic Medicine*, 71(7), 789.

14 For the origin of the term, see, for example: Maturana, H.R. & Varela, F.J. (1991). *Autopoiesis and cognition: The realization of the living* (Vol. 42). Springer Science & Business Media.

15 Luhmann, N. (1986). The autopoiesis of social systems. *Sociocybernetic Paradoxes*, 6(2), 172–192.

16 See https://www.ted.com/talks/eli_pariser_beware_online_filter_bubbles for a short version; for a slightly longer version: Pariser, E. (2011). *The filter bubble: What the Internet is hiding from you*. Penguin UK.

17 See, for example: Schmidt, A.L., Zollo, F., Del Vicario, M., Bessi, A., Scala, A., Caldarelli, G, & Quattrociocchi, W. (2017). Anatomy of news consumption on Facebook. *Proceedings of the National Academy of Sciences*, 201617052.

18 Kosinski, M., Stillwell, D. & Graepel, T. (2013). Private traits and attributes are predictable from digital records of human behavior. *Proceedings of the National Academy of Sciences*, 110(15), 5802-5805.

19 Christopher Wylie – on of the whizzkids behind the Cambridge Analytica method of working and its revelation – gave an account of the development and use of this poweful weapon ina fascinating interview in *De Standaard Weekend* of 14 and 15 July 2018.

20 Nuttin, J.M. (1985). Narcissism beyond Gestalt and awareness: The name letter effect. *European Journal of Social Psychology*, 15(3), 353–361.

21 For a short summary, see: Trivers, R. (2011). *Deceit and self-deception: Fooling yourself the better to fool others*. Penguin UK.

22 This questionnaire has its origins in models based on the psychological work of C.G. Jung. The most widespread version is the MBTI®. This was in turn the basis for the work of Keirsey, which we have taken as our starting point: Keirsey, D. & Bates, M.M. (1984). *Please understand me*. Prometheas Nemesis.

Chapter 6

1   Piff, P.K., Stancato, D.M., Côté, S., Mendoza-Denton, R. & Keltner, D. (2012). Higher social class predicts increased unethical behavior. *Proceedings of the National Academy of Sciences, 109*(11), 4086–4091.

2   Galinsky, A.D., Magee, J.C., Inesi, M.E. & Gruenfeld, D.H. (2006). Power and perspectives not taken. *Psychological Science, 17*(12), 1068–1074.

3   Van Kleef, G.A., Oveis, C., Van Der Löwe, I., LuoKogan, A., Goetz, J. & Keltner, D. (2008). Power, distress, and compassion: Turning a blind eye to the suffering of others. *Psychological Science, 19*(12), 1315–1322.

4   Kipnis, D. (1972). Does power corrupt? *Journal of Personality and Social Psychology* (psycnet.apa. org).

5   Keltner, D. (2017). *The Power Paradox: How we gain and lose influence.* Penguin.

6   See, for example: Gruenfeld, D.H., Inesi, M.E., Magee, J.C. & Galinsky, A.D. (2008). Power and the objectification of social targets. *Journal of Personality and Social Psychology, 95*(1), 111.

7   See, for example: De Waal, F. (2007). *Chimpanzee politics: Power and sex among apes.* JHU Press.

8   (http://www.ted.com/talks/paul_piff_does_money_make_you_mean)

9   Knegtmans, H., van Dijk, W.W., Mooijman, M., van Lier, N., Rintjema, S. & Wassink, A. (2018). The impact of social power on the evaluation of offensive jokes. *Humor, 31*(1), 85–104.

10 Piff, P.K., Kraus, M.W., Côté, S., Cheng, B.H. & Keltner, D. (2010). Having less, giving more: the influence of social class on prosocial behavior. *Journal of Personality and Social Psychology, 99*(5), 771.

11 Lammers, J., Stapel, D.A. & Galinsky, A.D. (2010). Power increases hypocrisy: Moralizing in reasoning, immorality in behavior. *Psychological Science, 21*(5), 737–744.

12 Tiger, L. (1970). Dominance in human societies. *Annual Review of Ecology and Systematics, 1*(1), 287–306 (zie ook https://hbr.org/2009/05/baboons).

13 Keltner, D., Gruenfeld, D.H. & Anderson, C., (2003). Power, approach, and inhibition. *Psychological Review* (psycnet.apa.org).

14 Nelissen, M. (2013). *Darwin in het nieuws. Of hoe de evolutie nog elke dag de voorpagina's haalt.* Lannoo.

15 See, for example: Abramson, L.Y., Seligman, M.E. & Teasdale, J.D. (1978). Learned helplessness in humans: Critique and reformulation. *Journal of Abnormal Psychology, 87*(1), 49. See also: Taylor, S.E. & Brown, J.D. (1988). Illusion and well-being: a social psychological perspective on mental health. *Psychological Bulletin, 103*(2), 193.

16 Fast, N.J., Gruenfeld, D.H., Sivanathan, N. & Galinsky, A.D. (2009). Illusory control: A generative force behind power's far-reaching effects. *Psychological Science, 20*(4), 502–508.

17 Galinsky, A.D., Gruenfeld, D.H. & Magee, J.C. (2003). From power to action. *Journal of Personality and Social Psychology, 85*(3), 453.

18 Brinol, P., Petty, R.E., Valle, C., Rucker, D.D. & Becerra, A. (2007). The effects of message recipients' power before and after persuasion: a self-validation analysis. *Journal of Personality and Social Psychology, 93*(6), 1040.

19 Galinsky, A.D., Magee, J.C., Gruenfeld, D.H., Whitson, J.A. & Liljenquist, K.A. (2008). Power reduces the press of the situation: implications for creativity, conformity, and dissonance. *Journal of Personality and Social Psychology, 95*(6), 1450.

20 Van Kleef, G.A., De Dreu, C.K., Pietroni, D. & Manstead, A.S. (2006). Power and emotion in negotiation: Power moderates the interpersonal effects of anger and happiness on concession making. *European Journal of Social Psychology, 36*(4), 557–581.

21 Overbeck, J.R. & Park, B. (2006). Powerful perceivers, powerless objects: Flexibility of powerholders' social attention. *Organizational Behavior and Human Decision Processes, 99*(2), 227–243.

22 Galinsky, A.D., Gruenfeld, D.H. & Magee, J.C. (2003). From power to action. *Journal of Personality and Social Psychology, 85*(3), 453.

23 Smith, P.K. & Trope, Y. (2006). You focus on the forest when you're in charge of the trees: power priming and abstract information processing. *Journal of Personality and Social Psychology, 90*(4), 578.

24 For an extensive anthology, see: Van der Vurst, J. (2015). *Moed. De kracht van bezieling.* Houtekiet.

25 Moshagen, M., Hilbig, B.E., & Zettler, I. (2018). The dark core of personality. *Psychological review.*

26 Smith, P.K., Jostmann, N.B., Galinsky, A.D. & Van Dijk, W.W. (2008). Lacking power impairs executive functions. *Psychological Science, 19*(5), 441–447.

27 Steele, C.M., Spencer, S.J. & Aronson, J. (2002). Contending with group image: The psychology of stereotype and social identity threat. *Advances in Experimental Social Psychology, 34,* 379–440.

28 Cuddy published a series of scientific articles about her field of research and gave a TED talk which is still amongst the top-10 most viewed talks of all time. For a full summary of her work in this area, see: Cuddy, A. (2015). *Presence: Bringing your boldest self to your biggest challenges.* Hachette UK.

29 Tracy, J.L. & Matsumoto, D. (2008). The spontaneous expression of pride and shame: Evidence for biologically innate nonverbal displays. *Proceedings of the National Academy of Sciences, 105*(33), 11655–11660.

30 See Grossman, P., Niemann, L., Schmidt, S. & Walach, H. (2004). Mindfulness-based stress reduction and health benefits: A meta-analysis. *Journal of Psychosomatic Research, 57*(1), 35–43, for a critical summary of the sound scientific studies that show the beneficial effects of mindfulness on the stress associated with medical conditions such as cancer, heart problems, pain, depression and anxiety.

Chapter 7

1 Fisher, R., Ury, W.L. & Patton, B. (2011). *Getting to yes: Negotiating agreement without giving in.* Penguin.

2 Ury, W. (2010). The walk from 'no' to 'yes'. *TED Talks.*

3 See, for example: Zeng, M. & Chen, X.P. (2003). Achieving cooperation in multiparty alliances: A social dilemma approach to partnership management. *Academy of Management Review, 28*(4), 587–605.

4 Sherif, M. (2010). *The robbers cave experiment: Intergroup conflict and cooperation [Orig. pub. as Intergroup conflict and group relations].* Wesleyan University Press.

5 Skitka, L.J., Bauman, C.W. & Sargis, E.G. (2005). Moral conviction: Another contributor to attitude strength or something more? *Journal of Personality and Social Psychology, 88*(6), 895.